The Teacher in American Society

This book is dedicated to Nel Noddings (philosopher, educational reformer, practitioner, and mensch) in appreciation of her contributions to the well-being of children and the field of education—and, of course, for her caring.

The Teacher in American Society

Eugene F. Provenzo, Jr.

University of Miami

Editor

Los Angeles | London | New Delhi
Singapore | Washington DC

For information:

SAGE Publications, Inc.
2455 Teller Road
Thousand Oaks,
   California 91320
E-mail: order@sagepub.com

SAGE Publications India Pvt. Ltd.
B 1/I 1 Mohan Cooperative
   Industrial Area
Mathura Road, New Delhi 110 044
India

SAGE Publications Ltd.
1 Oliver's Yard
55 City Road,
London EC1Y 1SP
United Kingdom

SAGE Publications
   Asia-Pacific Pte. Ltd.
33 Pekin Street #02-01
Far East Square
Singapore 048763

Printed in the United States of America

Library of Congress Cataloging-in-Publication Data

The teacher in American society: a critical anthology/edited by Eugene F. Provenzo, Jr.
   p. cm.
Includes bibliographical references and index.
ISBN 978-1-4129-6593-4 (pbk.)
   1. Teachers—United States. 2. Teaching—United States. 3. Education—United States. I. Provenzo, Eugene F.

LB1775.2.T425 2011
371.00973—dc22   2009032718

This book is printed on acid-free paper.

10   11   12   13   14   10   9   8   7   6   5   4   3   2   1

Acquisitions Editor:	Diane McDaniel
Editorial Assistant:	Ashley Conlon
Production Editor:	Brittany Bauhaus
Copy Editor:	Kim Husband
Typesetter:	C&M Digitals (P) Ltd.
Proofreader:	Eleni-Maria Georgiou
Indexer:	Diggs Publication Services, Inc.
Cover Designer:	Edgar Abarca
Marketing Manager:	Carmel Schrire

Contents

Preface   ix

Introduction   1

Part I. On Being a Teacher   9

1. Letter to a Young Teacher   13
   Joseph Featherstone

2. Selection From *Accident, Awareness, and Actualization*   25
   Nel Noddings

3. Respect, Liking, Trust, and Fairness   31
   Kathleen Cushman

Part II. Beginning to Teach   45

4. A Negro Schoolmaster in the New South   49
   W. E. B. Du Bois

5. Selection From *36 Children*   59
   Herbert Kohl

6. Selection From *Educating Esmé: Diary of a Teacher's First Year*   67
   Esmé Raji Codell

Part III. Teaching as the Practice of Freedom   75

7. Selection From *Dumbing Us Down: The Hidden Curriculum of Compulsory Schooling*   77
   John Taylor Gatto

8. Engaged Pedagogy   85
   bell hooks

Part IV. Teaching Others   93

9. The Silenced Dialogue: Power and Pedagogy in
    Educating Other People's Children   97
    Lisa D. Delpit

10. White Privilege and Male Privilege: A Personal Account
    of Coming to See Correspondences Through
    Work in Women's Studies   121
    Peggy McIntosh

11. Teaching Themes of Care   135
    Nel Noddings

Part V. Teaching as Work   147

12. Prologue From *Horace's Compromise*   149
    Theodore R. Sizer

13. Selection From *My Posse Don't Do Homework*   161
    LouAnne Johnson

14. "What Teachers Make, or Objection Overruled, or
    If things don't work out, you can always go to law school"   171
    Taylor Mali

Part VI. Teaching as Social Activism   175

15. Selection From *Death at an Early Age: The Destruction
    of the Hearts and Minds of Negro Children in the
    Boston Public Schools*   177
    Jonathan Kozol

16. "Should the Teacher Always Be Neutral?"   189
    George S. Counts

17. Selection From *Roll of Thunder, Hear My Cry*   197
    Mildred D. Taylor

Part VII. Myths and Stereotypes About Teaching   205

18. Selection From *To Teach: The Journey of a Teacher*   209
    William Ayers

19. Selections From *School Is Hell*: Lesson 6: The 9 Types
    of Grade School Teachers and Lesson 13: The 9
    Types of High School Teachers   223
    Matt Groening

Part VIII. Teaching and Sexuality   **227**

20. "The Teacher" From *Winesburg, Ohio*   231
      Sherwood Anderson

21. Selection From *Socrates, Plato, & Guys Like Me:*
Confessions of a Gay Schoolteacher   239
      Eric Rofes

Index   253

About the Editor   259

Preface

In this book, I have tried to provide an understanding of the teaching profession in the United States and of the purpose behind the work of teachers. I do so through the presentation and analysis of historical and sociological information, as well as by providing sources for reading from a wide range of historical, sociological, and literary sources. In addition, I reference films and other sources in popular culture, such as cartoons and YouTube videos, as a means of understanding not only the work and experience of teachers but also the perception of them in American society.

The approach used in this book is critical. Following this introduction, it is divided into eight parts. Each part includes two or three readings. A general overview is provided in each chapter introduction and then for each reading. At the end of each chapter introduction, a section titled "Linking to Popular Culture" is included. In this section are suggestions about movies and other popular culture sources that are relevant to the chapter. Questions are provided for each of the readings included in the book. These questions are located at the end of the introductions that precede each of the readings.

Underlying this book is the assumption that learning to teach well is not a science, but a deeply reflective and, ultimately, a qualitative act. Learning from the experiences and reflections of others is essential. Learning to ask and answer key questions about the experience of other teachers is also important. In doing so, understanding of the reader is extended to a wider range of cultures, traditions and experiences.

Acknowledgments

I wish to acknowledge the many people who contributed to this book. Its content was primarily shaped by an effort to reshape my course at the

University of Miami, *The Teacher and American Society* (TAL 603). Not having taught this course for nearly a decade, I returned to it in the fall of 2005 with the purpose of developing a new approach to the course, emphasizing the use of film and literature as primary sources.

Special thanks go to Manuel Bello, who provided excellent suggestions on several sources for this book. As always, his insights are greatly appreciated. Very special thanks to my wife Asterie Baker Provenzo, who remains my best friend and best critic.

I also thank the reviewers whose commentary helped to shape this manuscript:

Dwight Allen, *Old Dominion University*

Jennifer C. Herring, *University of Illinois–Springfield*

Sheena Choi, *Indiana–Purdue University Fort Wayne*

Dorothy Craig, *Middle Tennessee State University*

Elizabeth B. Day, *Santa Clara University*

Tarra Ellis, *University of North Carolina–Charlotte*

Justin Finney, *Columbus State University*

Jo Victoria Goodman, *Penn State University Harrisburg*

Cynthia Resor, *Eastern Kentucky University*

—*Eugene F. Provenzo, Jr.*
University of Miami
May 2009

Introduction

The *Oxford English Dictionary* (1989) defines the verb *teach* this way: "To show (a person) the way; to direct, conduct, convoy, guide (*to, from* a place); to send away; also, to direct or refer (*to* something)." This definition emphasizes the idea of the teacher as a guide, as someone who directs the learner to a better understanding of the world around them.

Implicit in this definition is the idea that the teacher must be reflective about teaching. People cannot guide or lead someone else without thinking about what they are doing, where they are going—in other words, being reflective and thoughtful about what they are doing. This idea of the teacher being reflective is explored in detail in the work of the educational theorist Donald Schön (1930–1997).

According to Schön, teaching is a profession that involves *reflective practice*. Instead of being thought of as a science, Schön argues that teaching needs to be thought of as *art* or *artistry*. In a 1987 address before the American Educational Research Association, he talked about teaching as "giving reason." This is a much more difficult task than one might think. In this context, Schön gives the example of an individual learning to ride a bicycle, something he describes as involving "reflection-in-action." According to him,

> This reflection-in-action is tacit and spontaneous and often delivered without taking thought, and is not a particularly intellectual activity. And yet it involves making new sense of surprises, turning thought back on itself to think in new ways about phenomena and about how we *think* about those phenomena. (Schön, 1987b).

In this context, teaching a person to ride a bicycle does involve technical issues. There is the gyroscopic effect of the wheels, for example, which keeps the rider upright, and which allows one to lean into a curve. But no one learning to ride a bicycle thinks too much about the science underlying how a bicycle works. Instead, the person practices riding, maybe uses training

1

wheels, maybe falls over a bit, and uses his or her senses to get the feel for how a bicycle functions and operates (Schön 1987b). That person learns the art rather than the science of riding a bike.

The art of riding a bicycle involves both practice and reflection. To successfully ride a bicycle, one needs to take many things into account. You must know where to place your feet and how to hold on to the handlebars. You must also judge the road and how the bike will do on a slick or dry pavement or how to go over a bump. This process involves what Schön (1987b) describes as "knowing-in-action." According to him,

> This capacity to respond to surprise through improvisation on the spot is what I mean by *reflection-in-action*. When a teacher turns her attention to giving kids reason for listening to what they say, then teaching itself becomes a form of reflection-in-action, and I think this formulation helps to describe what it is that constitutes teaching artistry. (Schön 1987b)

> Teaching in the form of reflection-in-action

> involves a surprise, a response to surprise by thought turning back on itself, thinking what we're doing as we do it, setting the problem of the situation anew, conducting an action experiment on the spot by which we seek to solve the new problems we've set, an experiment in which we test both our new way of seeing the situation, and also try to change that situation for the better. (Schön 1987b)

This is what a jazz musician does when he improvises, or an abstract painter does when she lets the paint flow in a drip. There is control and pattern, but there is also chance and surprise.

Schön believes that we teach best by being involved in "reflective practicum"—one in which we "learn by *doing*." In terms of the development and training of teachers, this involves educating them "in the capacity to teach reflectively and to think about their own reflection-in-action with kids." One learns to teach much as one learns to ride a bike, by sitting on its seat, grabbing the handlebars, and starting to ride. In teaching, however, this also includes having an understanding of the subject matter, judging the needs and abilities of the students one is working with, and jumping in and teaching them.

One might argue that there is little that we can do to prepare beginning teachers before they start teaching. This is incorrect. We can prepare beginning teachers by helping them to understand and reflect on the experience of others who have taught before them. In this context, literature, personal accounts, reflections on the art and craft of teaching, and popular films can provide an important means by which beginning teachers can follow Schön's model and function as reflective practitioners. The readings included in this book have been chosen because they provide beginning teachers with precisely these types of materials.

Closely related to the process of being a reflective practitioner is understanding precisely what it is that teachers do and how they are situated as intellectual workers within American society. Beginning teachers need to ask the questions: "What is a teacher?" "What does it mean for me to teach?"

Teaching is among the oldest of all professions. We have descriptions of teachers that date back over 4,000 years to ancient Sumer (modern southern Iraq). In Noah Kramer's (1988) classic study of firsts in history, *History Begins at Sumer: Thirty-Nine Firsts in Recorded History,* the work of a Sumerian scribe and teacher is described in detail. Essentially, much of what he does is not very different from what a contemporary teacher does: teach students skills, keep them on task, and discipline them when they misbehave, and so on.

Teachers are the single largest group of educated workers in the United States. There are 6.2 million teachers in America, from prekindergarten through the graduate university level. Preschool and kindergarten teachers represent 442,000 workers. Ninety-eight percent are women. There are 3.1 million elementary and middle school teachers. Seventy-eight percent are women. At the secondary level there are 772,000 teachers. Fifty-nine percent are women. Postsecondary education includes 1.1 million individuals, of whom 46% are women. Special education teachers number about 175,000, and other types of teachers and instructors number just over half a million (U.S. Census Bureau, 2008).

Teaching, particularly at the preschool, elementary, and middle school levels, is a profession dominated by women—what some researchers have referred to as a *feminized* profession. Teaching is also often referred to as a *smiling* profession. Essential to the idea of teaching is helping others. This is an important motivating force for most teachers. More than other fields, teachers are compensated by the satisfaction they receive from working with people. This seems to be a constant in the profession. When the sociologist Dan Lortie asked teachers in the mid-1960s what experience they found most satisfying, 86.2% reported, "The times I know I have reached a group of students and they have learned" (Lortie, 1964 and Kottkamp, et al., 1986, p. 565). When this question was asked of a nearly identical group of teachers 20 years later, the figure was 86.7% (Kottkamp, Provenzo, & Cohn, 1986).

Teaching is middle-class work. The highest average teacher salary for K–12 teachers in the United States is $54,300. The lowest salaries are in South Dakota, where the average is $31,000. The average salary across the nation is $44,700. Benefits, including retirement, tend to be good. Teachers are fairly secure in their jobs, and less subject to economic downturns than other sectors of the economy (U.S. Census Bureau, 2008).

Teaching, however, is also highly regulated. Unlike other professionals, such as lawyers, doctors, and engineers, teachers are controlled by people outside of their professional peer group—that is, school boards through agents such as school superintendents and building principals. In law, for example, if a lawyer is subject to censure or discipline, his or her actions are reviewed by the state legal bar, which is made up of lawyers who are peers. Likewise, doctors are reviewed by other doctors who make up the state medical board.

Other aspects of teaching make the profession different from medicine and law. Doctors and lawyers, in theory, can choose their own clientele. Thus, a lawyer can refuse to represent a client. This is technically true for doctors, although in reality, one cannot imagine an emergency room physician refusing to treat a patient who is critically ill. The opportunity to select with whom one works is not available to teachers. Teachers are assigned a group of children in their class or classes, and they are expected to work with them. They have little or no input on selecting whom they will teach.

The fact that teachers do not regulate themselves as a profession, compounded by the lack of control over selecting who they work with, has led theorists such as Dan Lortie to describe teaching as a "semi-profession" (Lortie, 1964). Certainly much that teachers do is professional in nature. When one is in the classroom working, one constantly makes independent decisions about how to best deliver instruction or how to meet the emotional and personal needs of a student. Likewise, planning a lesson calls for a type of independence and judgment typically associated with *professional practice*. Having said this, however, teachers do not have the autonomy and independence that doctors or lawyers have.

The semiprofessional status of teachers shapes their day-to-day experiences and what they can or cannot do in the classroom. Thus, in the case of Jonathan Kozol, working in an inner-city school in Boston in the mid-1960s (included in Part III of this work), his lack of professional autonomy led him to be subject to the intense scrutiny of his school's administration and to his ultimate dismissal from his position because of his beliefs about professional practice and those practices that were in place as part of the school system's administration.

Kozol (1967), like many of the other authors included in this book, found himself in the position of "educating other people's children." This concept is discussed in the work of the educational anthropologist, Lisa Delpit (see Part IV). Delpit (1995) argues in *Other People's Children* that many mainstream White middle-class teachers view minority and low-income children as "other" and "make them into damaged and dangerous caricatures of the vulnerable and impressionable beings before them" (p. xiii). According to Delpit, an unconscious "culture of power" exists in American schools in which teachers act as though they hold no cultural power or influence over the students they teach. As she explains,

> to act as if power does not exist is to ensure that the power status remains the same. To imply to children or adults . . . that it doesn't matter how you talk or how you write is to ensure their ultimate failure. I prefer to be honest with my students. I tell them that their language and cultural style is unique and wonderful but that there is a political power game that is also being played, and if they want to be in on that game there are certain games that they must play. (pp. 39–40)

Delpit's arguments are particularly important in light of the demographics of the teaching profession. Teachers in the United States are predominantly White-non-Hispanic (84.3%). The student population is 42% minority. Although minority teachers tend to teach more often in schools serving low-income and minority students, these same students are more likely to have a White-non-Hispanic teacher (Zumwalt and Craig, 2008, p. 411). This mismatch between White-non-Hispanic teachers and the low-income and minority students they teach is extremely important in light of the arguments made by Delpit.

How this translates into practice can be seen in the way White-non-Hispanic teachers use language versus the minority children whom they teach. Citing the work of Shirley Brice Heath and Catherine Snow, Delpit explains how White middle-class teachers provide children with different directives than their parents. In White middle-class culture, for example, children are often asked to do things in the form of a question, although in reality they are being given an order or directive. When a middle-class child is asked, "Is it time for your bath?" this is not necessarily a question but an order. In other words, what is really being said is, "Go take your bath." In contrast, in many minority and low-income African American groups the child would be told more directly to take a bath. There would be no use of a question.

These cultural differences have a potentially profound effect in the classroom. Students often do not understand the directives they get from their White-non-Hispanic teachers. They think that by being asked a question they are being given a choice, which in reality is not the case. Delpit recounts how:

> a black elementary school principal in Fairbanks, Alaska, reported to me that she has a lot of difficulty with black children who are placed in some white

teachers' classrooms. The teachers often send the children to the office for disobeying teacher directives. Their parents are frequently called in for conferences. The parents' response to the teacher is usually the same. "They do what
I say; if you just tell them what to do, they'll do it. I tell them at home that they
have to listen to what you say." (p. 36)

Many Black children expect authority figures to act with authority. When
a White teacher asks them if they would "like to do something" they assume
that the person who is instructing them has no power (Delpit, 1995).

Teachers function as what Henry Giroux (1992) describes as "border-
crossers." They must learn to work with their children, whose background,
both cultural and intellectual, may vary widely from one year to the next.
They need to work with families and parents and understand how different
values and norms may be at work—ones that need to be addressed if the
needs of the child being taught are to be met.

Teachers need to understand how schools and the classrooms in which they
work are part of larger bureaucratic and cultural systems. They need to understand what is acceptable or unacceptable in terms of the rules of the system and
of the local community in which they work. Being gay, and out of the closet, it
may be acceptable in many large urban settings but is not necessarily going to
be well received in more conservative communities. This is an issue addressed
directly by Eric Rofes (1985) in the selection included in Part VIII from his
book, *Socrates, Plato, & Guys Like Me: Confessions of a Gay Schoolteacher*.

As indicated by many of the selections included in this book, teaching is
hard work. In addition to preparing for class and grading, teachers are typically "on" for 6 to 7 hours a day. Elementary school teachers enter the
classroom and are confronted by dozens of students and a schedule that
gives little or no time between classes. They must constantly make on-the-
spot judgments and decisions with a highly fluid and demanding clientele.

Teachers must know their subject matter and keep themselves current in
their areas of expertise—a fact that is true for elementary and middle school
teachers as well as high school and college instructors. They need to adapt
to changing technologies. And they are also constantly required to react to
events that emerge in their schools and communities, and with the individual students they teach.

Teachers need to be psychologists and counselors. Jose's father dies unex-
pectedly in a car crash. Mary's father is laid off from work. A beloved pet is
lost, parents get divorced, a student is bullied and needs to be protected, and
so on. All of these types of things must be addressed by the typical teacher,
in addition to addressing the issues of teaching students new subjects and
information—the supposed primary reason for teaching in the first place.

Keep in mind that all of this takes place within the context of teachers' own lives—their own desires and needs and disappointments. Like the teacher Kate Swift in Sherwood Anderson's (1919) compelling story from his collection *Winesburg, Ohio* (Part VIII), teachers bring with them to the classroom their own personality and history, which profoundly shape what they can or cannot achieve in the classroom.

As you read the selections in this book, try to reflect on your own experiences in school and to project yourself into a life in the classroom. Think about the personal experiences of others and how the lives they have lived can inform you about your work. Consider how the various literary and popular culture sources included in these readings reflect realities in the lives of teachers and the classrooms in which they work. Think about how these sources can inform you. It is hoped that the following selections will provide you, the reader, a useful way to explore and further understand what it means to be a teacher.

References

Anderson, S. (1919). *Winesburg, Ohio: A group of tales of Ohio small town life.* New York: The Modern Library.

Delpit, L. (1995). *Other people's children.* New York: New Press.

Giroux, H. (1992). *Border crossings: Cultural workers and the politics of education.* New York: Routledge.

Kottkamp, R. B., Provenzo, E. F. Jr., & Cohn, M. (1986). Stability and change in a profession: Two decades of teacher attitudes, 1964–1984. *Phi Delta Kappan, 67*(8), 559–567.

Kozol, J. (1967). *Death at an early age: The destruction of the hearts and minds of Negro children in the Boston public schools.* Boston: Houghton Mifflin.

Kramer, N. (1988). *History begins at Sumer: Thirty-nine "firsts" in recorded history.* Philadelphia: University of Pennsylvania Press.

Lortie, D. C. (1975). *Schoolteacher: A sociological study.* Chicago: University of Chicago Press.

Oxford English dictionary. (1989). New York: Oxford University Press.

Rofes, E. (1985). *Socrates, Plato, & guys like me: Confessions of a gay schoolteacher.* Boston: Alyson.

Schön, D. (1983). *The reflective practitioner: How professionals think in action.* London: Temple Smith.

Schön, D. (1987a). *Educating the reflective practitioner.* San Francisco: Jossey-Bass.

Schön, D. (1987b). *Educating the reflective practitioner.* Paper presented at the meeting of the American Educational Research Association.

U.S. Census Bureau. (2008). Facts for features. Available online at: http://www .census.gov/Press-Release/www/releases/archives/facts_for_features_special_ editions/001737.html

Zumwalt, K., & Craig, E. (2008). Who is teaching? Does it matter? In Marilyn Cochran-Smith, Sharon Feiman-Nemser, & D. John McIntyre (Eds.), *Handbook of research on teacher education: Enduring questions in changing contexts* (p. 411). New York: Routledge.

PART I

On Being a Teacher

1. Letter to a Young Teacher
   Joseph Featherstone

2. Selection From *Accident, Awareness, and Actualization*
   Nel Noddings

3. Respect, Liking, Trust, and Fairness
   Kathleen Cushman

———————

B. Othanel Smith (1968) has written that in many regards teaching is the same from one culture to another—that is, "a natural social phenomenon" (Smith, 1968, p. 4). It involves an agent who interacts with students within a specific setting. Typically, he or she has little control over the size of the class that is taught, the social and cultural background of students, or their physical characteristics. What a teacher can do is deal with the students on a personal level, shape assignments and the way questions are asked, and shape the content of what is taught. Teaching is more art than science, an imprecise process of trial and error and successive approximation. Bill Ayers (1995), an author included in this book (see Chapter 7), well known political activist from the 1960s, and an experienced teacher at both the university and K–12 level describes teaching this way:

A life in teaching is a stitched-together affair, a crazy quilt of odd pieces and scrounged materials, equal parts invention and imposition. To make a life in teaching is largely to find your own way, to follow this or that thread, to work until your fingers ache, your mind feels as if it will unravel, and your eyes give out, and to make mistakes and then rework large pieces. It is sometimes tedious and demanding, confusing and uncertain, and yet it is as often creative and dazzling: Surprising splashes of color can suddenly appear at its center; unexpected patterns can emerge and lend the whole affair a sense of grace and purpose and possibility. (p. 1)

For most people, when teaching goes well, there are few more satisfying experiences. When it goes badly, it can be a nightmare.

The sociologist Dan Lortie (1989), in his book *Schoolteacher,* identifies five attractions to teaching that set it apart from other professionals. These include the following:

1. the *service theme,* serving other people and making a difference in their lives

2. the *interpersonal theme,* working with individuals and making a difference in their lives

3. the *continuation theme,* continuing positive experiences people have had in their earlier lives and education (a coach being involved in teaching people about sports, someone who liked literature, teaching English, etc.)

4. the *time compatibility theme,* having a job that is compatible with people's needs or desires (having summer breaks to allow one to travel, having a schedule that allows one the time to have a profession and also raise children); and

5. the *market benefit theme,* making an income on which to live (pp. 27–31).

Teachers entering the profession must address a number of personal and professional issues that go beyond Lortie's five main attractors. These include their moral and ethical stance. Historically, teachers have been held to a higher standard than other members of the society. The reasons for this are clear: They are public figures who deal with minors. As a result, indiscretions that are permissible in the more general public are not acceptable for teachers.

In the selections in Chapter 1, we begin by looking at the advice given by Joseph Featherstone, a master teacher educator, to a young beginning teacher. In the second reading, Kathleen Cushman (2004) interviews students about what it is that they feel teachers should do in their classrooms and how they should represent themselves and interact with their students. In other words, Cushman is dealing with how teachers should lead their daily lives in the classroom.

The final chapter concludes with a reading by the educational philosopher Nel Noddings (1997), who describes in detail how she constructed her life as an elementary and secondary school teacher, mother, and, eventually, university educator. Her reflections address the accidental developments in her life and career. She describes at length, for example, how disappointments often, in the end, served to her advantage (i.e., only being able to get an elementary position when she originally wanted to teach high school).

Further Readings: In addition to the "Letter to a Young Teacher" written by Joseph Featherstone included with this selection, an excellent similar work is Jonathan Kozol's *Letters to a Young Teacher* (Crown Publishers, 2007). Also of interest is Sonia Nieto's *Why We Teach* (Teachers College Press, 2005).

Linking to Popular Culture: There are numerous movies that describe the lives of teachers and their day-to-day work. In the movie *Dead Poets Society* (1989), a charismatic teacher at an elite New England boarding school challenges the conservative values of the school and its curriculum. The movie won an Academy Award for best screenplay and raises a number of interesting issues concerning how teachers can and should shape their students. This issue was also raised in the 1969 movie based on a Muriel Spark's novel of the same title, *The Prime of Miss Jean Brodie*. It explores the story of a private school teacher vicariously living through the personal experiences of her students. Moral and ethical issues are also raised in the 2002 movie *The Emperor's Club,* in which an idealistic prep school teacher attempts to redeem an incorrigible student. For historical photographs of teachers in the United States, go to the Prints and Photographs Catalogue at the Library of Congress (http://www.loc.gov/rr/print/catalog.html) and type "American Teachers" into the photographic search engine.

References

Ayers, W. (1995). *To teach: The journey of a teacher*. New York: Teachers College Press.

Featherstone, J. (1995). Letter to a young teacher. In W. Ayers (Ed.), *To become a teacher*. New York: Teachers College Press.

Lortie, D. C. (1975). *Schoolteacher: A sociological study*. Chicago: University of Chicago Press, 1975.

Smith, B. O. (1968). Toward a theory of teaching. In A. A. Bellack (Ed.), *Theory and research in teaching* (p. 23). New York: Teachers College, Bureau of Publications.

1

Letter to a Young Teacher

Joseph Featherstone

Joseph Featherstone is a professor at Michigan State University. He is a well known teacher educator, essayist, and former school principal. In his "Letter to a Young Teacher" (1995), Featherstone remembers his grandmother, the principal of a small elementary school in rural Pennsylvania, and her commitment to a social and political agenda. Featherstone argues that in a "confused political time" such as the one we live in, being a teacher requires, more than ever, the need for a political understanding and commitment.

Featherstone recognizes that schools have historically reflected the systematic inequality at work in the larger American society. He also maintains that schools have the potential—much as his grandmother believed—to be places where all people can be nurtured, grow, and develop. According to Featherstone, schools also need to be places where people can learn the joy of learning and creating. Students need to be able to experience a "movement of the spirit," not just the acquisition of pragmatic knowledge that leads to a job.

"What is to be taught?" in the curriculum is among the perennial questions Featherstone raises. The selection of course content is deeply political. Who and what get left out of what we teach? What gets left in? In the end, teaching and instruction are deeply cultural and political.

NOTE: Reprinted by permission of the Publisher. From William Ayers (Ed.), To Become a Teacher: Making a Difference in Children's Lives, New York: Teachers College Press. Copyright © 1995 by Teachers College, Columbia University. All rights reserved.

Featherstone distrusts business models of efficiency in education while at the same time espousing a democratic notion of a schooling in which high and elite culture is available to all students. Like John Dewey, Featherstone recognizes that schools are "embryonic democracies." What children learn in school about being part of a democratic system is carried with them into their adult lives.

Reading Featherstone's "Letter to a Young Teacher" raises the following questions:

1. To what extent should teachers be acting to change the world in terms of society and politics?

2. Should the type of education we provide our children in a democracy be different from what is found in other societies? If yes, why?

3. Is education in the United States truly equal?

4. How has the recent emphasis on standards in our schools diminished the ability of the schools to be places where children learn "grace, poetry and laughter"? Is this something teachers and schools need to be concerned about?

5. Who should determine what is taught in our schools?

6. Should models drawn from business and commerce dominate the discussion of how our schools should function?

7. How do you think schools should function to encourage the growth and development of democratic values and communities?

Dear Josie,

You asked me for some advice about starting out as a teacher, and what popped into my head first is an image of my grandmother. I never met her, but she remains a strong presence. She was the principal of a small, mostly immigrant elementary school in the Pennsylvania coal country. Like so many teachers then and now, the stories of her teaching got buried with her. She was one of many urban Irish Catholics who took part in the progressive educational and political movements of her day. I know that she was ambitious for kids' learning. The immigrant coal miners' children, whose families were often out of work, were to read high-class literature and poetry—she had a weakness for the English poet Browning. She also checked to see that kids brushed their teeth. She was a force in local and state politics, fighting for labor rights, pioneering in women's rights, and leading the movement to end child labor. She was the first woman elected to the state Democratic committee in Pennsylvania. I think she saw a direct link between politics and her practice in education: Both had as their aim the general progress of ordinary people. She was on the people's side, creating an expansive democratic vision of education based on the idea of a country that would work for everybody, not just for the rich.

This seems to me a perspective—a tradition, really—worth reminding ourselves about in a confused political time. Fewer teachers now put matters in terms of politics, although it seems to me that teaching in the United States today more than ever involves a political commitment. I would argue that, like my grandmother, you should think of yourself as a recruit on the people's side, working to build a democracy that doesn't yet exist but is part of the American promise. My grandmother would surely point out that there is important work to be done both in and out of classrooms, and that sometimes school matters get framed by wider social issues. I can hear her, for example, insisting that the biggest educational problem today is the growing despair of joblessness. And I'm sure that my grandmother would say that teachers today have a vital stake in a national health care system, for she always saw the connection between kids' learning and good health. Brushing your teeth and Browning were connected. Her image reminds me that society and its schools are both battlegrounds, on which different sides fight for rival visions of America and its possibilities. The real basics in education, she would argue, flow from the kind of country you want the kids to make when they grow up. She was voting for a real, rather than a paper, democracy. And she thought that teachers had a role to play in helping the people become more powerful.

New teachers often don't realize that there are sides to take, and that they are called upon to choose. The old idea that education is above politics is a useful half-truth—it helps keep the schools from being politicized. But it conceals the essentially political character of choices we make for kids. Do we see the children we teach today as low-paid workers for the global economy, or as the reserve army of the unemployed? If so, why be ambitious for their hearts and minds? Alternatively, we can frame fundamental aims: that we are creating a first-rate education for everybody's kids, so that as grownups they can make a democracy happen. My grandmother and many in her generation would say that schools should offer what students need to take part in a democratic society and its culture—a complex package for everybody's children that would equip them for full participation in work, culture, and liberty.

This is clearly an ambitious goal, rarely achieved in world history, let alone in America. Schools alone can never accomplish it. Still, our sense of the purpose of education matters, and for a long while too many of our schools have not believed in educating the people. The old Greeks said that some were born gold and others brass, and they designed education accordingly. A slave or a woman would not get a free man's education.

Over the centuries around the planet, a lot of the human race has agreed, establishing separate educations for rulers and ruled. Hewers of wood and drawers of water would not read Jane Austen in advanced placement English classes. In a democracy, however, the people are supposed to rule. They are, the old phrase has it, the equal of kings. So the people need an education commensurate with their potential political, economic, and cultural power. To give the children of ordinary people the kind of education once reserved for the children of the elites—to do this for the first time in history—is the dream of the builders of U.S. education like Horace Mann and my grandmother and thousands of others who triumphed and struggled and died in obscurity.

You are a newcomer to an historic struggle. Some of this you may have learned already, just by keeping your eyes open. You probably know that the United States has always been a deeply flawed democracy and that education has always mirrored the systematic inequality of society. There was no golden age when the United States did right by everybody's kids. This society still has vastly different expectations for well-off and poor kids. The gap seems to be growing, not shrinking. We are two educational nations. The schools for poor kids that you may visit and teach in will often look like schools in a desperately poor nation, not the world's most powerful country. Textbooks are old, the roof leaks, and there is a shortage of paper. People of color and women and immigrants had to fight their way into the educational feast and are still kept at the margins in many schools. But you also need to know that in each generation, strong teachers like my grandmother have worked with parents and communities to make democracy happen. Her ghost is silently cheering you on.

My grandmother was not alone in thinking that schools have a special responsibility for the progress of the people's culture. In taking a large, ambitious, ample—democratic—view of education's aims, she was opposing minimalist views that reduce children to tiny gears in the nation's great economic machine. She was opposing the oldest human superstition of all, the belief in fundamental inequality. She was also laying rude hands on the second oldest superstition, the belief that because there is never enough to go around, existing unfairness must be endured. My grandparents' generation had a healthy respect for policies that generate jobs for the people, but they never made the mistake of thinking that all of life is embraced by the equations of economists or the maxims of bankers and investors. The economy should serve human life and its needs, not the other way around. There is, the old progressives argued, no real wealth but life. Making a living ought to be a means to a wider end: making a life. And in fact, students educated to fit narrow economic grooves—management's view of what will suffice for today's workforce—will never be equipped to take part in debates and movements to change society and build a democratic economy in which everybody has a fair share and basic security.

The capacity to participate—in work, in politics, in the thought of the times—is really in the end a matter of cultural development. The key to the people's success will be the quality of their characters and their minds—the quality of their culture. It is this hardheaded grasp of the radical importance of culture that makes the progressives of my grandmother's generation worth listening to again today. Symbols and ideas and understanding have to become the property of the people if they are to ever gain any control over their lives and the lives of their children. Symbols and ideas and words and culture are no replacement for jobs or political power, but without them, people will easily lose their way. Many in my grandmother's generation admired Eugene Debs, who once said that he would not lead the people to the promised land, because if he could take them there, some other leader could convince them to leave.

Democratic teaching aims to make the people powerful in a host of ways, but perhaps most importantly in the realm of culture itself the web of meanings we weave with language and symbols out of our experience and the heritage of the past. In a democracy, people should be educated to be powerful, to tell their stories, to make their own voices heard, and to act together to defend and expand their rights. Culture might be said to be a shorthand word for all the ways that people and their imaginations and identities grow—how we construct the world and make ourselves at home in it, and then reinvent it fresh.

Schoolteachers of my grandmother's era had an almost mystical reverence for the word "growth." This is how you can tell that, for all their toughness (my aunt Mary had my grandmother in the fourth grade and said that she was really strict), they were romantics under the skin. In tough times, against heavy odds, with huge polyglot classes, they kept alive an idea of democratic education itself as a romance. This language doesn't fit our current skeptical mood and circumstance. It has an extravagant and sentimental sound—it's the language of possibility, democratic hope. The old progressives believed in a version of true romance. Some got these ideas from politics, some from religion, and some from poetry, believe it or not. My grandmother mixed her poetry and her politics into a potent brew. One of her favorite romantic poets, John Keats, put the argument for a romantic, democratic view of culture this way: now the human race looks like low bushes with here and there a big tree; spin from imaginative experience an "airy citadel" like the spider's web, "filling the air with beautiful circuiting," every human might become great, everybody would grow to the full height, and humanity "instead of being a wide heath of furze and briars with here and there a remote pine or oak, would become a grand democracy of forest trees."[1]

A forest of oak trees: This democratic and romantic view of a people's culture—articulated in the nineteenth century by poets like Keats and Walt Whitman and practical dreamers like Margaret Fuller, Elizabeth Cady Stanton, Margaret Haley, Jane Addams, W. E. B. Du Bois, Eugene Debs, and John Dewey—insists that the goal for which we struggle is a democratic culture in which everyone can grow to their full height and take part in the world of ideas, books, art, and music as well as work and politics. To hardheaded teachers like my grandmother, this was a version of true romance—true, because they knew that no kid grows on a diet of dry academic splinters and stunted expectations. If you teach kids just minimalist stuff—isolated skills, for example—they never get to practice and enact the real thing, culture itself. They get slices of the animal but not the whole live hog. They lose what Emily Dickinson called the thing with feathers—hope. In today's hard times, ruled by bastard pragmatism, it is important to insist that beauty is a human necessity, like water and food and love and work. The multiplication tables need memorizing. So do the French verbs. Not all learning is fun. But an idea of learning that leaves out grace and poetry and laughter will never take root in kids' hearts and souls. Education is in the end a movement of the spirit. This is the realism behind the old vision of education as true romance. Children require, finally, things that cannot be bought and sold, accomplishments that last a lifetime. They are asking for bread. Too many of our schools are giving them stones instead. From our point of view today, the school culture of my grandmother's generation may have been too genteel—a white schoolmarm culture that often ignored or disdained the experience of immigrants, women, and people of color. It was a monochromatic culture, tied into the many weaknesses of gentility. But what is impressive today about it is the depth of its democratic aspirations: the assumption that everyone can rise up on the wings of hope.

As today, Americans in the past argued over whose version of culture to teach. The tug-of-war over today's (quite recent) canons of literature and history is an inevitable aspect of being what Whitman called a people of peoples. I believe—though my grandmother might disagree—that such tugging and pulling is a sign of cultural vitality, part of a process of democratic change that Whitman described as "lawless as snowflakes." The

---

[1]This passage was quoted, significantly, by that romantic John Dewey (1934, p. 347) in *Art as Experience,* his great argument for a democratic approach to art and culture.

arguments over whose version of culture to teach will properly go on until the republic closes shop. A democracy educates itself by arguing over what to teach the next generation. But as grown-up groups struggle for each generation's balance of pride and recognition and representation and inclusion, we need to keep in mind how important it is for kids to be allowed to make and do culture, to participate in enacting live meanings and symbols. Opening up the school curriculum to the world's rainbows of cultures is a necessary step toward becoming a people of peoples, a real democracy. But it will not be much of a gain to substitute a new multicultural and multiracial orthodoxy for an older cultural orthodoxy. Nobody's version of the canon will matter if kids don't start reading real books sometime. Unless kids get a chance to make cultural meaning, and not passively absorb it, nothing will come alive. Anybody's version of culture can be delivered secondhand and dead. The real challenge is to help kids make cultural meanings come alive here and now, to act as creators and critics of culture, armed with the skills and discipline to—as Emerson put it—form and power. And what holds for kids surely holds for teachers too.

A romantic and democratic vision of human possibility may in the end be a practical thing for teachers—as real as radium, and even more valuable. Teaching is, after all, more like taking part in a religion or a political movement than anything else—the whole thing rests on what the old theologians called the virtue of hope. Its loss kills more kids than guns and drugs. The technocratic lingo of the educational managers and the boredom of today's colleges of education do no service to a profession that in the end requires true romance, the stuff that lights up the soul. Who would rise up on a cold, dark morning and go out to teach if the only goal were to raise the SAT scores? A democratic vision helps you not only in rethinking your purposes, in choosing the curriculum, for example, but also in making it through those February days when the radiators are banging and teaching school feels like the dark night of the soul. It says on the Liberty Bell, across the crack, that the people without vision shall perish. This should be a warning to us in an educational era dominated by dull experts, squinty-eyed economists, and frightened politicians. You will never survive your years as a teacher by listening to what passes for vision now in the United States.

The novelist Charles Dickens dramatized the basics—the fundamental democratic issues—in his novel about depressed times in nineteenth-century England, *Hard Times*. (Passages sound a lot like the United States in the 1990s.) Dickens introduces a capitalist named Mr. Gradgrind. Mr. Gradgrind, not at all coincidentally, runs a school for workers' kids. Gradgrind calls the kids by number, not by name, and insists on a curriculum limited to "facts, facts, facts." "You are not to wonder," he says to the children. Mr. Gradgrind stands for a minimalist and antiromantic political ideology that measures life by the profit margin and reduces humans to numbers. He is a utilitarian, like many of our current leaders in politics and education, for whom the bottom line is a religion. He believes only what can be measured and therefore misses out on human mystery and potential. To him, children are parts for the great economic machine. He sees a world composed of competing individual atoms. He fears the human imagination and the bonds of friendship.

Gradgrind wants kids and teachers to be passive recipients of the curriculum of "facts, facts, facts." They are not to wonder, because wondering makes trouble. Dickens argues that children's imagination is in fact a critical political issue, and that the imagination and the human heart require much more than calculations of profit and loss. He asks us to put true romance and human sympathy and the imagination back in our picture of education. Dickens is clear that Mr. Gradgrind's approach to education is a strategy of control: He wants passive labor, not active critical minds. Nothing could show more clearly the political implications of a minimalist, as opposed to an expansive and democratic, vision of culture.

Education is a battleground on which different visions of the future are struggling. Gradgrind offers a grim and colorless world of isolated, competing individuals in an environment whose skies are blackened and ruined by greed; he can never match the bright colors and laughter of communities of children.

Mr. Gradgrind is above all an enemy of the idea of culture for the people. He sees art and humor as absurd and dangerous frills. Children's imagination is a threat. He hates the circus, for example, which Dickens makes into a symbol of popular creativity. Mr. Gradgrind is not, alas, dead. He is everywhere today, in corporations, legislatures, governors' mansions, and central offices of school systems. I saw him on the evening news last night. He was wearing an expensive suit and was pointing to a wall chart. An hour later, he was flourishing a Bible. To fight today's versions of Mr. Gradgrind, teachers and the rest of us need to start imagining an expansive and democratic vision of education as true romance—not the romance of sentimentality and fakery and escape (the media have stuffed us all with too many such lies) but the true romance that knows that the heart is the toughest human muscle, the romance of respect for the people and what their children's minds are capable of.

To enact this true romance, we need to do many things. We need a democratic version of the humanities and the liberal arts from kindergarten through the university. At the university level, as in the schools, the older traditions of the "liberal arts" and the "humanities" and elite science and math are often preserves for privilege, crusted over with the practices and superstitions of human inequality. But the people's children deserve the best, and such subjects and traditions need to be rescued for them, not abandoned. Culture needs to be democratized, not abandoned. The people have a right to claim their heritage and take possession of what generations of leisure have given the privileged.

Underlying the daily work in schools, then, is the task of creating a democratic culture, a task that may take generations. Of course, a genuine people's culture, when it emerges, will look very different from the oily "people's cultures" concocted by the commissars in totalitarian regimes. To begin such work, teachers need to be able to see "culture" in its several meanings: what used to be called the "high" culture, the traditional symbols of academic learning, the great books and works of art and music; newcomers to the canon; and also the local webs of meaning and tradition arising out of the lives of students and communities. Today we want to interrogate the old "high" culture and ask who it included and who it left out. But in the end, we also want our kids to get access, to break into the old vaults as well as savor new treasures.

Instead of thinking of culture as a separate realm of "high" experience, an elite commodity, we want to show our kids the common continuum of human experience that reaches from the great works of art of all times and cultures to children's talk and imagining right now, to help students move back and forth from their experience to the experiences embodied in poems, artworks, and textbooks. Unlike my grandmother's generation, we want the visions of culture offered in our schools to be true rainbow bridges that the children crisscross daily in both directions—the home and neighborhood cultures on one end, and the wider worlds of culture on the other.

My grandmother had a vision of a teacher going forth to bring culture to the people. What we might add to that today is the image of the people and their children giving something back in a true exchange of gifts. Today we might be in a better position to see that culture making in the schools has to be a two-way street. The idea of culture embraced by the school must also reach out to embrace the cultures of the students and their families. As a Native American friend of mine says, you will be the children's teacher when you learn how to accept their gifts.

Gradgrind sees school as a small factory in which elite managers make decisions for the passive hands. This is also his model for politics. Does this sound familiar? Dickens, by contrast, sees education as taking part in a democratic community—groups of people who share imaginative participation. As a teacher on the side of the people, you need to make yourself a careful student of the care and feeding of small, provisional human communities, for these are where people learn to make cultural meaning together, to practice and create the people's culture. This is why John Dewey called schools "embryonic democracies" and why some of the old reformers called them "little commonwealths." Classroom communities require certain elements: learning to talk the talk, learning to listen respectfully, finding a voice, learning to make and criticize knowledge in a group, giving and taking, finding the blend of intellectual and emotional support that a good classroom group can provide, valuing the habits and skills of reading and writing that arise when speakers and writers and artists get responses from audiences and listeners and readers. The discipline that lasts comes from participation, and it is the discipline of freedom.

In practice, then, helping the people progress in cultural terms means the ongoing creation of provisional forms of community. In good schools, students are learning to make culture—the kind of broad, powerful, and purposeful meanings we associate with intellectual, artistic, scientific, and democratic communities—and to forge links between the kind of culture they are enacting in school and the cultures of their communities. In school subjects, they learn the discourse of many of the smaller worlds that make up the large world of culture, literacy, and the languages of math and science and the arts, as well as the logic of action required to go on making, remaking, and criticizing different kinds of community over a lifetime.

With her union background, my grandmother would warn you about Gradgrind's loneliness and the need for solidarity as an educational ideal. The Gradgrinds want you to stay isolated and to think of education and politics as mainly a matter of competition between individuals. Dickens and my grandmother tell you something different: that we are brothers and sisters, that we learn from one another, and that we will have to work out a common fate on a troubled and threatened planet. Not only that, but to the extent that we remain isolated, the Gradgrinds will prevail. Look at the way they have used the racial issue to divide the forces of democracy in the last 20 years.

Although individual students make the meanings, the business of taking part in culture always means participation in some kind of community, real or imagined. You are part of a music community, even when you play the guitar alone. Math skills and ideas have as their aim participation in the community of those who make, who "do," math. The old Greeks emphasized the communal side of math when they called it a performance art and—to our astonishment today—linked it with such communal arts as theater and dancing. They would be amazed to hear that we make kids study math solo, rather than reasoning together as a group.

I emphasize the community angle not to slight the individual—all education has to balance individual and social aims—but to stress the way that the individuality we prize so deeply in our students emerges from what they learn through community encounters with others, their families, peers, and teachers. Mr. Gradgrind doesn't get this. He preaches rugged individualism but is at bottom an enemy of true individuality. But students who haven't learned to listen won't have much of a chance of finding their distinctive voices; nor will students who have never spoken in class about something that really matters to them or made some significant choices at some important points about their own learning.

My grandmother's generation was in love with the idea of growth. It's easy to see the importance of growth for students, but how about for you? When you start teaching, you do not know enough, but you are also not culturally developed enough to be a model for your students. This might be particularly true if you come from a family that never had much access to "high" culture. Even if you got a lot of "culture," is it really yours, or is it a ragbag of secondhand experiences and unexplained views? How do you help your kids build the rainbow bridges back and forth? How can you sell them on literacy if you yourself don't read much and don't enjoy books? What about your identity as a teacher? What about the struggle for democracy? You might like the picture of the teacher going out to meet the people, but what do you really have to offer? This is a harsh question, but you have a big responsibility if you are signing up as a teacher. How do you start the lifetime work of becoming a practical intellectual who can help the people progress culturally?

The question of your own cultural development may in the end be the big question about your future as a teacher. With some attention, I think that you can begin to see how democracy is the underlying issue in our society today, and how education reflects a wider, worldwide struggle. It may be more difficult to see the democratic cultural challenge: to see that a lively discussion of *Frog and Toad* in the second grade is one step toward a people's culture. A vision helps, but it needs to come alive daily in your teaching practice. How can you start to become a practical intellectual who is able to bring culture to the people's children and able to accept their gifts back? This will never be easy. But don't despair, you aren't dead yet. There are lots of ways to begin expanding your own possession of culture, ranging from exploring your roots to developing your own literacies and your acquaintance with ideas, traditions, and symbols in a host of realms. My grandmother, with her message of solidarity, would urge you not to go it alone, to join up with other teachers and reach out to people in your community. Your own ability to nourish a learning community in your classrooms will be helped immeasurably if you yourself inhabit—and help create—genuine learning communities outside of class. The things you want for your students—the development of culture, interests, identities, and a voice—are all things that you need as a teacher. One or two genuine interests to share with kids are worth their weight in gold. Finding one or two ways to link your teaching to the wider struggle for democracy will show you the meaning of your work. Read Herbert Kohl's *Back to Basics* to begin to get a sense that history and democratic tradition are resources to draw on in the work of teaching. Learn something about your own history, because that can give you an important angle on where you stand in relation to culture making.

Culture is like—is another name for—growth and development and education itself. Like history, it has no end. Generations of thoughtful teachers have taken part in the long struggle. Now, just your luck, it's your turn. All the best.

* * *

P. S. I call you "Josie" because that's what W. E. B. Du Bois calls his student in his sketch of himself as a teacher in the rural South in *The Souls of Black Folk*. Josie has all the life and vitality of the people and craves a formal education, which she never gets, dying young. Du Bois was the young teacher going out to meet the people, and Josie was the people meeting the teacher. Both had something to offer in the exchange. The result for Du Bois was the complex educational goal in *The Souls of Black Folk:* to learn the ways and the powers of the wider culture represented by school learning and the classics, but to keep your soul and know your roots. Du Bois was the spiritual granddaddy of the civil rights generation—he died just as the 1963 March on Washington was taking place—but his vision of a democratic culture awaits our work. I know that the dreadful premature harvest of young Josies has not stopped, but I like to think that some are making their way into teaching, like you.

2

Selection From *Accident, Awareness, and Actualization*

Nel Noddings

Nel Noddings is a former high school math teacher and one of the country's most distinguished educational philosophers. The following selection is taken from a larger autobiographical account about her work as a teacher, philosopher, and feminist. Noddings was a mathematics major in college and always wanted to teach high school. When she began teaching, however, there were no secondary jobs available and she instead got a job teaching sixth grade. Her experiences teaching younger children were to have a profound effect on her.

Later in this book, we include a piece by Noddings outlining her belief that education and teaching must ultimately involve a philosophy of care. In this selection, she makes clear that students have individual needs that cannot be met only by the academic curriculum and high test scores.

As you read Noddings's (1997) work, consider the following questions:

1. What should be the aims and purposes of education? Whose aims and purposes should be met—the student's or the society's? Are their needs incompatible?

2. What is the difference between teaching and nurturing? Do most schools, as they currently operate, truly meet the needs of students?

When I finished college, no high school teaching jobs were available. Luckily, I had obtained an emergency elementary certificate, and so I was given a position teaching sixth grade. This was one of the most fortuitous accidents of my career as an educator. I thought I would hate teaching all that baby stuff. After all, I was trained as a high school math teacher, and I wanted to teach geometry and trigonometry. A wonderful thing happened. All the reading that started with Miss Christ and continued ever after became directly useful. All the fascination with Greece and Rome, with explorers and colonists, with maps and dates and charts and details swept over me in a great wave of childhood revisited. For example, in Miss Baker's seventh grade, I had written a play-script for Dickens's *A Christmas Carol*. I looked it over and found it adequate to direct my sixth graders in the school Christmas play.

These kids and I had such a good time that we stayed together for seventh and eighth grades. Each year we did the school play. We started a school paper and a safety patrol. We had class elections and planned activities democratically. Jim often stopped in after school and played basketball with the boys. Three of my boys were fatherless, and Jim went to Boy Scout father and son dinners with them. We taught the kids to dance. We went on hikes with them. I taught them to sing in parts. We did loads of art work. We read "Evangeline" and memorized quotations from it and from a host of other sources. The father of one of my boys greeted my husband on the train one morning with, "The pen is mightier than the sword!" I know I taught them math, too, but it was dull stuff compared with the other things we did. So far as I can tell after years of reflection, I wasn't really like any of my beloved teachers. Without giving up the enormous love I had for them, I was still doing things my own way and learning from my husband (an engineer who is terrific with kids) and from the kids themselves.

How did my first students do on achievement tests? Of course the school authorities were concerned about this. Was this group of children deprived because they did not go to junior high as all the other children in the district did? Apparently not; their achievement scores were the same as those of the junior high kids. However, their special teachers (they spent half a day a week at the junior high for classes such as shop, home ec, art, and music) rated them far higher on every affective measure. They were more cooperative, happier, friendlier, and more creative than their junior high peers. Both those years I was disappointed that they didn't do *better* than the junior high kids on the achievement tests but, with a fuller awareness now, I realize the results were just fine.

At the end of those lovely years, when Jim and I were about to move back to our childhood community with our first daughter, and I was preparing to take a high school job, I applied for a permanent teaching credential. I was told by a bureaucrat in the state department of education that I could not have one because my elementary credential had been good for only one year. She said, "You should not even have been paid for those two years." That woman knew nothing of my experience in those two years. She didn't even ask; she thought she was protecting the children of New Jersey from the sure evils that accompany teaching without a proper credential. Perhaps it is not surprising that today I have little interest in "professional" standards, teacher accreditation, and the host of stuffy, silly, and rigid regulations endorsed in the name of accountability. What a weak word that is anyway! When you teach kids for several years, you take on *responsibility* not only for their academic growth but for their growth as whole human beings. To induce that sense of truly awesome responsibility in teachers, we must give teachers respect and freedom and allow them to experience the joy that goes with the responsibility. That joy arises out of continuous learning and out of the reciprocal relationships in which both teacher and students grow.

Next, in the chain of fateful accidents that structured my life, came parenthood. Our first child was, in many ways, like me. She turned the house upside down with intellectual curiosity—books, science experiments, artwork, and creative writing everywhere. In her college years as a math major, she would often start telephone conversations with, "Mother, consider the following." And there would follow a mathematical problem of some kind, not a recitation of the week's social events.

However, we did not have just one child. We had five, and then we adopted five more. There were several influences in this decision. Believe it or not, we were deeply influenced by *Cheaper by the Dozen,* the story of the Gilbreth family. We, too, wanted a large family, but we became concerned with the population explosion (to which we had already contributed) and decided to extend our family by adoption. Jim had spent almost two years in Korea while he was in the army and came to love Korean kids. Both of us were greatly impressed by Pearl Buck and her work with Amer-Asian children. Thus, over a period of time, three Amer-Asian boys joined the family. And somewhere along the way, two teenage girls just "joined up" and became part of the family, too.

Experience with a large family of very different kids reinforced what I had started to learn with my sixth graders: People have widely different talents and interests. I had, for most of my early life, valued academic talent above all others. After all, consider what I had to do to earn my A in high school math! I think that, with some encouragement, I could have become an intellectual snob *magna cum laude,* but I was saved from that fate by a wonderful bunch of kids—kids who loved animals, played the piano, trumpet, and clarinet, danced, drew and painted, composed poetry, repaired old radios, made dresses and draperies, cooked, and played poker. We had an Eagle Scout and a couple of boys who would not even consider scouting. We had math majors and kids who hated math. We had two kids who demonstrated against the Vietnam War and one who joined the Air Force at that time (but, fortunately, did not go to Vietnam). They argued with one another about duty, decency, and democracy and brought home to us literally and forcefully how reasonable and decent people can differ and how lack of tolerance for ideological differences can lead to tragedy. Jim and I were both deeply opposed to that stupid and destructive conflict (the Vietnam War), but we also had great sympathy for the young men—just boys really, as in all wars—who felt that serving was their duty. I don't see how anyone could raise a large, diverse family without learning a lasting appreciation for the breadth of human talent and without acquiring a tragic sense of life. No cause but life itself could be great enough to sacrifice the beautiful possibilities in these young lives. When one comes to such a realization, there are no "sides"—just kids killing one another, kids who, through a different accident of fate, could have been members of my family or my sixth grade.

Again, it is no surprise that, in my current work, I urge educators to consider the full range of student capacities and ethicists to consider the full range of human response. Human beings are not just rational mechanisms. Indeed, as Miguel Unamuno (1954) pointed out:

> Man is said to be a reasoning animal. I do not know why he has not been defined as an affective or feeling animal. Perhaps that which differentiates him from other animals is feeling rather than reason. More often I have seen a cat reason than laugh or weep. Perhaps it weeps or laughs inwardly—but then perhaps, also inwardly, the crab resolves equations of the second degree. (p. 3)

Thus, although I believe that designing new and better curriculums for science and math education is an important task, I am disheartened when colleagues see nothing more urgent and even embrace the dreadful goal that our children must be "number one" in math and science by the year 2000. When kids are killing one another, when children are bearing children with no sense of how to raise them, when one in ten (or perhaps one in seven) children is on welfare, what can we be thinking in urging such a concentration on math and science? I am reminded here of Jerome Bruner's modest and insightful observation after the structure of the disciplines movement, in which he played such an important role, had produced so many rich and creative curriculums. Looking at the plight of our inner cities, he said simply, "Curriculum is not the answer." This does not mean, of course, that curriculum cannot be *part* of the answer, but curriculum theorists and designers today must look beyond the rigor, beauty, and internal structures of their disciplines. Schooling must address the real problems of contemporary life.

Much of what we are striving for today in education is guided by a well-intentioned but deeply flawed conception of equality. Because academic math has for so long been a gatekeeper for higher education, many of us believe all students should be exposed to it. Policymakers are not satisfied with counseling and granting opportunities. They want to prove their commitment by forcing all kids to take algebra and geometry. A few see that most adults do not in fact use algebra in their professional or private lives, and so they talk about a "new" algebra—mathematical study that will have relevance and induce an admirable, analytic habit of mind. But surely there are other subjects that might also induce admirable habits of mind if students were allowed to immerse themselves in them. Why not question math's status as a gatekeeper instead of forcing everyone to study it?

There are at least two strong arguments against forcing all students to take algebra. (Notice that I say "take," not "study" or "learn," because one cannot force people to study or learn.) Both arise, for me, out of the personal experiences I have been describing. First, many kids—probably most—are just not inclined toward serious mathematics. Common sense should direct us to memories of our own school days. How many of our friends really liked math? How many understood it? As a teacher, I could always get some honest achievement out of most of my students, and good teachers all over the country do this year after year. But probably only 20 to 30 percent of our students really understand what it's all about, and 10 percent or so should be studying math in far greater depth than we allow now. We are so bound and determined to achieve equality that we ignore reality, and, paradoxically, we commit a great sin against equality itself. We confuse equality with sameness.

Human talents are wonderfully broad, and, if we are really concerned with equality, those talents should be treated with equal respect. Students need to understand what it means to live in a mathematicized world, which means that they need to know something about the political and social uses of mathematics, but it is not clear how much mathematics they must be able to do in order to achieve this understanding. Indeed they might learn the mathematics they need better through the study of social problems that really interest them.

At bottom the present crusade for equality is deeply, although not intentionally, disrespectful. It aims to cast all students in the mold of a traditional, successful, white male—of a hypothetical male really, for most actual, even affluent, boys have not fitted the mold comfortably. In talking this way, I seem to be in the minority today, but prominent educators in the past urged us to think about what we are doing when we force the same curriculum on everyone. John Dewey, in *Democracy and Education,* said of education:

> The general aim translates into the aim of regard for individual differences among children. Nobody can take the principle of consideration of native powers into account without being struck by the fact that these powers differ in different individuals. The difference applies not merely to their intensity, but even to their quality and arrangement. As Rousseau said: "Each individual is born with a distinctive temperament. . . . We indiscriminately employ children of different bents on the same exercises; their education destroys the special bent and leaves a dull uniformity. Therefore after we have wasted our efforts in stunting the true gifts of nature we see the short-lived and illusory brilliance we have substituted die away, while the natural abilities we have crushed do not revive." (p. 116)

My perspective on aims and equality has been deeply influenced by the work of John Dewey, but it has also been formed by reflection on my life as a mother, student, mathematics teacher, and philosopher. The personal dimension has, perhaps, been more important than any philosophical argument. . . .

3

Respect, Liking, Trust, and Fairness

Kathleen Cushman

In this selection from *Fires in the Bathroom,* Kathleen Cushman (2004) interviews students about their perceptions of teachers and their interactions with students. What is made clear from the very beginning of the piece is that life in the classroom is a two-way process that involves the teacher interacting with students. While this point seems perfectly obvious, it is often forgotten in personal accounts and in the research literature, where the emphasis is usually on the teacher's perspective. What is particularly interesting about this piece is how it provides the reader with the opportunity to understand the feelings of the students with whom teachers are working with on a day-to-day basis.

The students Cushman interviews provide invaluable suggestions for both beginning and experienced teachers. They provide suggestions on how to make sure that teachers have the respect of their students and on whether it is important for students to like their teacher or for their teacher to like them. Much of the essay deals with techniques for building mutual respect and trust in the classroom and discusses the bargains and agreements that need to be made between teachers and students so that the classroom can run smoothly.

NOTE: Cushman, K. (2004). *Fires in the bathroom: Advice for teachers from high school students* (pp. 17–35). New York: The New Press.

As you read Cushman's work, consider the following questions:

1. What do teachers need to do to gain the respect of their students?

2. Is being liked by students necessary in order to work well with them? Should teachers be their students' friends?

3. Do teachers need to like their students?

4. What boundaries do teachers need to establish with their students?

5. What role does fairness play in the instruction of students?

6. What are the basic things that students expect from their teachers?

"If you see the teacher respect students, you'll follow that role model."

In the high school classroom, respect and trust travel a two-way street between teacher and student—and have everything to do with learning. Students say that if a teacher sets a steady example of fairness and respect they respond positively whether or not they like a teacher personally. If they trust a teacher to do the job with competence and without bias, they are willing to fulfill their part of the deal: to pay attention, do the work, and play by the rules.

There was this guy who coached track. If he told you to do twenty laps and the guys were complaining, he would say: "Okay, do five." If you were tired, he would say, "Okay, you can stop." He would take you out for pizza after practice. He was a cool coach; they all loved him. But when the time for the meets came, they never won anything. So they got a new coach. The new coach, if he says, "Do fifty laps," and they say, "We don't wanna," he'll say, "Oh, no? Then do fifty-two!" They hated him because he made them work so hard. But when the time for the meets came, they won every single time. They learned the difference between respecting and liking.—ALEXIS

Being able to trust your teacher and be trusted is important. One student in my school was homeless. The principal wasn't like, "Let's go to your house and talk to your mom." He was like, "If you need a safe place to stay, I know someone you can talk to." He doesn't want you to feel embarrassed. When they have teacher conferences, he does not tell other people private things you have told him. If you're gay, if you're getting beat up, if you're not eating, if you're dealing with identity problems, you can tell him! Because you *know* that it is affecting your work. You can talk about it with him, and he'll keep giving you chances, even if you keep messing up. If going to homework lab after school doesn't work, he'll try something else.—ALEXIS

How can new high school teachers, who sometimes look and feel quite close to their students in age, strike that balance of respect, trust, and fairness? How does mutual respect in high school show itself—and what, if anything, does it have to do with how much a student and teacher like each other? What builds trust between teachers and students, and what breaks it down? At a time when students are just developing into adults, how much leeway do they need to make mistakes?

I'm not adult enough to get a job and have my own apartment, but I'm adult enough to make decisions on my own, know right from wrong, have ideas about the world. That's why it's hard to be a teenager—it's like a middle stage.—VANCE

If I have to go to the bathroom, and you tell me not to go, I'm going to go anyway. I'm not trying to be disrespectful, but certain teachers ask me to do something that compromises myself, and I'll say no. It has its effects—then you don't call on me, or you have an expression on your face. You're attacking me back in class. You shouldn't show that it bothers you. It shouldn't have to show in front of other students. Don't ignore me. I'm a student. Yeah, I should have respected you, but you're thirty or forty years old, an adult—you should rise above it, not continue the animosity. No teacher should be rolling their eyes at me.—ALEXIS

One group of student co-authors made up the following rules of thumb they thought applied equally to teachers and students:

If You're Looking for Respect . . .

Show up on time.

Take your responsibility seriously, whatever it is. Do what you agreed to do.

Don't insult people's intelligence.

Respect others' right to a separate identity, even if it's not the one you choose.

Don't assume you know everything about someone.

Be careful what you say. Don't make jokes until you know people well enough.

Do Students Need to Like a Teacher?

Everyone likes some people better than others, including students and teachers. But in general kids want teachers to put good teaching ahead of popularity.

It's okay if kids hate you at first. If you care about your teaching, we'll get past that. We're not going to be receptive to someone so quickly—we're kind of young in our thinking.—MIKA

To a certain extent you have to have a personality that students respond to. But that doesn't mean you have to be our best friend, because that will cause our education to suffer. I hate to admit it, but respect and authority are part of the job. Kids expect adults to give us directions and boundaries, but it's a balance.—VANCE

Students often like a teacher who has something in common with them, who seems approachable, or who is closer to their generation and more familiar with youth culture. Though they don't need to know a lot about a teacher's private life, they appreciate a degree of openness and humor.

I relate to one teacher well and a lot of people don't. She is somewhat like me (very sarcastic and moody at times), and I think that's why we click. We talk like we're buddies, and she's always encouraging me.—ALEXIS

The teacher should fill out the same questionnaire and share his answers with the students. Let them laugh at him a little. There's nothing like laughing at a teacher.—LAURALIZ

Liking a teacher can help with learning.

It kind of ruins a subject if you don't like the teacher. I never liked history at all. But this year I have a really cool teacher, and so even if it's hard, even if I don't do well on tests, I'm starting to like it more.—BOSUNG

I really hate calculus, but I really like the teacher so I really work hard and do my homework.—TIFFANY

I have to somewhat like the teacher to be able to learn—to know I can go to that person and ask for help when I need it, and he will be okay with it. —LAURALIZ

But most students are also ready to learn from teachers they may not like on a personal level. Whether or not they like them, they gain more from teachers who care about their material and commit themselves to students' learning.

I don't have to act like I like you, and you don't have to act like you like me, in order for me to learn and you to teach. [I don't like] the way my math teacher teaches, but I know that the way he comes into a classroom, he wants the students to leave knowing math. This makes me open my mind to what he has to say and how he's trying to say it. I'm going to learn whether or not the teacher and I are friends. As long as a teacher is real and the student is real and they are acting in a respectful way, there can be a give-and-take relationship with information.—MIKA

I liked my Spanish teacher most. She was a good teacher but she would get off the subject and talk about other things—she was very easily distracted. She was funny and I like funny teachers. But I learned more from my global studies teacher. He is a great teacher—very serious and strict. He really cares about students; you can tell he likes to teach. He sticks to the subject. It wasn't easy to distract him. When he's done with the lesson he'll make one joke and that will be it—and it will relate to the subject.—LAURALIZ

Must Teachers Like Students?

It matters to students that teachers like being in their company.

It's not as important for a teacher to like the students as it is for the students to think the teacher likes them. Students feel more comfortable and motivated in classes where they think the teacher likes them.—DARYL

But when teachers appear to like some students more than others, they feel uncomfortable, whether or not they count among the favored.

I would rather not know if I'm a teacher's favorite. It puts me in a weird position. When we're having a test or something, other students will come up to me and say, "Why don't you ask if we can not have it—she likes YOU."—TIFFANY

My French teacher has a very disturbing habit of calling some of his students his "advanced" students. This gives those that are not "advanced" a feeling of lesser value, and feelings of anger come up. He creates a barrier between himself and students, and even between students in the class.—BOSUNG

If teachers don't like students, the students can also tell, and it affects their learning. Even the suspicion that a teacher holds a bias sometimes grows into students feeling that they can't do anything right.

If the teacher doesn't like you, they won't say, "You can do it," or push you to your full potential. If you miss a day at school, they won't say what you missed and help you out.—MONTOYA

My friend said one little thing, and now that's the end of her. The teacher wrote her off, so she has a zero now and I have a 65 and we have done nothing different.—LAURALIZ

Most students would rather stay somewhere in the middle, not singled out for favor or disfavor. They may not feel comfortable making a personal connection until after a course has ended.

> When I'm their student, I go to them for help and nothing else—it's just something I have. After I'm not their student anymore, I might go to them just to talk; I tell them how my new teacher is, and how I like my new class.—MARIBEL

The Importance of Self-Respect

Students respect teachers who are comfortable with themselves. Even when teachers come from a different background than students do, if they convey self-respect, kids will respond.

> A student has enough common sense to see something in the teacher that they connect with. The teacher doesn't have to throw it to them—the student will choose to make the connection because they see it.—ALEXIS

> The teacher has to not be afraid to show himself, and at the same time maintain a boundary. Don't try to look like me, talk like me, dress like me, put your hair in cornrows. The minute you try to broadcast about yourself in order to make a connection with the kid, that's the minute it fails, because we can sniff out that kind of thing. If you just keep teaching, you will eventually reach someone. We'll put in the effort to connect with you.—VANCE

And they want teachers to act like adults, confident and authoritative.

> If you start as an authority figure, the relationships will come. You can get friendly later on. And you can be friendly and still be strict. You have to let them know that you're not one of their peers.—BOSUNG

> If you are too friendly with the students, when things get out of control and you try to get authoritative, they're like, "yeah, whatever," and don't pay any attention.—TIFFANY

Fairness Builds Trust and Respect

Students know that by coming to school they are making a bargain with teachers, and they want it to be a fair one. Here's how they define it:

The Bargain We Make with Teachers

If you will . . .	Then we will . . .
Show you know and care about the material	Believe the material can be important for us to learn
Treat us as smart and capable of challenging work	Feel respected and rise to the challenge of demanding work
Allow us increasing independence but agree with us on clear expectations	Learn to act responsibly on our own, though we will sometimes make mistakes in the process
Model how to act when you or we make mistakes	Learn to take intellectual risks; learn to make amends when we behave badly
Show respect for our differences and individual styles	Let you limit some of our freedoms in the interest of the group
Keep private anything personal we tell you	Trust you with information that could help you teach us better

Whether they are "hard" or "easy" teachers, the adults who win student trust and respect are the ones perceived as scrupulously fair in carrying out this usually unspoken bargain. From the very first day, students are alert for signals of whether the teacher will uphold it—and that will largely determine whether they in turn will do their part. Our students listed the following things they hope their teachers will do:

Let us know what to expect from you and the class.

When you ask us about ourselves on the first day, answer our questions, too. You don't have to reveal anything you consider private (like whether you have a girlfriend/boyfriend), but we should know certain things from the start. Do you give a zero when homework is not turned in on time? Do you count class participation as part of the final grade?

Some Things We Want to Know on the First Day

What will we be studying or doing during this course?

What can we expect for pop quizzes, tests, essays, or projects?

Do you give a lot of homework?

What is your grading system?

Is this class going to be fun? If not, what will make it interesting?

Will you be available to help us outside class?

Know your material.

It feels like we're being punished when the teacher doesn't know the subject well enough to help students. The student has to move on the next year to a higher level, and they'll be stumped in the next year. It's kind of not fair.—ANDRES

I had a math and chemistry teacher that didn't know either subject. If you were quiet, you got an A, and if you were talking, you wouldn't do well. It kind of makes me angry in a way, because when you get to college you'll be stuck. It's okay for a teacher to learn, but they shouldn't take your time to learn it.—MAHOGANY

Push us to do our best—

I had a math teacher who was always on your case: "Write out the problem, turn in your work, you can do it." I didn't like the way he pushed me. But later I thought he was a good teacher—the little things, like "make sure you don't forget to write it all out"—those are the things you need to remember.—DIANA

My algebra teacher, when I got a C in his class, he was upset. He just pushed me to keep my head outa them boys and into the books. He made me go to tutoring after school to keep my grades up.—PORSCHE

—and push us equally.

I have a teacher who pushes the "good" students a lot more than the not-so-good students. Like when a straight-A student doesn't do the work, he'll give that person lectures, but when a lower-grade student doesn't do the work, he'll just give up, like he didn't expect it anyway.—DIANA

Some teachers give more of themselves to students who succeed rather than fail. It feels like they're saying, "You're not worth my time because I'm dealing with students who have more potential than you." I don't feel that "go-go-go!" from them.—ALEXIS

Do your part.

You have teachers that are not even responsible. They're not even in class—they leave you there. They give you the assignment and just walk around the halls.—PORSCHE

One teacher made us redo an assignment that I was sure that I had already done, then claimed that we had done it all wrong, just to cover up for the fact that he had lost the assignments. It was an insult to my pride, a waste of time, and a blatant lie. "Because I said so," or "Because I am the teacher," are also not good explanations for punishments. Teachers must be clear and fair, or students will be hurt or angry.—BOSUNG

Make sure everyone understands.

Give the slower students among us a chance without putting them on the spot.

When you have a question, it's better if the teacher comes and stands by your desk instead of saying "What do you need?" from across the room.—PORSCHE

[Some teachers] don't care whether you're smart or dumb. They don't talk to you; if you're failing a class they don't ask you "What's the matter?" They let you fail, and they don't give you makeup work.—MONTOYA

Grade us fairly.

If someone gives you a bad grade, they should tell you exactly why. I have this Spanish teacher that grades Latino kids so hard it's impossible for them to get A's no matter how hard you try.—DIANA

Sometimes [favoritism] shows in their opinions on papers and comments on grades—which is the worst thing, because students always compare their grades with each other.—MARIBEL

Am I Playing Favorites? A Reflective Exercise for Teachers

Pick out a representative mix of students from your class. Using copies of this questionnaire or blank pages in a notebook or journal, answer the following questions.

Student's name _____

Things I like about the student
Personal choices (clothes, hair, posture, language, cooperation)

Academic choices (does work, participates)

Things that annoy me about the student
Personal choices (clothes, hair, posture, language, rule-breaking)

Academic choices (does work, participates)

Positive attention I paid the student today *(circle any that apply)*

- Called on in an encouraging way
- Asked how things are going
- Trusted with an important responsibility
- Asked his or her thoughts on a question that matters
- Acknowledged good work or helpful contribution by student
- Responded to something in the student's writing

Negative attention I paid the student today

- Used sarcasm in class to make my point with the student
- Criticized in class
- Did not offer specific encouragement to speak
- Imposed behavior sanctions (gave detention, sent to office, etc.)

Most recent grade(s) I gave the student _____

After you have completed the questionnaire for several students, look over the results and reflect in writing on the following questions:

1. Did students with lower grades have more "personal choices" that annoyed me?

2. Did students with higher grades receive more positive attention from me?

3. What could I do to increase positive attention to students whose choices annoy me?

Understand that we make mistakes.

Because of something that happened in ninth grade, she won't sit down with me and talk to me about anything. So I do the same back to her—I don't smile at her or respect her. Teachers need to make allowance for the fact that we change from year to year and even from week to week. Sometimes I'm just acting hotheaded, I need to clear the air and then come back and apologize. I can acknowledge the things I do wrong.—ALEXIS

We're some moody-ass people right now!—MIKA

We're growing.—VANCE

Don't denigrate us, especially in public. One teacher would say out loud, "You're getting a D," or other negative things in front of other students, disrespecting them.—MAHOGANY

I respect this one teacher, but I feel like she doesn't respect me. She'll say things in front of the class that make me feel bad, like "you didn't do this" or "you did this wrong."—DIANA

Keep your biases to yourself.

This gay kid in my class was putting something on his lips, and the teacher said, "You don't need to put on lip gloss in class!" If a girl put on lip gloss in class, he wouldn't say that. Then the boys in class felt like they could laugh at that kid. If the teacher could make comments, they felt like they could, too.—TIFFANY

By the looks of a kid, some teachers think he'll be a troublemaker. People say, "They're black, they do drugs," that kind of thing. If the teacher judges kids like that, the kids start saying the teacher's racist and they have less respect for that teacher.—MARIBEL

Don't treat us like little kids.

Teenagers don't think of themselves as children, even from the ninth grade. Teachers should realize that they're working with kids who feel that they are somewhat adults and don't like to be treated as little kids, even though in actuality they are kids. In my mind you're not my parent, you're my teacher. That line goes but so far. Don't overstep your boundary.—ALEXIS

Part of a teacher's job is giving teenagers the practice at that independence—not just controlling the kids in their classes but actually giving them more ability to try things out for themselves.—MAHOGANY

Listen to what we think.

Some teachers have a way of making themselves more approachable. They do not seem like hard, old teachers who sternly instruct the class; a student can go up and carry out a conversation without feeling awkward. This gives the class a more comfortable and accepting atmosphere to learn in.—BOSUNG

Sometimes my teachers ask me things like, "What grade do you think I'm going to give you if you didn't do the work?" Then they get upset if I seem to actually be thinking of what the answer might be. A lot of times I'm not interested in the work.—DIANA

We Wish a Teacher Would Ask

you like extra credit?

Will you be able to do homework over the weekend?

How would you like to make up your homework/projects?

How are you feeling—do you want to do your work right now, or for homework?

Do you need a ride to and from school?

Do you have lunch money?

What could I be doing to help you learn better?

Care what's going on with us.

Some teachers start to fill a void that maybe isn't being addressed at home. Teachers are our de facto parents for the seven or so hours you're with them. I don't really have a father, so I guess it's important talking to a guy who seems to know what's going on in the world, respects you, knows what's going on with you.—VANCE

School lets you find some adults you can connect with. There might be something really important, like pregnancy, that you can't talk to your parents about, but you know you have to talk to adults about. I have one of these relationships with my adviser. I think I trust him because I see him so often; he's my teacher for two classes, and I have a free [period] with him.—ANDRES

Don't betray our confidences.

You want to be able to trust a teacher. You don't want to be telling them your problem and then have them go to other teachers and say you have a problem, or tell your mom you should see a psychiatrist. Some teachers, it's like you tell them something and then there's a microphone attached to them.—PORSCHE

If you have that trust with a teacher, it could go kind of wrong. They might look down on you because you did something that you're not telling other people. It makes you wonder if it will affect how you do in their class.—ANDRES

Sometimes the chance to stand in each other's shoes can build respect between teachers and students.

In the very beginning of the class, our teacher had us write for homework one night about how we would teach a history class if we were teachers. She didn't use what I wrote down, but it got the students to recognize how hard it was to teach it.—HILARY

One day we had to plan a lesson. She gave us a topic, and we had to research it and make a lesson plan. Each day the students got to teach, and we got to see where she was coming from, in terms of having everyone in the class pay attention and learn from you. That changed our class a lot—now every time we get disruptive, she reminds us how we felt in that situation.—MAHOGANY

Fairness Affects Classroom Behavior

A teacher's fairness, trust, and respect have a lot of influence on how students feel about themselves and about their teachers. But they also have an important effect on students' behavior in the classroom.

The worst thing for a teacher is to be considered unfair, because students then try to take advantage of it. If you're the favorite one, you think you can get away with certain things. If you're the "down" one, sometimes you can shut yourself off, or try to control the class instead of the teacher.—MARIBEL

If you hurt me with your words, I'm gonna say or do something that I know is gonna hurt you.—ALEXIS

Summary

How to Show Respect, Trust, and Fairness

- Let us know what to expect from you and from the class.
- Know your material.
- Push us to do our best—and push us equally.
- Do your part.
- Make sure everyone understands.
- Grade us fairly.
- Understand that we make mistakes.
- Don't denigrate us.
- Keep your biases to yourself.
- Don't treat us like little kids.
- Listen to what we think.
- Care what's going on with us.
- Don't betray our confidences.

PART II

Beginning to Teach

4. A Negro Schoolmaster in the New South
   W. E. B. Du Bois

5. Selection From *36 Children*
   Herbert Kohl

6. Selection From *Educating Esmé: Diary of a Teacher's First Year*
   Esmé Raji Codell

Teachers have a somewhat unusual perspective as professionals. Their involvement with their clientele is very personal and intense. They typically spend the entire year with a single group of students, and then when the year is done, they start over with an entirely new group of people. Each year they have to begin again, reestablish their authority, and gain the trust of the people with whom they are working.

There are few more stressful moments in a teacher's career than teaching the first day of school. This is a particular challenge the first time one teaches, but it is hard even for experienced teachers who have many classes and years behind them. Walking into a classroom at the beginning of the year with a new class involves learning about one's students, setting rules and boundaries, and beginning to understand what can or cannot be done in a specific learning environment.

One needs to go cautiously at the beginning of the school year. There is an old axiom in the teaching literature about "not smiling until Christmas." The idea is that one should not give up too much control in the first few months of working with a class. The idea is probably a good one, if not taken to too much of an extreme.

The following chapter includes selections from W. E. B. Du Bois (1968) account of teaching for the first time in a rural African American school in the late 1880s, "A Negro Schoolmaster in the New South;" Herb Kohl's (1968) *36 Children,* in which he describes his first day of teaching students in a Harlem slum school in the mid-1960s; and Esmé Raji Codell's (1999) account of teaching in an inner-city public school in Chicago, *Educating Esmé.*

Further Readings: Lucia Downing (1868–1945) provides an extremely interesting account of working as a young teacher in a one-room school in rural Vermont. She was 14 years old and had little experience when she began teaching in 1882. Her experience was consistent with other 19th-century accounts of teachers in one-room schools. See Lucia B. Downing, "Teaching in the Keeler 'Deestrict' School," *Vermont Quarterly, A Magazine of History, XIX*(4), 233–40. For a history of one-room schools in the United States, read Andrew Gulliford's *America's Country Schools* (1996).

For a description more similar to Du Bois' experience, see Booker T. Washington's description of being a beginning teacher included in *My Larger Education: Being Chapters from My Experience* (Doubleday, Page, 1911).

Linking to Popular Culture: The experience of teaching in a one-room school-house with African American children is beautifully depicted in Pat Conroy's autobiographical novel, *The Water is Wide* (New York: Bantam Books, 1972), which was based on his work as a teacher on Daufuskie Island off the coast of South Carolina. In 1974, the movie *Conrack* (starring John Voight) was made based on the book. In 2006, Jeff Hephner and Alfre Woodard starred in a remake of the film that was produced as a Hallmark Hall of Fame television movie. In many regards, the issues and tensions faced by Du Bois as a teacher in his country school at the end of the 1880s were the same as those faced by Conroy in a similar setting in the mid-1960s.

One of the funniest works describing the first year of teaching is Bel Kaufman's novel *Up the Down Staircase* (Barker, 1965). The novel is set in a fictional high school in New York City. While somewhat dated, it provides insights into the process of entering the classroom for the first time. A 1967 film starring Sandy Dennis, based on the novel, is worth viewing. *To Sir, with Love* (1967) provides a sentimental introduction to the experiences of a British West Indian teacher working in a working-class school in London. The film is based on a novel of the same title by E. R. Braithwaite. Michelle Pfeiffer is the star of the 1995 movie *Dangerous Minds,* which is based on LouAnne Johnson's autobiographical account of teaching bussed-in inner-city students in an affluent school in East Palo Alto, California.

Often, films like the ones mentioned above tell us more about society's perceptions of teachers and schools than about the actual work of teachers. In the case of Michelle Pfieffer's character in *Dangerous Minds,* many of the activities she undertakes as a teacher would simply not be allowed in a well run school. Not able to reach her students through the traditional curriculum, for example, she drops the school's required materials, after only the first day, and proceeds to teach her students about poetry by having them read the lyrics to Bob Dylan songs. Later in the film she takes her students on a field trip to an amusement park without school or parental clearance, and then, to protect a young male student involved in a gang rivalry, she has him stay overnight in her apartment (she is a divorced single woman). Actions such as these are not acceptable from a professional point of view. (She could have arranged for her student to be protected by the police or a school administrator without having him stay with her.) Consider, while viewing some of these films, how teachers and their work are a socially constructed phenomenon in American culture.

On YouTube's (http://www.youtube.com/) search engine, type "one-room schoolhouses" to find numerous sources on one-room schools, including vintage films from the 1930s of children in classrooms, as well as various documentaries on the restoration and preservation of one-room schools in the United States. For historical photographs of one-room schools in the United States, go to the Prints and Photographs Catalogue at the Library of Congress (http://www.loc.gov/rr/print/catalog.html) and type "one-room school" into the photographic search engine.

References

Gulliford, A. (1996). *America's country schools*. Niwot: University Press of Colorado.

Codell, E. R. (1999). *Educating Esmé: Diary of a teacher's first year.* Chapel Hill, NC: Algonquin Books.

Du Bois, W. E. B. (1968). *The autobiography of W. E. B. DuBois: A soliloquy on viewing my life from the last decade of its first century.* New York: International.

Kohl, H. (1968). *36 children.* New York: New American Library.

4

A Negro Schoolmaster in the New South

W. E. B. Du Bois

W. E. B. Du Bois was the first African American to receive his doctorate from Harvard University. He was a pioneer political activist, historian, and sociologist. The following piece was originally published in the January 1899 issue of the *Atlantic Monthly* magazine and later as Chapter IV "Of the Meaning of Progress," in his classic 1903 book *The Souls of Black Folk*. In this essay, Du Bois recounts his experience teaching in a rural Tennessee school during two summer vacations from Fisk University in 1886 and 1887.

Raised in Western Massachusetts, Du Bois' experience as a beginning teacher in rural Tennessee introduced him, for the first time, to the experiences of poor rural Blacks in the South. During this experience, he "touched the very shadow of slavery." Du Bois (1968) explained his experience in this way:

> I determined to know something of the Negro in the country districts; to go out and teach during the summer vacation. I was not compelled to do this, for my scholarship was sufficient to support me, but that was not the point. I had heard about the country in the South as the real seat of slavery. I wanted to know it. I walked out into east Tennessee ten or more miles a day until at last in a little valley near

NOTE: Du Bois, W. E. B. (1899, January). A Negro schoolmaster in the New South. *Atlantic Monthly, LXXXIII*, 99–104.

Alexandria I found a place where there had been a Negro public school only once since the Civil War; and there for two successive terms during the summer I taught at $28 and $38 a month. (p. 114)

Du Bois' experience fits into the category of what Henry Giroux (1992) describes as teachers being "border crossers." Like an anthropologist or sociologist, Du Bois went into what was essentially a foreign community, adapted to it, carefully observed, and learned. It was his first encounter with the poverty of the Black rural south. In his autobiography, he writes the following:

All the appointments of my school were primitive; a windowless log cabin, hastily manufactured benches; no blackboard; almost no books; long, long distances to walk. And on the other hand, I heard the sorrow songs sung with primitive beauty and grandeur. I saw the hard, ugly drudgery of country life and the writhing of landless ignorant peasants. I saw the race problem at its lowest terms. (p. 117)

Du Bois was clearly transformed by this experience as a beginning teacher. His personal account provides a unique insight into the idea of the teacher crossing cultural borders. As you read Du Bois' essay, keep in mind the following questions:

1. To what extent does teaching for the first time in almost any community provide an opportunity for reflection and growth?

2. How does teaching involve the crossing of social and cultural borders?

References

Du Bois, W. E. B. (1968). *The autobiography of W. E. B. Du Bois: A soliloquy on viewing my life from the last decade of its first century.* New York: International.

Giroux, H. (1992). *Border crossings: Cultural workers and the politics of education.* New York: Routledge.

Once upon a time I taught school in the hills of Tennessee, where the broad dark vale of the Mississippi begins to roll and crumple to greet the Alleghanies. I was a Fisk student then, and all Fisk men think that Tennessee—beyond the Veil—is theirs alone, and in vacation time they sally forth in lusty bands to meet the country school commissioners. Young and Happy, I too went, and I shall not soon forget that summer, ten years ago.

First, there was a teachers' Institute at the county-seat; and there distinguished guests of the superintendent taught the teachers fractions and spelling and other mysteries,—white teachers in the morning, Negroes at night. A picnic now and then, and a supper, and the rough world was softened by laughter and song. I remember how—But I wander.

4. A Negro Schoolmaster in the New South

There came a day when all the teachers left the Institute, and began the hunt for schools. I learn from hearsay (for my mother was mortally afraid of fire-arms) that the hunting of ducks and bears and men is wonderfully interesting, but I am sure that the man who has never hunted a country school has something to learn of the pleasures of the chase. I see now the white, hot roads lazily rise and fall and wind before me under the burning July sun; I feel the deep weariness of heart and limb, as ten, eight, six miles stretch relentlessly ahead; I feel my heart sink heavily as I hear again and again, "Got a teacher? Yes." So I walked on and on,—horses were too expensive,—until I had wandered beyond railways, beyond stage lines, to a land of "varmints" and rattlesnakes, where the coming of a stranger was an event, and men lived and died in the shadow of one blue hill. Sprinkled over hill and dale lay cabins and farmhouses, shut out from the world by the forests and the rolling hills toward the east. There I found at last a little school. Josie told me of it; she was a thin, homely girl of twenty, with a dark brown face and thick, hard hair. I had crossed the stream at Watertown, and rested under the great willows; then I had gone to the little cabin in the lot where Josie was resting on her way to town. The gaunt farmer made me welcome, and Josie, hearing my errand, told me anxiously that they wanted a school over the hill; that but once since the war had a teacher been there; that she herself longed to learn,—and thus she ran on, talking fast and loud, with much earnestness and energy.

Next morning I crossed the tall round hill, lingered to look at the blue and yellow mountains stretching toward the Carolinas; then I plunged into the wood, and came out at Josie's home. It was a dull frame cottage with four rooms, perched just below the brow of the hill, amid peach trees. The father was a quiet, simple soul, calmly ignorant, with no touch of vulgarity. The mother was different,—strong, bustling, and energetic, with a quick, restless tongue, and an ambition to live "like folks." There was a crowd of children. Two boys had gone away. There remained two growing girls; a shy midget of eight; John, tall, awkward, and eighteen; Jim, younger, quicker, and better looking; and two babies of indefinite age. Then there was Josie herself. She seemed to be the centre of the family: always busy at service or at home, or berry-picking; a little nervous and inclined to scold, like her mother, yet faithful, too, like her father. She had about her certain fineness, the shadow of an unconscious moral heroism that would willingly give all of life to make life broader, deeper and fuller for her and hers. I saw much of this family afterward, and grew to love them for their honest efforts to be decent and comfortable, and for their knowledge of their own ignorance. There was with them no affectation. The mother would scold the father for being so "easy;" Josie would roundly rate the boys for carelessness; and all knew that it was a hard thing to dig a living out of a rocky side hill.

the school. I remember the day I rode horseback out to the com-
house, with a pleasant young white fellow, who wanted the white
road ran down the bed of a stream; the sun laughed and the water
jingled, and we rode on. "Come in," said the commissioner,—"come in. Have
a seat. Yes, that certificate will do. Stay to dinner. What do you want a
month?" Oh, thought I, this is lucky; but even then fell the awful shadow of
the Veil, for they ate first, then I—alone.

The schoolhouse was a log hut, where Colonel Wheeler used to shelter his
corn. It sat in a lot behind a rail fence and thorn bushes, near the sweetest
of spring. There was an entrance where a door once was, and within, a massive rickety fireplace; great chinks between the logs served as windows.
Furniture was scarce. A pale blackboard crouched in the corner. My desk
was made of three boards, reinforced at critical points, and my chair, bor-
rowed from the landlady, had to be returned every night. Seats for the
children,—these puzzled me much. I was haunted by a New England vision
of neat little desks and chairs, but, alas, the reality was rough plank benches
without backs, and at times without legs. They had the one virtue of making naps dangerous,—possibly fatal, for the floor was not to be trusted.

It was a hot morning late in July when the school opened. I trembled when
I heard the patter of little feet down the dusty road, and saw the growing row
of dark solemn faces and bright eager eyes facing me. First came Josie and her
brothers and sisters. The longing to know, to be a student in the great school
at Nashville, hovered like a star above this child woman amid her work and
worry, and she studied doggedly. There were the Dowells from their farm
over toward Alexandria: Fanny, with her smooth black face and wondering
eyes; Martha, brown and dull; the pretty girl wife of a brother, and the
younger brood. There were the Burkes, two brown and yellow lads, and one
haughty-eyed girl. Fat Reuben's little chubby girl came, with golden face and
old gold hair, faithful and solemn. 'Thenie was on hand early,—a jolly, ugly,
good-hearted girl, who slyly dipped snuff and looked after her little bow-
legged brother. When her mother could spare her, 'Tildy came,—a midnight
beauty, with starry eyes and tapering limbs; and her brother, correspondingly
homely. And then the big boys: the hulking Lawrences; the lazy Neills, unfa-
thered sons of mother and daughter; Hickman, with a stoop in his shoulders;
and the rest.

There they sat, nearly thirty of them, on the rough benches, their faces
shading from a pale cream to a deep brown, the little feet bare and swing-
ing, the eyes full of expectation, with here and there a twinkle of mischief,
and the hands grasping Webster's blue-back spelling-book. I loved my
school, and the fine faith the children had in the wisdom of their teacher was
truly marvelous. We read and spelled together, wrote a little, picked flowers,

sang, and listened to stories of the world beyond the hill. At times the school would dwindle away, and I would start out. I would visit Mun Eddings, who lived in two very dirty rooms, and ask why little Lugene, whose flaming face seemed ever ablaze with the dark red hair uncombed, was absent all last week, or why I missed so often the inimitable rags of Mack and Ed. Then the father, who worked Colonel Wheeler's farm on shares, would tell me how the crops needed the boys; and the thin, slovenly mother, whose face was pretty when washed, assured me that Lugene must mind the baby. "But we'll start them again next week." When the Lawrences stopped, I knew that the doubt of the old folks about book-learning had conquered again, and so, toiling up the hill, and getting as far into the cabin as possible, I put Cicero pro Archia Poeta in the simplest English with local applications, and usually convinced them—for a week or so.

On Friday nights I often went home with some of the children; sometimes to Doc Burke's farm. He was a great, loud, thin Black, ever working, and trying to buy the seventy-five acres of hill and dale where he lived; but people said that he would surely fail, and the "white folks would get it all." His wife was a magnificent Amazon, with saffron face and shining hair, uncorseted and barefooted, and the children were strong and beautiful. They lived in a one-and-a-half-room cabin in the hollow of the farm, near the spring. The front room was full of great fat white beds, scrupulously neat; and there were bad chromos on the walls, and a tired centre-table. In the tiny back kitchen I was often invited to "take out and help" myself to fried chicken and wheat biscuit, "meat" and corn pone, string beans and berries. At first I used to be a little alarmed at the approach of bedtime in the one lone bed-room, but embarrassment was very deftly avoided. First, all the children nodded and slept, and were stowed away in one great pile of goose feathers; next, the mother and the father discreetly slipped away to the kitchen while I went to bed; then, blowing out the dim light, they retired in the dark. In the morning all were up and away before I thought of awakening. Across the road, where fat Reuben lived, they all went outdoors while the teacher retired, because they did not boast the luxury of a kitchen.

I liked to stay with the Dowells, for they had four rooms and plenty of good country fare. Uncle Bird had a small, rough farm, all woods and hills, miles from the big road; but he was full of tales,—he preached now and then,—and with his children, berries, horses, and wheat he was happy and prosperous. Often, to keep the peace, I must go where life was less lovely; for instance, 'Tildy's mother was incorrigibly dirty, Reuben's larder was limited seriously, and herds of untamed bedbugs wandered over the Eddingses' beds. Best of all I loved to go to Josie's, and sit on the porch, eating peaches, while the mother bustled and talked: how Josie had bought the sewing-machine;

how Josie worked at service in winter, but that four dollars a month was "mighty little" wages; how Josie longed to go away to school, but that it "looked like" they never could get far enough ahead to let her; how the crops failed and the well was yet unfinished; and, finally, how "mean" some of the white folks were.

For two summers I lived in this little world; it was dull and humdrum. The girls looked at the hill in wistful longing, and the boys fretted, and haunted Alexandria. Alexandria was "town,"—a straggling, lazy village of houses, churches, and shops, and an aristocracy of Toms, Dicks, and Captains. Cuddled on the hill to the north was the village of the colored folks, who lived in three or four room unpainted cottages, some neat and homelike, and some dirty. The dwellings were scattered rather aimlessly, but they centered about the twin temples of the hamlet, the Methodist and the Hard-Shell Baptist churches. These, in turn, leaned gingerly on a sad-colored schoolhouse. Hither my little world wended its crooked way on Sunday to meet other worlds, and gossip, and wonder, and make the weekly sacrifice with frenzied priest at the altar of the "old-time religion." Then the soft melody and mighty cadences of Negro song fluttered and thundered. I have called my tiny community a world, and so its isolation made it; and yet there was among us but a half-awakened common consciousness, sprung from common joy and grief, at burial, birth, or wedding; from a common hardship in poverty, poor land, and low wages; and, above all, from the sight of the Veil that hung between us and Opportunity. All this caused us to think some thoughts together; but these, when ripe for speech, were spoken in various languages. Those whose eyes thirty and more years before had seen "the glory of the coming of the Lord" saw in every present hindrance or help a dark fatalism bound to bring all things right in His own good time. The mass of those to whom slavery was a dim recollection of childhood found the world a puzzling thing: it asked little of them, and they answered with little, and yet it ridiculed their offering. Such a paradox they could not understand, and therefore sank into listless indifference, or shiftlessness, or reckless bravado. There were, however, some such as Josie, Jim, and Ben,— they to whom War, Hell, and Slavery were but childhood tales, whose young appetites had been whetted to an edge by school and story and half-awakened thought. Ill could they be content, born without and beyond the World. And their weak wings beat against their barriers,— barriers of caste, of youth, of life; at last, in dangerous moments, against everything that opposed even a whim. The ten years that follow youth, the years when first the realization comes that life is leading somewhere,—these were the years that passed after I left my little school. When they were past, I came by chance once more to the walls of Fisk University, to the halls of the chapel of melody. As I lingered there in the joy and pain of meeting old school friends, there swept over me a sudden longing to pass again beyond the blue hill, and to see the homes and the school of other days, and to learn how life had gone with my school-children; and I went.

Josie was dead, and the gray-haired mother said simply, "We've had a heap of trouble since you've been away." I had feared for Jim. With a cultured parentage and a social caste to uphold him, he might have made a venturesome merchant or a West Point cadet. But here he was, angry with life and reckless; and when Farmer Durham charged him with stealing wheat, the old man had to ride fast to escape the stones which the furious fool hurled after him. They told Jim to run away; but he would not run, and the constable came that afternoon. It grieved Josie, and great awkward John walked nine miles every day to see his little brother through the bars of Lebanon jail. At last the two came back together in the dark night. The mother cooked supper, and Josie emptied her purse, and the boys stole away. Josie grew thin and silent, yet worked the more. The hill became steep for the quiet old father, and with the boys away there was little to do in the valley. Josie helped them sell the old farm, and they moved nearer town. Brother Dennis, the carpenter, built a new house with six rooms; Josie toiled a year in Nashville, and brought back ninety dollars to furnish the house and change it to a home.

When the spring came, and the birds twittered, and the stream ran proud and full, little sister Lizzie, bold and thoughtless, flushed with the passion of youth, bestowed herself on the tempter, and brought home a nameless child. Josie shivered, and worked on, with the vision of schooldays all fled, with a face wan and tired,—worked until, on a summer's day, some one married another; then Josie crept to her mother like a hurt child, and slept—and sleeps.

I paused to scent the breeze as I entered the valley. The Lawrences have gone; father and son forever, and the other son lazily digs in the earth to live. A new young widow rents out their cabin to fat Reuben. Reuben is a Baptist preacher now, but I fear as lazy as ever, though his cabin has three rooms; and little Ella has grown into a bouncing woman, and is ploughing corn on the hot hillside. There are babies a plenty, and one half-witted girl. Across the valley is a house I did not know before, and there I found, rocking one baby and expecting another, one of my schoolgirls, a daughter of Uncle Bird Dowell. She looked somewhat worried with her new duties, but soon bristled into pride over her neat cabin, and the tale of her thrifty husband, the horse and cow, and farm they were planning to buy.

My log schoolhouse was gone. In its place stood Progress, and Progress, I understand, is necessarily ugly. The crazy foundation stones still marked the former site of my poor little cabin, and not far away, on six weary boulders, perched a jaunty board house, perhaps twenty by thirty feet, with three windows and a door that locked. Some of the window glass was broken, and part of an old iron stove lay mournfully under the house. I peeped through the window half reverently, and found things that were more familiar. The blackboard had grown by about two feet, and the seats were still without backs. The county owns the lot now, I hear, and every year there is a session of school. As I sat by the spring and looked on the Old and the New I felt glad, very glad, and yet—

After two long drinks I started on. There was the great double log house on the corner. I remembered the broken, blighted family that used to live there. The strong, hard face of the mother, with its wilderness of hair, rose before me. She had driven her husband away, and while I taught school a strange man lived there, big and jovial, and people talked. I felt sure that Ben and 'Tildy would come to naught from such a home. But this is an odd world; for Ben is a busy farmer in Smith County, "doing well, too," they say, and he had cared for little 'Tildy until last spring, when a lover married her. A hard life the lad had led, toiling for meat, and laughed at because he was homely and crooked. There was Sam Carlon, an impudent old skinflint, who had definite notions about niggers, and hired Ben a summer and would not pay him. Then the hungry boy gathered his sacks together, and in broad daylight went into Carlon's corn; and when the hard-fisted farmer set upon him, the angry boy flew at him like a beast. Doc Burke saved a murder and a lynching that day.

The story reminded me again of the Burkes, and an impatience seized me to know who won in the battle, Doc or the seventy-five acres. For it is a hard thing to make a farm out of nothing, even in fifteen years. So I hurried on, thinking of the Burkes. They used to have a certain magnificent barbarism about them that I liked. They were never vulgar, never immoral, but rather rough and primitive, with an unconventionality that spent itself in loud guffaws, slaps on the back, and naps in the corner. I hurried by the cottage of the misborn Neill boys. It was empty, and they were grown into fat, lazy farm hands. I saw the home of the Hickmans, but Albert, with his stooping shoulders, had passed from the world. Then I came to the Burkes' gate and peered through; the inclosure looked rough and untrimmed, and yet there were the same fences around the old farm save to the left, where lay twenty five other acres. And lo! the cabin in the hollow had climbed the hill and swollen to a half-finished six-room cottage.

The Burkes held a hundred acres, but they were still in debt. Indeed, the gaunt father who toiled night and day would scarcely be happy out of debt, being so used to it. Some day he must stop, for his massive frame is showing decline. The mother wore shoes, but the lionlike physique of other days was broken. The children had grown up. Rob, the image of his father, was loud and rough with laughter. Birdie, my school baby of six, had grown to a picture of maiden beauty, tall and tawny. "Edgar is gone," said the mother, with head half bowed,—"gone to work in Nashville; he and his father couldn't agree."

Little Doc, the boy born since the time of my school, took me horseback down the creek next morning toward Farmer Dowell's. The road and the stream were battling for mastery, and the stream had the better of it. We splashed and waded, and the merry boy, perched behind me, chattered and laughed. He showed me where Simon Thompson had bought a bit of ground and a home; but his daughter Lana, a plump, brown, slow girl, was not there. She had married as man and a farm twenty miles away. We wound on down the stream till we came to a gate that I did not recognize, but the boy insisted that it was "Uncle Bird's." The farm was fat with the growing crop. In that little valley was a strange stillness as I rode up; for death and marriage had stolen youth, and left age and childhood there. We sat and talked that night, after the chores were done. Uncle Bird was grayer, and his eyes did not see so well, but he was still jovial. We talked of acres bought,—one hundred and twenty-five,—of the new guest chamber added, of Martha's marrying. Then we talked of death: Fanny and Fred were gone; a shadow hung over the other daughter, and when it lifted she was to go to Nashville to school. At last we spoke of the neighbors, and as night fell Uncle Bird told me how, on a night like that, 'Thenie came wandering back to her home over yonder, to escape the blows of her husband. And next morning she died in the home that her little bow-legged brother, working and saving, had bought for their widowed mother.

My journey was done, and behind me lay hill and dale, and Life and Death. How shall man measure Progress there where the dark-faced Josie lies? How many heartfuls of sorrow shall balance a bushel of wheat? How hard a thing is life to the lowly, and yet how human and real! And all this life and love and strife and failure,—is it the twilight of nightfall or the flush of some faint-dawning day?

Thus sadly musing, I rode to Nashville in the Jim Crow car.

5

Selection From *36 Children*

Herbert Kohl

Herbert Kohl is the author of more than 30 books on education. A philosophy major at Harvard as an undergraduate, he began his teaching career in Harlem in 1962. Since he began his career nearly 50 years ago, he has been among the most thoughtful voices in American education, often taking to task American schools for failing to fully meet the needs of minority students.

Kohl published *36 Children,* his account of teaching in a slum school in Harlem, in 1968. It is a classic account that describes not only the failure of the public school to meet the needs of poor minority students but also the possibilities that are open to a determined teacher who wants to make a difference in the lives of the students he or she teaches.

In this selection, Kohl (1968) writes about the first day of a new school year and working with the students in his class. There are expectations and fears on both sides. Both Kohl and the 36 children he has been assigned to work with approach each other cautiously. Kohl, who is White and middle-class, is working with students who are poor and Black. As the day progresses, boredom quickly sets in among the students as Kohl tries to connect with them. It all becomes a bit uncomfortable and frightening. He explains how, as he droned on, "the weight of Harlem and my whiteness and strangeness" began to hang in the air.

NOTE: "Teaching", from *36 Children* by Herbert Kohl, copyright © 1967 by Herbert Kohl. Used by permission of Dutton Signet, a division of Penguin Group (USA) Inc.

Kohl's experience on his first day points to the fact that simply being prepared in terms of lesson plans and rubrics is not enough to be an effective teacher. Going into a new classroom involves entering into new cultural territory. You must observe and listen carefully, adapt, and change as you begin to understand the complex reality of the classroom.

Kohl was eventually highly successful in his work with his 36 children, but it did not happen automatically, nor did the possibilities for what could be done seem that promising after the first day.

As you read the selection that follows consider the following questions:

1. To what extent must a teacher discover what his or her students are about and what their cultural roots are each time he or she teaches a new class?

2. What do students bring to the classroom? What does the teacher bring to the classroom?

3. How does one cope with the sense that one is not necessarily reaching one's students?

4. What do you do the night before you teach your second day?

My alarm clock rang at seven thirty, but I was up and dressed at seven. It was only a fifteen-minute bus ride from my apartment on 90th Street and Madison Avenue to the school on 119th Street and Madison.

There had been an orientation session the day before. I remembered the principal's words. "In times like these, this is the most exciting place to be, in the midst of ferment and creative activity. Never has teaching offered such opportunities . . . we are together here in a difficult situation. They are not the easiest children, yet the rewards are so great—a smile, loving concern, what an inspiration, a felicitous experience."

I remembered my barren classroom, no books, a battered piano, broken windows and desks, falling plaster, and an oppressive darkness.

I was handed a roll book with thirty-six names and thirty-six cumulative record cards, years of judgments already passed upon the children, their official personalities. I read through the names, twenty girls and sixteen boys, the 6–1 class, though I was supposed to be teaching the fifth grade and had planned for it all summer. Then I locked the record cards away in the closet. The children would tell me who they were. Each child, each new school year, is potentially many things, only one of which the cumulative record card documents. It is amazing how "emotional" problems can disappear, how the dullest child can be transformed into the keenest and the brightest into the most ordinary when the prefabricated judgments of other teachers are forgotten.

The children entered at nine and filled up the seats. They were silent and stared at me. It was a shock to see thirty-six black faces before me. No preparation helped. It is one thing to be liberal and talk, another to face something and learn that you're afraid.

The children sat quietly, expectant. Everything must go well; we must like each other.

Hands went up as I called the roll. Anxious faces, hostile, indifferent, weary of the ritual, confident of its outcome.

The smartest class in the sixth grade, yet no books.

"Write about yourselves, tell me who you are." (I hadn't said who I was, too nervous.)

Slowly they set to work, the first directions followed—and if they had refused?

Then arithmetic, the children working silently, a sullen, impenetrable front. *To talk to them, to open them up this first day.*

"What would you like to learn this year? My name is Mr. Kohl."

Silence, the children looked up at me with expressionless faces, thirty-six of them crowded at thirty-five broken desks. This is the smartest class?

Explain: they're old enough to choose, enough time to learn what they'd like as well as what they have to.

Silence, a restless movement rippled through the class. Don't they understand? There must be something that interests them, that they care to know more about.

A hand shot up in the corner of the room.

"I want to learn more about volcanoes. What are volcanoes?"

The class seemed interested. I sketched a volcano on the blackboard, made a few comments, and promised to return.

"Anything else? Anyone else interested in something?"

Silence, then the same hand.

"Why do volcanoes form?"

And during the answer:

"Why don't we have a volcano here?"

A contest. The class savored it, I accepted. Question, response, question. I walked toward my inquisitor, studying his mischievous eyes, possessed and possessing smile. I moved to congratulate him, my hand went happily toward his shoulder. I dared because I was afraid.

His hands shot up to protect his dark face, eyes contracted in fear, body coiled ready to bolt for the door and out, down the stairs into the streets.

"But why should I hit you?"

They're afraid too!

Hands relaxed, he looked torn and puzzled. I changed the subject quickly and moved on to social studies—How We Became Modern America.

"Who remembers what America was like in 1800?"

A few children laughed; the rest barely looked at me.

"Can anyone tell me what was going on about 1800? Remember, you studied it last year. Why don't we start more specifically? What do you think you'd see if you walked down Madison Avenue in those days?"

A lovely hand, almost too thin to be seen, tentatively rose.

"Cars?"

"Do you think there were cars in 1800? Remember that was over a hundred and fifty years ago. Think of what you learned last year and try again. Do you think there were cars then?"

"Yes . . . no . . . I don't know."

She withdrew, and the class became restless as my anger rose.

At last another hand.

"Grass and trees?"

The class broke up as I tried to contain my frustration.

"I don't know what you're laughing about—it's the right answer. In those days Harlem was farmland with fields and trees and a few houses. There weren't any roads or houses like the ones outside, or street lights or electricity. There probably wasn't even a Madison Avenue."

The class was outraged. It was inconceivable to them that there was a time their Harlem didn't exist.

"Stop this noise and let's think. Do you believe that Harlem was here a thousand years ago?"

A pause, several uncertain Noes.

"It's possible that the land was green then. Why couldn't Harlem also have been green a hundred and fifty or two hundred years ago?"

No response. The weight of Harlem and my whiteness and strangeness hung in the air as I droned on, lost in my righteous monologue. The uproar turned into sullen silence. A slow nervous drumming began at several desks; the atmosphere closed as intelligent faces lost their animation. Yet I didn't understand my mistake, the children's rejection of me and my ideas. Nothing worked, I tried to joke, command, play—the children remained joyless until the bell, then quietly left for lunch.

There was an hour to summon energy and prepare for the afternoon, yet it seemed futile. What good are plans, clever new methods and materials, when the children didn't—wouldn't—care or listen? Perhaps the best solution was to prepare for hostility and silence, become the cynical teacher,—untaught by his pupils, ungiving himself, yet protected.

At one o'clock, my tentative cynicism assumed, I found myself once again unprepared for the children who returned and noisily and boisterously avoided me. Running, playing, fighting—they were alive as they tore about the room. I was relieved, yet how to establish order? I fell back on teacherly words.

"You've had enough time to run around. Everybody please go to your seats. We have work to begin."

No response. The boy who had been so scared during the morning was flying across the back of the room pursued by a demonic-looking child wearing black glasses. Girls stood gossiping in little groups, a tall boy fantasized before four admiring listeners, while a few children wandered in and out of the room. I still knew no one's name.

"Sit down, we've got to work. At three o'clock you can talk all you want to."

One timid girl listened. I prepared to use one of the teacher's most fearsome weapons and last resources. Quickly white paper was on my desk, the blackboard erased, and numbers from 1 to 10 and 11 to 20 appeared neatly in two columns.

"We're now going to have an *important* spelling test. Please, young lady"—I selected one of the gossipers—"what's your name? Neomia, pass out the paper. When you get your paper, fold it in half, put your heading on it, and number carefully from one to ten and eleven to twenty, exactly as you see it on the blackboard."

Reluctantly the girls responded, then a few boys, until after the fourth, weariest, repetition of the directions the class was seated and ready to begin—I thought.

Rip, a crumpled paper flew onto the floor. Quickly I replaced it; things had to get moving.

Rip, another paper, rip. I got the rhythm and began quickly, silently replacing crumpled papers.

"The first word is anchor. The ship dropped an anchor. Anchor."

"A what?"

"Where?"

"Number two is *final*. *Final* means last, final. Number three is *decision*. He couldn't make a *decision* quickly enough."

"What decision?"

"What was number two?"

"*Final*."

I was trapped.

"Then what was number one?"

"*Anchor*."

"I missed a word."

"Number four is *reason*. What is the *reason* for all this noise?"

"Because it's the first day of school."

"Yeah, this is too hard for the first day."

"We'll go on without any comments whatever. The next word is ——"

"What number is it?"

"—— direction. What direction are we going? *Direction.*"

"What's four?"

The test seemed endless, but it did end at two o'clock. What next? Once more I needed to regain my strength and composure, and it was still the first day.

"Mr. Kohl, can we please talk to each other about the summer? We won't play around. Please, it's only the first day."

"I'll tell you what, you can talk, but on the condition that everyone, I mean *every single person in the room,* keeps quiet for one whole minute."

Teacher still had to show he was strong. To prove what? The children succeeded in remaining silent on the third attempt; they proved they could listen. Triumphant, I tried more.

"Now let's try for thirty seconds to think of one color."

"You said we could talk!"

"My head hurts, I don't want to think anymore."

"It's not fair!"

It wasn't. A solid mass of resistance coagulated, frustrating my need to command. The children would not be moved.

"You're right, I'm sorry. Take ten minutes to talk and then we'll get back to work."

For ten minutes the children talked quietly; there was time to prepare for the last half hour. I looked over my lesson plans: Reading, 9 to 10; Social Studies, 10 to 10:45, etc., etc. How absurd academic time was in the face of the real day. *Where to look?*

"You like it here, Mr. Kohl?"

I looked up into a lovely sad face.

"What do you mean?"

"I mean do you like it here, Mr. Kohl, what are you teaching us for?" *What?*

"Well, I . . . not now. Maybe you can see me at three and we can talk. The class has to get back to work. All right, everybody back to your seats, get ready to work."

She had her answer and sat down and waited with the rest of the class. They were satisfied with the bargain. Only it was I who failed then; exhausted, demoralized, I only wanted three o'clock to arrive.

"It's almost three o'clock and we don't have much time left."

I dragged the words out, listening only for the bell.

"This is only the first day, and of course we haven't got much done. I expect more from you during the year . . ." The class sensed the maneuver and fell nervous again. "Take out your notebooks and open to a clean page. Each day except Friday you'll get homework."

My words weighed heavy and false; it wasn't my voice but some common tyrant or moralizer, a tired old man speaking.

"There are many things I'm not strict about but homework is the one thing I insist upon. In my class everybody always does homework. I will check your work every morning. Now copy the assignment I'm putting on the blackboard, and then when you're finished, please line up in the back of the room."

What assignment? What lie now? I turned to the blackboard, groping for something to draw the children closer to me, for something to let them know I cared. *I did care!*

"Draw a picture of your home, the room you live in. Put in all the furniture, the TV, the windows and doors. You don't have to do it in any special way but keep in mind that the main purpose of the picture should be to show someone what your house looks like."

The children laughed, pointed, then a hand rose, a hand I couldn't attach to a body or face. They all looked alike. I felt sad, lonely.

"Do you have to show your house?"

Two boys snickered. *Are there children ashamed to describe their homes?* Have I misunderstood again? The voice in me answered again.

"Yes."

"I mean . . . what if you can't draw, can you let someone help you?"

"Yes, if you can explain the drawing yourself."

"What if your brother can't draw?"

"Then write a description of your apartment. Remember, *everybody always* does homework in my classes."

The class copied the assignment and lined up, first collecting everything they'd brought with them. The room was as empty as it was at eight o'clock. Tired, weary of discipline, authority, school itself, I rushed the class down the stairs and into the street in some unacknowledged state of disorder.

The bedlam on 119th Street, the stooped and fatigued teachers smiling at each other and pretending they had had no trouble with their kids relieved my isolation. I smiled too, assumed the comfortable pose of casual success, and looked down into a mischievous face, the possessed eyes of the child who had thought I would hit him, Alvin, who kindly and thoughtfully said: "Mr. Kohl, how come you let us out so early today? We just had lunch . . ."

Crushed, I walked dumbly away, managed to reach the bus stop and make my way home. As my weariness dissolved, I only remembered of that first day Alvin and the little girl who asked if I liked being "there."

6

Selection From
Educating Esmé

Diary of a Teacher's First Year

Esmé Raji Codell

Esmé Raji Codell's (1999) *Educating Esmé: Diary of a Teacher's First Year* recalls her first year as a teacher in a public school in Chicago. The wildly enthusiastic Codell's efforts on her first day contrast, in interesting ways, to Herbert Kohl's experience more than 30 years earlier in New York City. Humor and enthusiasm infect her approach and clearly propel her through the school year and its demands. The idea of the classroom as a fun place for both students and their teacher suggests some of the rewards involved in being a teacher on a day-to-day basis, as well as the obvious progress students have made by the end of the school year. As you read this selection, consider the following questions:

1. How important is setting the tone in a classroom? Are bulletin boards and other types of displays worth the effort? If yes, why?

2. How does humor work to the advantage of a teacher like Ms. Codell?

3. How does one best measure the progress one makes with students?

September 18

Sorry I haven't written. A lot has been going on, as you can probably imagine.

Setting up my classroom, at long last, was very exciting. I put up a bulletin board with a big red schoolhouse shape *without* windows (those would come later) that said, "New School . . . You're What Makes It Special." There was a tree covered with apples. Each apple had a number on it. *Thunk, thunk, thunk,* it was so gratifying, stapling it to the board. Then I had to arrange the chairs. I noticed other teachers arranging the desks so children would be sitting in cooperative, small groups. I kept thinking that that was politically correct, I should do it like that. But somehow it took all the romance out of the first day of school, when you're supposed to feel very formal and alien, a day when your thoughts are very new and personal. So I decided to be more traditional and put the desks in rows. Besides, I want to seem really mean for a while. I bought black pointy lace-up boots, like a witch, to wear for the first day, to add to the dramatic effect.

I put up another bulletin board that said, "Solving Conflicts: 1. Tell person what you didn't like. 2. Tell person how it made you feel. 3. Tell person what you want in the future. 4. Person responds with what they can do. Congratulations! You are a Confident Conflict Conqueror!" I didn't make this up. I learned it from a Jewish guy my age I observed teaching at a Good News Christian private school. We are going to have conflict resolution meetings every Friday, to be mediated eventually by the kids. I also put up a smiley-faced mobile of "Kind Words."

The third bulletin board I made was a cutout of King Kong on top of an aluminum-foil Empire State Building, with the caption "King Kong Says Reach for the Top!" and on the floors of the Empire State it says, "Listen," "Think," "Work carefully," and "Check your work." I left space to hang their best papers.

I made a "clothesline" with four articles of fake clothing made of poster board covered with ribbons and sequins and stuff, hung on a rope with clothespins. Each article of clothing has a pocket in back that holds either a fun puzzle or artwork activity or an at-your-desk game. Across the clothes is written "If . . . you . . . finish . . . early."

There is a spelling center with spelling games, a typewriter, an electric wiggle pen, a box of cornmeal and sponge letters with tempera paint for kids to practice their spelling words. There is also an art center with bins of new, juicy markers, craft books and real art books with pictures of naked people (isn't it nice to have already drawn in!), and goodies such as glitter, old wrapping paper, colored glues.

My *piece de resistance* is my 3D papier mache poster with five multieth-nic kids' heads sticking out that says, "Welcome to Cool School." One of the kids is wearing a real pair of purple sunglasses. I like the girl with steel-wool red hair. I had to make the kids' heads out of wire first. It took a lot of work to make, but it is gorgeous, if I do say so myself. If I was a kid and saw this, I would just die.

The older teachers shook their heads and told me my room looked over-stimulating, which means they are totally jealous because I have the most insanely beautiful classroom ever, of all time. Oh, God! I have beautiful por-traits of explorers over the chalkboard, the cloakroom has a cutout panorama of an international open-air market, and there's a learning center with flags of all nations. I'm sorry, this room is so fun it's sickening. I feel sorry for any kid who is not in this room.

So, First Day. As they entered, they each took a numbered apple off of the bulletin board and matched it to the numbered apples taped to the desks. This is how they were seated temporarily. I passed out my list of nec-essary supplies, in English and Spanish. Of the thirty kids, all were black except for about five Mexican kids and one girl who is from Pakistan and one from the Philippines. Then I looked them over and thought, *This is my destiny, to have this group of children before me. As they were growing aging to be fifth graders, I was training, and now we meet, in this unique place and time.* The moment felt holy.

I gave them my speech about how mean I was and how I've taught foot-ball players and cowboys and dinosaurs and Martians, so a few fifth graders aren't too challenging, but I need the money, so I'd give it a shot. I told them that they were going to work harder than they ever have in their whole lives, so if they want extra credit, they should get a head start on sweating. I told them if they didn't have their supplies by Monday, they already will have earned a check on their report card for preparedness. I showed them my one Golden Rule: "Treat others the way you would like to be treated;" written out in gold glitter.

Then I gave them red and white paper and showed them how to make a little book that looks like a window. Inside they each wrote and illustrated a little composition, "Old School, New School," about how they liked where they came from and how they felt coming here. Then I hung their work on the big red schoolhouse cutout on the bulletin board, so now the school had little windows you could open and read.

Here are two of my favorites:

"I was so scare I hide under the bed [drawing of two eyes under the bed]. And then I meet nice teacher [drawing of me with curly hair and pearls, smiling ear to ear—after all the trouble I went to be nasty!]:"

"My name is Samantha. And I like my old school because I liked old teachers from 0–4. When I first started school she was mean. But then when I got to know she was nice. And all the other teacher I thought was mean. But once got to know them they were nice. And now I's the New School with a new teacher. And she says she's the meanest teacher in the west but I know she's not. I think just saying that to make us good, kind."

November 19

The kids like the Greek myths. We've been studying them for a few weeks. They were impressed that Cronus ate his children. I think some of them have fathers who have dispositions like Cronus. They loved the story of the kidnapping of Persephone, especially when I ripped open the pomegranate, fruit of the dead, and red juice dribbled down my wrists. Ohhhhhh!

They are tracing and cutting out the shape of their bodies and coloring them in—creating themselves as their favorite gods. This dispelled some of their anger that none of the Greek gods were black. In the middle, they are attaching compositions of who is the god they can most relate to and why. I am waiting for a parent to accuse me of having them worship false idols. Mr. Turner walked in as all thirty-one kids were on the floor, laughing, cutting, and coloring in a fabulous mess. They didn't stop because he entered.

"There's no control!" he mourned.

"There absolutely is!" I raised my thumb, which is the signal for attention, and like a magic trick, within twelve seconds every mouth was closed, thirty-one thumbs were in the air to show they got my signal, and all eyes were on us.

"Just checking," I explained. The kids went back to work.

It's not that I'm so great or that they love me so much. It's just that I'm consistent, and they know if they do not follow my guidelines, I will be a dragon lady. Still, I loved seeing Mr. Turner's face just then.

January 7

This whole week at school has been very good. I kept waiting for something bad to happen, but nothing did. The only kind of bad thing: It was snowing so beautifully outside, first snow kind of snow, powdery, glittering, ivory, the neighborhood was frosted and perfect. So I took all thirty-one kids outside, just around the square block, to see which trees were deciduous and which were coniferous. I told Ms. Coil that I was going, but she didn't mention it to anyone. We left from the side door and tried to re-enter from the front door, but it was locked. Mr. Turner happened to be near the door. Wow! He spazzed that we were outside. The liability! etc. He comes goose-stepping over to the door. His face was all crumpled, his forehead in a pulled seam.

"Here comes that faggot," Vanessa remarked upon seeing his approach.

"Don't insult faggots," I countered.

I got reprimanded but played dumb. Ha-ha! Sky's the limit, since I bet this will be my only year teaching.

Today was especially cool. I got my Happy Box back, for one thing. Some kid said he found it in a public park, under a bush. I gave him the five dollar reward. The other teachers said I shouldn't have given him squat, that he probably took it in the first place. Even if he did, I think he's learned a valuable lesson about extortion, and that deserves to be rewarded.

The other fab thing was that the Slick Boys rap group came and did a Just Say No assembly at our school today. They had huge amps and "hoochie girls" rubbing their crotches and oscillating. It was great, of course, but I couldn't help thinking that school assemblies sure have changed since I was a kid. They did all their hip-hop dancing and blabbing incoherently into the microphones. Music was blaring at a deafening volume, but hey, rock and roll! They brought kids onstage to dance as they performed. I tried to get my kids into it. I was in the aisle, getting kids to clap along and root for them or whatever, when one of the rapper guys brought me by the hand onstage. Wow, the kids went bananas to see a teacher with the Slick Boys.

A roar went up, so I totally kicked it and did my *Soul Train* thing like I do at home! My class was laughing so hard, to see me do the "Humpty Dumpty"! Zykrecia shouted, "Madame Esmé got the moves! She got it going on!" and hopped onstage with me. When they saw us enjoying ourselves, a lot of other kids followed. It was my dream come true, I was an R&B pedagogue. I was very happy. The other teachers were kind of shocked, but what the hell! You only live once—in Western culture anyway.

January 11

Miss Clark is the special education teacher. She keeps a lot of charts with gold stars. She's blond and thin and gorgeous. She makes them brownies when they all master a multiplication table. Isn't that nice? The kids eat her alive.

She tried to do a whole class lesson on her own, to make it up to me for blowing off helping my class as much as she's supposed to. I was in the back of the room getting some paperwork done. "I'm invisible," I told them. "Treat Miss Clark like she's your homeroom teacher."

Unfortunately, they did. They weren't paying good attention and defied her, even though she kept saying please. Then she said, "Now we're going to do the nine-times tables."

"What'll you give us?" asked Kirk.

My mouth dropped open. I put down my pen.

Even more shockingly, Miss Clark answered, "Stickers."

"What'll you get! What'll you *get!*" I roared, suddenly becoming visible. "You'll get an education, that's what you'll get! Which is more than you deserve, for the rotten way you've been treating Miss Clark! You aren't getting *stickers,* you aren't getting *brownies,* you aren't getting *please and thank you,* you're getting to work, and you'll work double the assignment that Miss Clark gives you, I'll be checking on it. Now, who else wants to get something?"

Nobody else did. I thought I'd hear a chorus of tongue-clucking, but I didn't hear a peep. Everyone got to work. A couple of kids even quietly apologized as they passed Miss Clark to go to lunch.

Alone together, Miss Clark wept dainty tears from her luxurious lashes. "I just want them to like me," she squeaked.

"It's not our job to be liked," I reminded her. "It's our job to help them be smart." Secretly, I thought, Who gives a rat's ass if they like us? Sometimes I can hardly stand them!

June 28

Last day of school. Had the kids write letters to the next class of fifth graders. It was neat to see what the kids remembered most. I like Asha's letter:

The things you will learn are fractions, the preamble, the Bill of Rights, Beethoven, and explorers, enventers, learn about planets like Saturn. You also will learn about solar power. You might read *King Matt, Tikki Tikki Tembo, The Wish Giver, Number the Stars, The Empty Pot, The Hundred Dresses, What's So Funny Ketu, Herschel and the Hanukkah Goblins, The Sneetches, The Bat-Poet* and *The Big Orange Splot.*

The rules are no saying shut up or bad language.

You should be good in Madame Esme's class cause she can be real mean.

Zykrecia wrote:

In my class our rules are never say shut up to anyone, don't talk back to the teacher but we sometimes do it anyway and no chewing gum but we do that anyway. My advice is to try hard on your work and be real nice and listen and cooperate with your teacher and classmates . . . and just because someone's messing with you don't have to beat them up unless you want to.

Zowela:

If you guys are worried if she's mean don't be because she is one of the most nicest teacher I ever had. If your nice to her she will be nice to you. I am giving you my word that you will have a wonderful time in fifth grade. The teacher gives you jobs. Every week she changes your job. Let me tell you that my favorites are messenger, postal worker, lunch ticket passer, line captain, jokester. She read us this book that has about 300 pages called King Matt, maybe she will read it to you someday. One more thing that I know you will love is the Happy Box. If you answer a question that she thinks is hard you get it. It's filled with toys, stickers, bookmarks. Believe me, you will love this room.

Esther could barely write, she was crying nonstop and saying God bless me.

In the back of the room, Rochelle's mom, a really helpful parent, was working on a surprise for me. It was a gold scarf with all the children's signatures under the inscription:

Mme. Esmé;

You taught us:

math, spelling, to enjoy reading, science, art, music. To enhance our written words, to speak with good diction.

You taught us: to be kind to our brothers and sisters (mankind), how to hold our heads up high. To not just try but try our best.

You must wonder and ask, "Did I do O.K.?"

The answer is NO!!!—You did Great!

Of course, I cried. There was so much I wanted to say. But the sands of the hourglass fell, and they left me single file. . . .

PART III

Teaching as the Practice of Freedom

7. Selection From *Dumbing Us Down: The Hidden Curriculum of Compulsory Schooling*
   John Taylor Gatto

8. Engaged Pedagogy
   bell hooks

Why do people become teachers? As discussed earlier, for many it is a calling—one involving the need to serve and to nurture young people. For some, this can take the form of nurturing and helping students or actually involve working for social justice as an activist. For others, it is a means of gaining authority and power. Many people feel called to teaching as a profession; others come to it by accident or happenstance.

In this chapter, we look at writings by two different teachers—the first an experienced public school teacher, the second a university professor and cultural and feminist scholar. Both John Taylor Gatto (1992) and bell hooks (the pen name of Gloria Jean Watkins; 1994) are critical and reflective thinkers and social critics. Gatto spent his teaching career working in precollegiate instruction; hooks taught at the university level. Like Joseph Featherstone (1995), both consider teaching a political and social act, one involving the practice of freedom—a theme particularly emphasized in the selection by hooks.

Such an approach may seem perfectly obvious in a democratic society, but in fact it is a reality that may be rarer in schools than we would like to admit. More than a hundred years ago, the great French sociologist Emile Durkheim (1858–1917) (2005) concluded that schools are first and foremost institutions that exist for the benefit of the society of which they are a part. Essentially, their purpose is to create stable and compliant populations that will not necessarily challenge the existing social order and that will perpetuate the culture and its values. Such an idea, in many regards, challenges the principles inherent in a democracy in which personal freedom and equality are emphasized as part of the pursuit of democratic principles.

Theorists such as the Brazilian educator Paulo Freire (1921–1997), who bell hooks cites at length, maintain that teaching is a liberatory process—one ultimately involved in the practice of freedom. As such, teaching in a Freireian context is inherently democratic.

Further Readings: John Taylor Gatto's work, in many regards, represents a continuation of romantic critics of education and compulsory schooling such as Paul Goodman in his books *Growing Up Absurd* (Random House, 1960) and *Compulsory Mis-education* (Horizon Press, 1964) and Ivan Illich in *Deschooling Society* (Harper, 1971). The majority of Paulo Freire's most important ideas can be found in his book *The Pedagogy of the Oppressed* (Continuum, 2007), which was first published in 1970.

Linking to Popular Culture: The idea of teaching as the practice of freedom is a theme that shows up in numerous films. It can be seen at work in the previously discussed movie *Dead Poets Society,* a film about a teacher who attempts to construct a community in an oppressive environment. A popular personal account of using the classroom to emphasize the process of schooling as liberation is Erin Gruwell's book *The Freedom Writers Diary: How a Teacher and 150 Teens Used Writing to Change Themselves and the World Around Them* (Broadway Books, 1999), which became the basis of the 2007 movie of the same name. Nowhere is the idea of schools being oppressive and undemocratic institutions conveyed in a funnier way than in Matt Groening's (the creator of *The Simpsons*) cartoon book *School Is Hell* (Random House, 2007). Selections of Groening's cartoons are included in Chapter 19 of this work.

References

Durkheim, E. (2005). *Selected Writings on Education*. New York: Routledge.

Featherstone, J. (1995). Letter to a young teacher. In W. Ayers (Ed.), *To become a teacher.* New York: Teachers College Press.

Gatto, J. T. (1992). *Dumbing us down: The hidden curriculum of compulsory schooling.* Gabriola Island, BC: New Society.

hooks, b. (1994). *Teaching to transgress: Education as the practice of freedom.* New York: Routledge.

Selection From
Dumbing Us Down

The Hidden Curriculum of
Compulsory Schooling

John Taylor Gatto

John Taylor Gatto (1935–) is an author and former New York City and New York State Teacher of the Year. Critical of compulsory schooling, he is part of a tradition of romantic critics of schooling that extends back to the 1960s and includes figures such as Paul Goodman and Ivan Illich.

The following selection is taken from Gatto's 1992 book *Dumbing Us Down: The Hidden Curriculum of Compulsory Schooling*. In the essay that follows, Gatto describes growing up as a young boy along the banks of the Monongahela River in a simpler time than the one in which we live. He writes that he "learned to teach from being taught by everyone in town." In his memoir, he recalls how he gave up a successful career in the corporate world to enter the seemingly more problematic field of teaching.

Gatto's personal account brings home to the reader how a single teacher can make a difference in the life of a child. Describing a little girl named Milagros

NOTE: Gatto, J. T. (1992). *Dumbing us down: The hidden curriculum of compulsory schooling*. Gabriola Island, British Columbia, Canada: New Society; © 1992 John Taylor Gatto.com.

(a nonnative speaker of English) who had been misidentified as a poor reader, he confronts the bureaucracy of the school where he is teaching in order to have her assigned to an advanced class, one reflecting her true level of ability.

As you read Gatto's essay, keep in mind the following questions:

1. What role does community play in the teaching of children and the teaching of teachers?

2. Do some teachers have the potential to make more of a difference in the lives of children than others? If yes, what is it that makes them different?

3. What does Gatto mean when he says at the end of this selection, "Ah, Milagros, is it just possible that I was your Monongahela River?"

In the beginning I became a teacher without realizing it. At the time, I was growing up on the banks of the green Monongahela River forty miles southwest of Pittsburgh, and on the banks of that deep green and always mysterious river I became a student too, master of the flight patterns of blue dragonflies and cunning adversary of the iridescent ticks that infested the riverbank willows.

"Mind you watch the ticks, Jackie!" Grandmother Mossie would call as I headed for the riverbank, summer and winter, only a two-minute walk from Second Street, where I lived across the trolley tracks of Main Street and the Pennsylvania Railroad tracks that paralleled them. I watched the red and yellow ticks chewing holes in the pale green leaves as I ran to the riverbank. On the river I drank my first Iron City at eight, smoked every cigarette obtainable, and watched dangerous men and women make love there at night on blankets—all before I was twelve. It was my laboratory: I learned to watch closely and draw conclusions there.

How did the river make me a teacher? Listen. It was alive with paddle-wheel steamers in center channel, the turning paddles churning up clouds of white spray, making the green river boil bright orange where its chemical undercurrent was troubled; from shore you could clearly hear the loud *thump thump thump* on the water. From all over town young boys ran gazing in awe. A dozen times a day. No one ever became indifferent to them because nothing important can ever really be boring. You can see the difference, can't you? Between those serious boats and the truly boring spacecraft of the past few decades, just flying junk without a purpose a boy can believe in; it's hard to feign an interest even now that I teach for a living and would like to pretend for the sake of the New York kids who won't have paddle-wheelers in their lives. The rockets are dull toys children in Manhattan put aside the day after Christmas, never to touch again; the riverboats were serious magic, clearly demarcating the world of boys from the world of men. Levi-Strauss would know how to explain.

In Monongahela by that river everyone was my teacher. Daily, it seemed to a boy, one of the mile-long trains would stop in town to take on water and coal or for some mysterious reason; the brakeman and engineer would step among snot-nosed kids and spin railroad yarns, let us run in and out of box-cars, over and under flatcars, tank cars, coal cars, and numbers of other spe-cialty cars whose function we memorized as easily as we memorized enemy plane silhouettes. Once a year, maybe, we got taken into the caboose that reeked of stale beer to be offered a bologna on white bread sandwich. The anonymous men lectured, advised, and inspired the boys of Monongahela—it was as much their job as driving the trains.

Sometimes a riverboat would stop in mid-channel and discharge a crew, who would row to shore, lying their skiff to one of the willows. That was the excuse for every rickety skiff in the twelve-block-long town to fill up with kids, pulling like Vikings, sometimes with sticks instead of oars, to raid the "Belle of Pittsburgh" or "The Original River Queen." Some kind of natural etiquette was at work in Monongahela. The rules didn't need to be written down: if men had time they showed boys how to grow up. We didn't whine when our time was up—men had work to do—we understood that and scampered away, grateful for the flash of our own futures they had had time to reveal, however small it was. I was arrested three times growing up in Monongahela, or rather, picked up by the police and taken to jail to await a visit from Pappy to spring me. I wouldn't trade those times for anything. The first time I was nine, caught on my belly under a parked car at night, half an hour after curfew; in 1943 blinds were always drawn in the Monongahela Valley for fear Hitler's planes would somehow find a way to reach across the Atlantic to our steel mills lin-ing both banks of the river. The Nazis were apparently waiting for a worried mother to go searching for her child with a flashlight after curfew, then *whammo!* down would descend the Teutonic air fleet!

Charlie was the cop's name. Down to the lockup we went—no call to mother until Charlie diagrammed the deadly menace of Goering's Luftwaffe. What a geopolitics lesson that was! Another time I speared a goldfish in the town fishpond and was brought from jail to the library, where I was sen-tenced to read for a month about the lives of animals. Finally, on VJ Day—when the Japanese cried "Uncle!"—I accepted a dare and broke the window of the police cruiser with a slingshot. Confessing, I suffered my first encounter with employment to pay for the glass, becoming sweep-up boy in my grand-father's printing office at fifty cents a week. After I went away to Cornell, I saw Monongahela and its green river only one more time, when I went there after my freshman year to give blood to my dying grandfather, who lay in the town hospital, as strong in his dying as he had ever been in his living. In another room my grandmother lay dying. Both passed within twenty-four hours, my grandad, Harry Taylor Zimmer, Sr., taking my blood to his grave in the cemetery there. My family moved again and again and again, but in my own heart I never left Monongahela, where I learned to teach from being taught by everyone in town, where I learned to work from being asked to shoulder my share of responsibility, even as a boy, and where I learned to find adventures I made myself from the everyday stuff around me—the river and the people who lived alongside it.

In 1964, I was making a lot of money. That's what I walked away from to become a teacher. I was a copywriter on the fast track in advertising, a young fellow with a knack for writing thirty-second television commercials. My work required about one full day a month to complete, the rest of the time being spent in power breakfasts, after-work martinis at Michael's Pub, keeping up with the shifting fortunes of about twenty agencies in order to gauge the right time to jump ship for more money, and endless parties that always seemed to culminate in colossal headaches.

It bothered me that all the urgencies of the job were generated externally, but it bothered me more that the work I was doing seemed to have very little importance—even to the people who were paying for it. Worst of all, the problems this work posed were cut from such a narrow spectrum that it was clear that past, present, and future were to be of a piece: a twenty-nine-year-old man's work was no different from a thirty-nine-year-old man's work, or a forty-nine-year-old man's work (though there didn't seem to be any forty-nine-year-old copywriters—I had no idea why not).

"I'm leaving," I said one day to the copy chief.

"Are you nuts, Jack? You'll get profit sharing this year. We can match any offer you've got. Leaving for who?"

"For nobody, Dan. I mean I'm going to teach junior high school."

"When you see your mother next, tell her for me she raised a moron. Christ! Are you going to be sorry! In New York City we don't have schools; we have pens for lost souls. Teaching is a scam, a welfare project for losers who can't do anything else!"

Round and round I went with my advertising colleagues for a few days. Their scorn only firmed my resolve; the riverboats and trains of Monongahela were working inside me. I needed something to do that wasn't absurd more than I needed another party or a new abstract number in my bankbook.

And so I became a junior high school substitute teacher, working the beat from what's now Lincoln Center to Columbia, my alma mater, and from Harlem to the South Bronx. After three months the dismal working conditions, the ugly rooms, the torn books, the repeated instances of petty complaints from authorities, the bells, the buzzers, the drab teacher food in the cafeterias, the unpressed clothing, the inexplicable absence of conversation about children among the teachers (to this day, after twenty-six years in the business, I can honestly say I have never once heard an extended conversation about children or about teaching theory in any teachers' rooms I've been in) had just about done me in.

In fact, on the very first day I taught I was attacked by a boy waving a chair above his head. It happened in the infamous junior school Wadleigh, on 113th Street. I was given the eighth grade typing class—seventy-five students and typewriters—with this one injunction: "Under no circumstances are you to allow them to type. You lack the proper license. Is that understood?" A man named Mr. Bash said that to me. It couldn't have taken more than sixty seconds from the time I closed the door and issued the order not to type for one hundred and fifty hands to snake under the typewriter covers and begin to type. But not all at once-that would have been too easy. First, three machines began to *clack clack* from the right rear. Quick, who were the culprits? I would race to the corner screaming *stop!*—when suddenly, from behind my back, three other machines would begin! Whirling as only a young man can do, I caught one small boy in the act. Then, to a veritable symphony of machines clicking, bells ringing, platens being thrown, I hoisted the boy from his chair and announced at the top of my foolish lungs I would make an example of this miscreant.

"Look out!" a girl shouted, and I turned toward her voice just in time to see a large brother of the little fellow I held heading toward me with a chair raised above his head. Releasing his brother, I seized a chair myself and raised it aloft. A standoff! We regarded each other at a distance of about ten feet for what seemed forever, the class jeering and howling, when the room door opened and Assistant Principal Bash, the very man who'd given the no-typing order, appeared.

"Mr. Gatto, have these children been typing?"

"No, sir," I said, lowering my chair, "but I think they want to. What do you suggest they do instead?"

He looked at me for signs of impudence or insubordination for a second, then, as if thinking better of rebuking this upstart, he said merely, "Fall back on your resources," and left the room.

Most of the kids laughed—they'd seen this drama enacted before.

The situation was defused, but silently I dubbed Wadleigh the "Death School." Stopping by the office on my way home, I told the secretary not to call me again if they needed a sub.

The very next morning my phone rang at 6:30. "Are you available for work today, Mr. Gatto?" said the voice briskly.

"Who is this?" I asked suspiciously. (Ten schools were using me for sub work in those days, and each identified itself at once.)

"The law clearly states, Mr. Gatto, that we do not have to tell you who we are until you tell us whether you are available for work."

"Never mind," I bellowed, "there's only one school who'd pull such crap! The answer is no! I am never available to work in your pigpen school!" And I slammed the receiver back onto its cradle.

But the truth was none of the sub assignments were boat rides; schools had an uncanny habit of exploiting substitutes and providing no support for their survival. It's likely I'd have returned to advertising if a little girl, desperate to free herself from an intolerable situation, hadn't drawn me into her personal school nightmare and shown me how I could find my own significance in teaching, just as those strong men in the riverboats and trains had found their own significance, a currency all of us need for our self-esteem.

It happened this way. Occasionally, I'd get a call from an elementary school. This particular day it was a third grade assignment at a school on 107th Street, which in those days was nearly one hundred percent non-Hispanic in its teaching staff and 99% Hispanic in its student body.

Like many desperate teachers, I killed most of the day listening to the kids read, one after another, and expending most of my energy trying to shut the audience up. This class had a very low ranking, and no one was able to put more than three or four words together without stumbling. All of a sudden, though, a little girl named Milagros sailed through a selection without a mistake. After class I called her over to my desk and asked why she was in this class of bad readers. She replied that "they" (the administration) wouldn't let her out because, as they explained to her mother, she was really a bad reader who had fantasies of being a better reader than she was. "But look, Mr. Gatto, my brother is in the sixth grade, and I can read every word in his English book better than he can!"

I was a little intrigued, but truthfully not much. Surely the authorities knew what they were doing. Still, the little girl seemed so frustrated I invited her to calm down and read to me from the sixth grade book. I explained that if she did well, I would take her case to the principal. I expected nothing.

Milagros, on the other hand, expected justice. Diving into "The Devil and Daniel Webster," she polished off the first two pages without a gulp. My God, I thought, this is a real reader. What is she doing here? Well, maybe it was a simple accident, easily corrected. I sent her home, promising to argue her case. Little did I suspect what a hornet's nest my request to have Milagros moved to a better class would stir up.

"You have some nerve, Mr. Gatto. I can't remember when a substitute ever told me how to run my school before. Have you taken specialized courses in reading?"

"No."

"Well then, suppose you leave these matters to the experts!"

"But the kid can read!"

"What do you suggest?"

"I suggest you test her, and if she isn't a dummy, get her out of the class she's in!"

"I don't like your tone. None of our children are dummies, Mr. Gatto. And you will find that girls like Milagros have many ways to fool amateurs like yourself. This is a matter of a child having memorized one story. You can see if I had to waste my time arguing with people like you I'd have no time left to run a school."

But, strangely, I felt self-appointed as the girl's champion, even though I'd probably never see her again.

I insisted, and the principal finally agreed to test Milagros herself the following Wednesday after school. I made it a point to tell the little girl the next day. By that time I'd come to think that the principal was probably right she'd memorized one story—but I still warned her she'd need to know the vocabulary from the whole advanced reader and be able to read any story the principal picked, without hesitation. My responsibility was over, I told myself.

The following Wednesday after school I waited in the room for Milagros' ordeal to be over. At 3:30 she shyly opened the door of the room.

"How'd it go?" I asked.

"I don't know," she answered, "but I didn't make any mistakes. Mrs. Hefferman was very angry, I could tell."

I saw Mrs. Hefferman, the principal, early the next morning before school opened. "It seems we've made a mistake with Milagros," she said curtly. "She will be moved, Mr. Gatto. Her mother has been informed."

Several weeks later, when I got back to the school to sub, Milagros dropped by, telling me she was in the fast class now and doing very well. She also gave me a sealed card. When I got home that night, I found it, unopened, in my suitcoat pocket. I opened it and saw a gaudy birthday card with blue flowers on it. Opening the card, I read, "A teacher like you cannot be found. Signed, Your student, Milagros."

That simple sentence made me a teacher for life. It was the first praise I ever heard in my working existence that had any meaning. I never forgot it, though I never saw Milagros again and only heard of her again in 1988, twenty-four years later. Then one day I picked up a newspaper and read:

OCCUPATIONAL TEACHER AWARD

Milagros Maldonado, United Federation of Teachers, has won the Distinguished Occupational Teacher Award of the State Education Department for "demonstrated achievement and exemplary professionalism." A secretarial studies teacher at Norman Thomas High School, New York City, from which she graduated, Miss Maldonado was selected as a Manhattan Teacher of the Year in 1985 and was nominated the following year for the Woman of Conscience Award given by the National Council of Women.

Ah, Milagros, is it just possible that I was your Monongahela River? No matter, a teacher like you cannot be found.

8

Engaged Pedagogy

bell hooks

bell hooks (1952–) is a well known feminist who has written extensively on education. In the essay that follows, hooks (1994) argues that teaching should involve what she describes as "the practice of freedom." Her model of practice, which she maintains anyone can learn, is based on the work of the Brazilian educator Paulo Freire (1921–1997) and the Vietnamese Buddhist monk Thich Nhat Hanh (1926–).

Both Freire and Hanh demand that teaching involve not just the recitation and memorizing of knowledge, but also the active participation of those who are learning. In this context, both want to link their understanding and awareness of the world with actual practice. For the teacher, this involves engaging in teaching as a dialogue in which both teacher and student participate and in which both are active in the process of learning.

Although hooks writes this essay from the perspective of a university-level teacher, it is included here because it has significant relevance to elementary and secondary school teachers.

As you read hooks, consider the following questions:

1. What does it mean to teach in a "liberatory" fashion? With which models of the professorate as teacher does it conflict?

2. What is the role of self-actualization in hooks's model of teaching?

3. What does hooks mean by the term *engaged pedagogy*?

4. Why, if hooks's model of teaching is to be effective, is it necessary that the teacher be vulnerable along with the student?

To educate as the practice of freedom is a way of teaching that anyone can learn. That learning process comes easiest to those of us who teach who also believe that there is an aspect of our vocation that is sacred; who believe that our work is not merely to share information but to share in the intellectual and spiritual growth of our students. To teach in a manner that respects and cares for the souls of our students is essential if we are to provide the necessary conditions where learning can most deeply and intimately begin.

Throughout my years as student and professor, I have been most inspired by those teachers who have had the courage to transgress those boundaries that would confine each pupil to a rote, assembly-line approach to learning. Such teachers approach students with the will and desire to respond to our unique beings, even if the situation does not allow the full emergence of a relationship based on mutual recognition. Yet the possibility of such recognition is always present.

Paulo Freire and the Vietnamese Buddhist monk Thich Nhat Hanh are two of the "teachers" who have touched me deeply with their work. When I first began college, Freire's thought gave me the support I needed to challenge the "banking system" of education, that approach to learning that is rooted in the notion that all students need to do is consume information fed to them by a professor and be able to memorize and store it. Early on, it was Freire's insistence that education could be the practice of freedom that encouraged me to create strategies for what he called "conscientization" in the classroom. Translating that term to critical awareness and engagement, I entered the classrooms with the conviction that it was crucial for me and every other student to be an active participant, not a passive consumer. Education as the practice of freedom was continually undermined by professors who were actively hostile to the notion of student participation. Freire's work affirmed that education can only be liberatory when everyone claims knowledge as a field in which we all labor. That notion of mutual labor was affirmed by Thich Nhat Hanh's philosophy of engaged Buddhism, the focus on practice in conjunction with contemplation. His philosophy was similar to Freire's emphasis on "praxis"—action and reflection upon the world in order to change it.

In his work Thich Nhat Hanh always speaks of the teacher as a healer. Like Freire, his approach to knowledge called on students to be active participants, to link awareness with practice. Whereas Freire was primarily concerned with the mind, Thich Nhat Hanh offered a way of thinking about pedagogy which emphasized wholeness, a union of mind, body, and spirit. His focus on a holistic approach to learning and spiritual practice enabled me to overcome years of socialization that had taught me to believe a classroom was diminished if students and professors regarded one another as "whole" human beings, striving not just for knowledge in books, but knowledge about how to live in the world.

During my twenty years of teaching, I have witnessed a grave sense of dis-ease among professors (irrespective of their politics) when students want us to see them as whole human beings with complex lives and experiences rather than simply as seekers after compartmentalized bits of knowledge. When I was an undergraduate, Women's Studies was just finding a place in the academy. Those classrooms were the one space where teachers were will-ing to acknowledge a connection between ideas learned in university settings and those learned in life practices. And, despite those times when students abused that freedom in the classroom by only wanting to dwell on personal experience, feminist classrooms were, on the whole, one location where I witnessed professors striving to create participatory spaces for the sharing of knowledge. Nowadays, most women's studies professors are not as com-mitted to exploring new pedagogical strategies. Despite this shift, many students still seek to enter feminist classrooms because they continue to believe that there, more than in any other place in the academy, they will have an opportunity to experience education as the practice of freedom.

Progressive, holistic education, "engaged pedagogy" is more demanding than conventional critical or feminist pedagogy. For, unlike these two teaching practices, it emphasizes wellbeing. That means that teachers must be actively committed to a process of self-actualization that promotes their own wellbeing if they are to teach in a manner that empowers students. Thich Nhat Hanh emphasized that "the practice of a healer, therapist, teacher or any helping professional should be directed toward his or herself first, because if the helper is unhappy, he or she cannot help many people." In the United States it is rare that anyone talks about teachers in university settings as healers. And it is even more rare to hear anyone suggest that teachers have any responsibility to be self-actualized individuals.

Learning about the work of intellectuals and academics primarily from nineteenth-century fiction and nonfiction during my pre-college years, I was certain that the task for those of us who chose this vocation was to be holistically questing for self-actualization. It was the actual experience of college that disrupted this image. It was there that I was made to feel as though I was terribly naive about "the profession." I learned that far from being self-actualized, the university was seen more as a haven for those who are smart in book knowledge but who might be otherwise unfit for social interaction. Luckily, during my undergraduate years I began to make a distinction between the practice of being an intellectual/teacher and one's role as a member of the academic profession.

It was difficult to maintain fidelity to the idea of the intellectual as someone who sought to be whole—well-grounded in a context where there was little emphasis on spiritual well-being, on care of the soul. Indeed, the objectification of the teacher within bourgeois educational structures seemed to denigrate notions of wholeness and uphold the idea of a mind/body split, one that promotes and supports compartmentalization.

This support reinforces the dualistic separation of public and private, encouraging teachers and students to see no connection between life practices, habits of being, and the roles of professors. The idea of the intellectual questing for a union of mind, body, and spirit had been replaced with notions that being smart meant that one was inherently emotionally unstable and that the best in oneself emerged in one's academic work. This meant that whether academics were drug addicts, alcoholics, batterers, or sexual abusers, the only important aspect of our identity was whether or not our minds functioned, whether we were able to do our jobs in the classroom. The self was presumably emptied out the moment the threshold was crossed, leaving in place only an objective mind—free of experiences and biases. There was fear that the conditions of that self would interfere with the teaching process. Part of the luxury and privilege of the role of teacher/professor today is the absence of any requirement that we be self-actualized. Not surprisingly, professors who are not concerned with inner wellbeing are the most threatened by the demand on the part of students for liberatory education, for pedagogical processes that will aid them in their own struggle for self-actualization.

Certainly it was naive for me to imagine during high school that I would find spiritual and intellectual guidance in university settings from writers, thinkers, scholars. To have found this would have been to stumble across a rare treasure. I learned, along with other students, to consider myself fortunate if I found an interesting professor who talked in a compelling way. Most of my professors were not the slightest bit interested in enlightenment. More than anything they seemed enthralled by the exercise of power and authority within their mini-kingdom, the classroom.

This is not to say that there were not compelling, benevolent dictators, but it is true to my memory that it was rare—absolutely, astonishingly rare—to encounter professors who were deeply committed to progressive pedagogical practices. I was dismayed by this; most of my professors were not individuals whose teaching styles I wanted to emulate.

My commitment to learning kept me attending classes. Yet, even so, because I did not conform—would not be an unquestioning, passive student—some professors treated me with contempt. I was slowly becoming estranged from education. Finding Freire in the midst of that estrangement was crucial to my survival as a student. His work offered both a way for me to understand the limitations of the type of education I was receiving and to discover alternative strategies for learning and teaching. It was particularly disappointing to encounter white male professors who claimed to follow Freire's model even as their pedagogical practices were mired in structures of domination, mirroring the styles of conservative professors even as they approached subjects from a more progressive standpoint. When I first encountered Paulo Freire, I was eager to see if his style of teaching would embody the pedagogical practices he described so eloquently in his work. During the short time I studied with him, I was deeply moved by his presence, by the way in which his manner of teaching exemplified his pedagogical theory. (Not all students interested in Freire have had a similar experience.) My experience with him restored my faith in liberatory education. I had never wanted to surrender the conviction that one could teach without reinforcing existing systems of domination. I needed to know that professors did not have to be dictators in the classroom.

While I wanted teaching to be my career, I believed that personal success was intimately linked with self-actualization. My passion for this quest led me to interrogate constantly the mind/body split that was so often taken to be a given. Most professors were often deeply antagonistic toward, even scornful of, any approach to learning emerging from a philosophical standpoint emphasizing the union of mind, body, and spirit, rather than the separation of these elements. Like many of the students I now teach, I was often told by powerful academics that I was misguided to seek such a perspective in the academy. Throughout my student years I felt deep inner anguish. Memory of that pain returns as I listen to students express the concern that they will not succeed in academic professions if they want to be well, if they eschew dysfunctional behavior or participation in coercive hierarchies. These students are often fearful, as I was, that there are no spaces in the academy where the will to be self-actualized can be affirmed. This fear is present because many professors have intensely hostile responses to the vision of liberatory education that connects the will to know with the will to become. Within professorial circles, individuals often complain bitterly that students want classes to be "encounter groups." While it is utterly unreasonable for students to expect classrooms to be therapy sessions, it is appropriate for them to hope that the knowledge received in these settings will enrich and enhance them.

Currently, the students I encounter seem far more uncertain about the project of self-actualization than my peers and I were twenty years ago. They feel that there are no clear ethical guidelines shaping actions. Yet, while they despair, they are also adamant that education should be liberatory. They want and demand more from professors than my generation did. There are times when I walk into classrooms overflowing with students who feel terribly wounded in their psyches (many of them see therapists), yet I do not think that they want therapy from me. They do want an education that is healing to the uninformed, unknowing spirit. They do want knowledge that is meaningful. They rightfully expect that my colleagues and I will not offer them information without addressing the connection between what they are learning and their overall life experiences.

This demand on the students' part does not mean that they will always accept our guidance. This is one of the joys of education as the practice of freedom, for it allows students to assume responsibility for their choices. Writing about our teacher/student relationship in a piece for the *Village Voice*, "How to Run the Yard: Off-Line and into the Margins at Yale," one of my students, Gary Dauphin, shares the joys of working with me as well as the tensions that surfaced between us as he began to devote his time to pledging a fraternity rather than cultivating his writing:

> People think academics like Gloria [my given name] are all about difference: but what I learned from her was mostly about sameness, about what I had in common as a black man to people of color; to women and gays and lesbians and the poor and anyone else who wanted in. I did some of this learning by reading but most of it came from hanging out on the fringes of her life. I lived like that for a while, shuttling between high points in my classes and low points outside. Gloria was a safe haven . . . Pledging a fraternity is about as far away as you can get from her classroom, from the yellow kitchen where she used to share her lunch with students in need of various forms of sustenance.

This is Gary writing about the joy. The tension arose as we discussed his reason for wanting to join a fraternity and my disdain for that decision. Gary comments, "They represented a vision of black manhood that she abhorred, one where violence and abuse were primary ciphers of bonding and identity." Describing his assertion of autonomy from my influence he writes, "But she must have also known the limits of even her influence on my life, the limits of books and teachers."

Ultimately, Gary felt that the decision he had made to join a fraternity was not constructive, that I "had taught him openness" where the fraternity had encouraged one-dimensional allegiance. Our interchange both during and after this experience was an example of engaged pedagogy.

Through critical thinking—a process he learned by reading theory and actively analyzing texts—Gary experienced education as the practice of freedom. His final comments about me: "Gloria had only mentioned the entire episode once after it was over, and this to tell me simply that there are many kinds of choices, many kinds of logic. I could make those events mean whatever I wanted as long as I was honest." I have quoted his writing at length because it is testimony affirming engaged pedagogy. It means that my voice is not the only account of what happens in the classroom.

Engaged pedagogy necessarily values student expression. In her essay, "Interrupting the Calls for Student Voice in Liberatory Education: A Feminist Poststructuralist Perspective," Mimi Orner employs a Foucauldian framework to suggest that

> Regulatory and punitive means and uses of the confession bring to mind curricular and pedagogical practices which call for students to publicly reveal, even confess, information about their lives and cultures in the presence of authority figures such as teachers.

When education is the practice of freedom, students are not the only ones who are asked to share, to confess. Engaged pedagogy does not seek simply to empower students. Any classroom that employs a holistic model of learning will also be a place where teachers grow, and are empowered by the process. That empowerment cannot happen if we refuse to be vulnerable while encouraging students to take risks. Professors who expect students to share confessional narratives but who are themselves unwilling to share are exercising power in a manner that could be coercive. In my classrooms, I do not expect students to take any risks that I would not take, to share in any way that I would not share. When professors bring narratives of their experiences into classroom discussions it eliminates the possibility that we can function as all-knowing, silent interrogators. It is often productive if professors take the first risk, linking confessional narratives to academic discussions so as to show how experience can illuminate and enhance our understanding of academic material. But most professors must practice being vulnerable in the classroom, being wholly present in mind, body, and spirit.

Progressive professors working to transform the curriculum so that it does not reflect biases or reinforce systems of domination are most often the individuals willing to take the risks that engaged pedagogy requires and to make their teaching practices a site of resistance. In her essay, "On Race and Voice: Challenges for Liberation Education in the 1990s," Chandra Mohanty writes

> that resistance lies in self-conscious engagement with dominant, normative discourses and representations and in the active creation of oppositional

analytic and cultural spaces. Resistance that is random and isolated is clearly not as effective as that which is mobilized through systemic politicized practices of teaching and learning. Uncovering and reclaiming subjugated knowledge is one way to lay claims to alternative histories. But these knowledges need to be understood and defined pedagogically, as questions of strategy and practice as well as of scholarship, in order to transform educational institutions radically.

Professors who embrace the challenge of self-actualization will be better able to create pedagogical practices that engage students, providing them with ways of knowing that enhance their capacity to live fully and deeply.

PART IV

Teaching Others

9. The Silenced Dialogue: Power and Pedagogy in *Educating Other People's Children*
   Lisa D. Delpit

10. White Privilege and Male Privilege: A Personal Account of Coming to See Correspondences Through Work in Women's Studies
    Peggy McIntosh

11. Teaching Themes of Care
    Nel Noddings

One of the most interesting things about teaching is that it forces individuals to work across different cultures and traditions. This is what the educational theorist Henry Giroux (1992) means when he talks about the "teacher as border crosser." Teachers cross many different borders in their work. They may cross from one neighborhood to another in the town where they live. They may teach children who are racially different than themselves, who speak a language other than English in their homes, who practice a different religion, or who come from a very different social and economic class.

Think about almost any classroom that you have ever been in. How many different religions were represented by the students? What races were represented? Difference defines the United States and its people and so, in turn, its classrooms.

Teachers, however, are to a large degree a relatively homogeneous group. They are overwhelmingly White and middle class. In terms of race, only 16% of teachers are people of color, yet 42% of public K–12 students are non-White (U.S. Department of Education, 2005). In terms of social class, the fact that teachers by definition of their salary and status are middle class means that a large number of their students come from different social strata than they do. This is what Lisa Delpit (1988), the author of the first selection in this section, refers to as teaching other people's children.

Research shows that White teachers consider White and Asian students to be more teachable than Black or Latino students. They often assume that the parents of these children do not value education as much as other groups do. White teachers refer children of color to special education more often than children who come from the same background as themselves.

White teachers often do not see themselves as privileged because of their race or "Whiteness." Included in this chapter is an essay by Peggy McIntosh (1988) about the concept of White privilege and male privilege in which she points to the ways in which privilege operates for certain groups versus others (whose holidays are celebrated in school, whose cultural traditions are recognized, whose poets and novelists are read, etc.). In terms of teachers teaching others, obviously this is a critical question.

The last selection included in this section, by Nel Noddings (1995), addresses the question of care. At first it may not seem to fit this section. It questions what we should care about in schools, what we should teach, and what we should value. In this context, understanding "other people's children" and the cultures and the values they find important is essential.

Further Readings: William Gibson's 1957 play *The Miracle Worker* provides an outstanding example of the teacher crossing borders—both cultural and personal. In the story, which is based on the life of Helen Keller, Annie Sullivan saves the main character, who is both deaf and blind, from a life of isolation and loneliness. The play was made into an Academy Award-winning movie starring Anne Bancroft and Patty Duke in 1962.

Linking to Popular Culture: There are many movies that focus on the theme of the teacher as teaching others and of the teacher as border crosser. Among the most well known is the 1967 film *To Sir, With Love* starring Sidney Poitier as a first-time Black teacher working with lower-class White students in the East End of London. The earlier mentioned 1974 film *Conrack*, based on Pat Conroy's autobiographical novel *The Water Is Wide*, is outstanding in describing what it is like to reach across cultural barriers and traditions while trying to teach. The 1986 film *Children of a Lesser God* tells the story of a speech teacher, played by William

Hurt, who falls in love with a deaf former student at the school where he teaches. Marlee Matlin, who plays opposite Hurt, won the Academy Award for her performance—the first deaf actor to win the award.

References

Delpit, L. (1988). The silenced dialogue: Power and pedagogy in educating other people's children. *Harvard Educational Review, 58*(3), 280–298.

Giroux, H. (1992). *Border crossings: Cultural workers and the politics of education.* New York: Routledge.

McIntosh, P. (1988). *White privilege and male privilege: A personal account of coming to see correspondences through work in women's studies.* Working Paper 189, Wellesley College Center for Research for Women.

Noddings, N. (1995). Teaching themes of care. *Phi Delta Kappan, 76,* 675–679.

U.S. Department of Education. (2005). *The condition of education, 2005.* Washington, DC: National Center for Educational Statistics.

9

The Silenced Dialogue

Power and Pedagogy in Educating Other People's Children

Lisa D. Delpit

In the following article, Lisa Delpit (1988) looks at the "culture of power" that operates within schools and the significance of teachers often coming from different social and cultural backgrounds than those of the students with whom they work.

Reading Delpit's piece raises the following questions:

1. What is the significance of Delpit's title, "The Silenced Dialogue," for this article?

2. Who has power in American society and in its classrooms? How is this power manifested?

3. How are power and its codes transmitted across a culture? Who gets included and who gets excluded?

4. Why do those in power not always realize that they have power?

5. Is there an advantage for those in power in not recognizing or knowing that they have power?

NOTE: Lisa D. Delpit, "The Silences Dialogue: Power and Pedagogy in Educating other People's Children," Harvard Educational Review, Col. 58, No. 3, August 1988, pp. 280–298. Copyright © by the President and Fellows of Harvard College. All rights reserved. For more information, please visit www.harvardeducationalreview.org.

A Black male graduate student who is also a special education teacher in a predominantly Black community is talking about his experiences in predominantly White university classes:

> There comes a moment in every class where we have to discuss "The Black Issue" and what's appropriate education for Black children. I tell you, I'm tired of arguing with those White people, because they won't listen. Well, I don't know if they really don't listen or if they just don't believe you. It seems like if you can't quote Vygotsky or something, then you don't have any validity to speak about your *own* kids. Anyway, I'm not bothering with it anymore, now I'm just in it for a grade.

A Black woman teacher in a multicultural urban elementary school is talking about her experiences in discussions with her predominantly White fellow teachers about how they should organize reading instruction to best serve students of color:

> When you're talking to White people they still want it to be their way. You can try to talk to them and give them examples, but they're so headstrong, they think they know what's best for *everybody,* for *everybody's* children. They won't listen, White folks are going to do what they want to do *anyway.*
>
> It's really hard. They just don't listen well. No, they listen, but they don't *hear*—you know how your mama used to say you listen to the radio, but you *hear* your mother? Well they don't *hear* me.
>
> So I just try to shut them out so I can hold my temper. You can only beat your head against a brick wall for so long before you draw blood. If I try to stop arguing with them I can't help myself from getting angry. Then I end up walking around praying all day "Please Lord, remove the bile I feel for these people so I can sleep tonight." It's funny, but it can become a cancer, a sore.
>
> So, I shut them out. I go back to my own little cubby, my classroom, and I try to teach the way I know will work, no matter what those folk say. And when I get Black kids, I just try to undo the damage they did.
>
> I'm not going to let any man, woman, or child drive me crazy—White folks will try to do that to you if you let them. You just have to stop talking to them, that's what I do. I just keep smiling, but I won't talk to them.

A soft-spoken Native Alaskan woman in her forties is a student in the Education Department of the University of Alaska. One day she storms into a Black professor's office and very uncharacteristically slams the door. She plops down in a chair and, still fuming, says, "Please tell those people, just don't help us anymore! I give up. I won't talk to them again!"

And finally, a Black woman principal who is also a doctoral student at a well-known university on the West Coast is talking about her university experiences, particularly about when a professor lectures on issues concerning educating Black children:

> If you try to suggest that that's not quite the way it is, they get defensive, then you get defensive, then they'll start reciting research.
>
> I try to give them my experiences, to explain. They just look and nod. The more I try to explain, they just look and nod, just keep looking and nodding. They don't really hear me.
>
> Then, when it's time for class to be over, the professor tells me to come to his office to talk more. So I go. He asks for more examples of what I'm talking about, and he looks and nods while I give them. Then he says that that's just my experiences. It doesn't really apply to most Black people.
>
> It becomes futile because they think they know everything about everybody. What you have to say about your life, your children, doesn't mean anything. They don't really want to hear what you have to say. They wear blinders and earplugs. They only want to go on research they've read that other White people have written.
>
> It just doesn't make any sense to keep talking to them.

Thus was the first half of the title of this text born—"The Silenced Dialogue." One of the tragedies in the field of education is that scenarios such as these are enacted daily around the country. The saddest element is that the individuals that the Black and Native American educators speak of in these statements are seldom aware that the dialogue has been silenced. Most likely the White educators believe that their colleagues of color did, in the end, agree with their logic. After all, they stopped disagreeing, didn't they?

I have collected these statements since completing a recently published article (Delpit, 1986). In this somewhat autobiographical account, entitled "Skills and Other Dilemmas of a Progressive Black Educator," I discussed my perspective as a product of a skills-oriented approach to writing and as a teacher of process-oriented approaches. I described the estrangement that I and many teachers of color feel from the progressive movement when writing-process advocates dismiss us as too "skills oriented." I ended the article suggesting that it was incumbent upon writing-process advocates—or indeed, advocates of any progressive movement—to enter into dialogue with teachers of color, who may not share their enthusiasm about so-called new, liberal, or progressive ideas.

In response to this article, which presented no research data and did not even cite a reference, I received numerous calls and letters from teachers, professors, and even state school personnel from around the country, both Black and White. All of the White respondents, except one, have wished to talk more about the question of skills versus process approaches—to support or reject what they perceive to be my position. On the other hand, *all* of the non-White respondents have spoken passionately on being left out of the dialogue about how best to educate children of color.

How can such complete communication blocks exist when both parties truly believe they have the same aims? How can the bitterness and resentment expressed by the educators of color be drained so that the sores can heal? What can be done?

I believe the answer to these questions lies in ethnographic analysis, that is, in identifying and giving voice to alternative world views. Thus, I will attempt to address the concerns raised by White and Black respondents to my article "Skills and Other Dilemmas" (Delpit, 1986). My charge here is not to determine the best instructional methodology; I believe that the actual practice of good teachers of all colors typically incorporates a range of pedagogical orientations. Rather, I suggest that the differing perspectives on the debate over "skills" versus "process" approaches can lead to an understanding of the alienation and miscommunication, and thereby to an understanding of the "silenced dialogue."

In thinking through these issues, I have found what I believe to be a connecting and complex theme: what I have come to call "the culture of power." There are five aspects of power I would like to propose as given for this presentation:

1. Issues of power are enacted in classrooms.

2. There are codes or rules for participating in power; that is, there is a "culture of power."

3. The rules of the culture of power are a reflection of the rules of the culture of those who have power.

4. If you are not already a participant in the culture of power, being told explicitly the rules of that culture makes acquiring power easier.

5. Those with power are frequently least aware of—or least willing to acknowledge—its existence. Those with less power are often most aware of its existence.

The first three are by now basic tenets in the literature of the sociology of education, but the last two have seldom been addressed. The following discussion will explicate these aspects of power and their relevance to the schism between liberal educational movements and that of non-White, non-middle-class teachers and communities.[1]

1. *Issues of power are enacted in classrooms.*

These issues include: the power of the teacher over the students; the power of the publishers of textbooks and of the developers of the curriculum to determine the view of the world presented; the power of the state in enforcing compulsory schooling; and the power of an individual or group to determine another's intelligence or "normalcy." Finally, if schooling prepares people for jobs, and the kind of job a person has determines her or his economic status and, therefore, power, then schooling is intimately related to that power.

2. *There are codes or rules for participating in power; that is, there is a "culture of power."*

The codes or rules I'm speaking of relate to linguistic forms, communicative strategies, and presentation of self; that is, ways of talking, ways of writing, ways of dressing, and ways of interacting.

3. *The rules of the culture of power are a reflection of the rules of the culture of those who have power.*

This means that success in institutions—schools, workplaces, and so on—is predicated upon acquisition of the culture of those who are in power. Children from middle-class homes tend to do better in school than those from non-middle-class homes because the culture of the school is based on the culture of the upper and middle classes—of those in power. The upper and middle classes send their children to school with all the accoutrements of the culture of power; children from other kinds of families operate within perfectly wonderful and viable cultures but not cultures that carry the codes or rules of power.

---

[1]Such a discussion, limited as it is by space constraints, must treat the intersection of class and race somewhat simplistically. For the sake of clarity, however, let me define a few terms: "Black" is used herein to refer to those who share some or all aspects of "core black culture" (Gwaltney, 1980, p. xxiii), that is, the mainstream of Black America—neither those who have entered the ranks of the bourgeoisie nor those who are participants in the disenfranchised underworld. "Middle-class" is used broadly to refer to the predominantly White American "mainstream." There are, of course, non-White people who also fit into this category; at issue is their cultural identification, not necessarily the color of their skin. (I must add that there are other non-White people, as well as poor White people, who have indicated to me that their perspectives are similar to those attributed herein to Black people.)

4. *If you are not already a participant in the culture of power, being told explicitly the rules of that culture makes acquiring power easier.*

In my work within and between diverse cultures, I have come to conclude that members of any culture transmit information implicitly to co-members. However, when implicit codes are attempted across cultures, communication frequently breaks down. Each cultural group is left saying, "Why don't those people say what they mean?" as well as, "What's wrong with them, why don't they understand?"

Anyone who has had to enter new cultures, especially to accomplish a specific task, will know of what I speak. When I lived in several Papua New Guinea villages for extended periods to collect data, and when I go to Alaskan villages for work with Alaskan Native communities, I have found it unquestionably easier—psychologically and pragmatically— when some kind soul has directly informed me about such matters as appropriate dress, interactional styles, embedded meanings, and taboo words or actions. I contend that it is much the same for anyone seeking to learn the rules of the culture of power. Unless one has the leisure of a lifetime of "immersion" to learn them, explicit presentation makes learning immeasurably easier.

And now, to the fifth and last premise:

5. *Those with power are frequently least aware of—or least willing to acknowledge—its existence. Those with less power are often most aware of its existence.*

For many who consider themselves members of liberal or radical camps, acknowledging personal power and admitting participation in the culture of power is distinctly uncomfortable. On the other hand, those who are less powerful in any situation are most likely to recognize the power variable most acutely. My guess is that the White colleagues and instructors of those previously quoted did not perceive themselves to have power over the non-White speakers. However, either by virtue of their position, their numbers, or their access to that particular code of power of calling upon research to validate one's position, the White educators had the authority to establish what was to be considered "truth" regardless of the opinions of the people of color, and the latter were well aware of that fact.

A related phenomenon is that liberals (and here I am using the term "liberal" to refer to those whose beliefs include striving for a society based upon maximum individual freedom and autonomy) seem to act under the assumption that to make any rules or expectations explicit is to act against liberal principles, to limit the freedom and autonomy of those subjected to the explicitness.

I thank Fred Erickson for a comment that led me to look again at a tape by John Gurnperz on cultural dissonance in cross-cultural interactions.[2] One of the episodes showed an East Indian interviewing for a job with an all White committee. The interview was a complete failure, even though several of the interviewers appeared to really want to help the applicant. As the interview rolled steadily downhill, these "helpers" became more and more indirect in their questioning, which exacerbated the problems the applicant had in performing appropriately. Operating from a different cultural perspective, he got fewer and fewer clear clues as to what was expected of him, which ultimately resulted in his failure to secure the position.

I contend that as the applicant showed less and less aptitude for handling the interview, the power differential became ever more evident to the interviewers. The "helpful" interviewers, unwilling to acknowledge themselves as having power over the applicant, became more and more uncomfortable. Their indirectness was an attempt to lessen the power differential and their discomfort by lessening the power-revealing explicitness of their questions and comments.

When acknowledging and expressing power, one tends towards explicitness (as in yelling to your 10-year-old, "Turn that radio down!"). When de-emphasizing power, there is a move toward indirect communication. Therefore, in the interview setting, those who sought to help, to express their egalitarianism with the East Indian applicant, became more and more indirect—and less and less helpful—in their questions and comments.

In literacy instruction, explicitness might be equated with direct instruction. Perhaps the ultimate expression of explicitness and direct instruction in the primary classroom is Distar. This reading program is based on a behaviorist model in which reading is taught through the direct instruction of phonics generalizations and blending. The teacher's role is to maintain the full attention of the group by continuous questioning, eye contact, finger snaps, hand claps, and other gestures, and by eliciting choral responses and initiating some sort of award system.

When the program was introduced, it arrived with a flurry of research data that "proved" that all children—even those who were "culturally deprived"—could learn to read using this method. Soon there was a strong response, first from academics and later from many classroom teachers, stating that the program was terrible.

---

[2] "*Multicultural Britain: Crosstalk,*" National Centre of Industrial Language Training, Commission for Racial Equality, London, England, John Twitchin, Producer.

What I find particularly interesting, however, is that the primary issue of the conflict over Distar has not been over its instructional efficacy—usually the students did learn to read—but the expression of explicit power in the classroom. The liberal educators opposed the methods—the direct instruction, the explicit control exhibited by the teacher. As a matter of fact, it was not unusual (even now) to hear of the program spoken of as "fascist."

I am not an advocate of Distar, but I will return to some of the issues that the program—and direct instruction in general—raises in understanding the differences between progressive White educators and educators of color.

To explore those differences, I would like to present several statements typical of those made with the best of intentions by middle-class liberal educators. To the surprise of the speakers, it is not unusual for such content to be met by vocal opposition or stony silence from people of color. My attempt here is to examine the underlying assumptions of both camps.

"I want the same thing for everyone else's children as I want for mine."

To provide schooling for everyone's children that reflects liberal, middle-class values and aspirations is to ensure the maintenance of the status quo, to ensure that power, the culture of power, remains in the hands of those who already have it. Some children come to school with more accoutrements of the culture of power already in place—"cultural capital," as some critical theorists refer to it (for example, Apple, 1979)—some with less. Many liberal educators hold that the primary goal for education is for children to become autonomous, to develop fully who they are in the classroom setting without having arbitrary, outside standards forced upon them. This is a very reasonable goal for people whose children are already participants in the culture of power and who have already internalized its codes.

But parents who don't function within that culture often want something else. It's not that they disagree with the former aim, it's just that they want something more. They want to ensure that the school provides their children with discourse patterns, interactional styles, and spoken and written language codes that will allow them success in the larger society.

It was the lack of attention to this concern that created such a negative outcry in the Black community when well-intentioned White liberal educators introduced "dialect readers." These were seen as a plot to prevent the schools from teaching the linguistic aspects of the culture of power, thus dooming Black children to a permanent outsider caste. As one parent demanded, "My kids know how to be Black—you all teach them how to be successful in the White man's world."

Several Black teachers have said to me recently that as much as they'd like to believe otherwise, they cannot help but conclude that many of the "progressive" educational strategies imposed by liberals upon Black and poor children could only be based on a desire to ensure that the liberals' children get sole access to the dwindling pool of American jobs. Some have added that the liberal educators believe themselves to be operating with good intentions, but that these good intentions are only conscious delusions about their unconscious true motives. One of Black anthropologist John Gwaltney's (1980) informants reflects this perspective with her tongue-in-cheek observation that the biggest difference between Black folks and White folks is that Black folks *know* when they're lying!

Let me try to clarify how this might work in literacy instruction. A few years ago I worked on an analysis of two popular reading programs, Distar and a progressive program that focused on higher-level critical thinking skills. In one of the first lessons of the progressive program, the children are introduced to the names of the letter *m* and *e*. In the same lesson they are then taught the sound made by each of the letters, how to write each of the letters, and that when the two are blended together they produce the word *me*.

As an experienced first-grade teacher, I am convinced that a child needs to be familiar with a significant number of these concepts to be able to assimilate so much new knowledge in one sitting. By contrast, Distar presents the same information in about forty lessons.

I would not argue for the pace of the Distar lessons; such a slow pace would only bore most kids—but what happened in the other lesson is that it merely provided an opportunity for those who already knew the content to exhibit that they knew it, or at most perhaps to build one new concept onto what was already known. This meant that the child who did not come to school already primed with what was to be presented would be labeled as needing "remedial" instruction from day one; indeed, this determination would be made before he or she was ever taught. In fact, Distar was "successful" because it actually *taught* new information to children who had not already acquired it at home. Although the more progressive system was ideal for some children, for others it was a disaster.

I do not advocate a simplistic "basic skills" approach for children outside of the culture of power. It would be (and has been) tragic to operate as if these children were incapable of critical and higher-order thinking and reasoning. Rather, I suggest that schools must provide these children the content that other families from a different cultural orientation provide at home. This does not mean separating children according to family background, but instead, ensuring that each classroom incorporate strategies appropriate for all the children in its confines.

And I do not advocate that it is the school's job to attempt to change the homes of poor and non-White children to match the homes of those in the culture of power. That may indeed be a form of cultural genocide. I have frequently heard schools call poor parents "uncaring" when parents respond to the school's urging, that they change their home life in order to facilitate their children's learning, by saying, "But that's the school's job." What the school personnel fail to understand is that if the parents were members of the culture of power and lived by its rules and codes, then they would transmit those codes to their children. In fact, they transmit another culture that children must learn at home in order to survive in their communities.

> "Child-centered, whole language, and process approaches are needed in order to allow a democratic state of free, autonomous, empowered adults, and because research has shown that children learn best through these methods."

People of color are, in general, skeptical of research as a determiner of our fates. Academic research has, after all, found us genetically inferior, culturally deprived, and verbally deficient. But beyond that general caveat, and despite my or others' personal preferences, there is little research data supporting the major tenets of process approaches over other forms of literacy instruction, and virtually no evidence that such approaches are more efficacious for children of color (Siddle, 1986).

Although the problem is not necessarily inherent in the method, in some instances adherents of process approaches to writing create situations in which students ultimately find themselves held accountable for knowing a set of rules about which no one has ever directly informed them. Teachers do students no service to suggest, even implicitly, that "product" is not important. In this country, students will be judged on their product regardless of the process they utilized to achieve it. And that product, based as it is on the specific codes of a particular culture, is more readily produced when the directives of how to produce it are made explicit.

If such explicitness is not provided to students, what it feels like to people who are old enough to judge is that there are secrets being kept, that time is being wasted, that the teacher is abdicating his or her duty to teach. A doctoral student in my acquaintance was assigned to a writing class to hone his writing skills. The student was placed in the section led by a White professor who utilized a process approach, consisting primarily of having the students write essays and then assemble into groups to edit each others' papers. That procedure infuriated this particular student. He had many angry encounters with the teacher about what she was doing. In his words:

> I didn't feel she was teaching us anything. She wanted us to correct each others' papers and we were there to learn from her. She didn't teach anything, absolutely nothing.
>
> Maybe they're trying to learn what Black folks knew all the time. We understand how to improvise, how to express ourselves creatively. When I'm in a classroom, I'm not looking for that, I'm looking for structure, the more formal language.
>
> Now my buddy was in [a] Black teacher's class. And that lady was very good. She went through and explained and defined each part of the structure. This [White] teacher didn't get along with that Black teacher. She said that she didn't agree with her methods. But *I* don't think that White teacher *had* any methods.

When I told this gentleman that what the teacher was doing was called a process method of teaching writing, his response was, "Well, at least now I know that she *thought* she was doing *something. I* thought she was just a fool who couldn't teach and didn't want to try."

This sense of being cheated can be so strong that the student may be completely turned off to the educational system. Amanda Branscombe, an accomplished White teacher, recently wrote a letter discussing her work with working-class Black and White students at a community college in Alabama. She had given these students my "Skills and Other Dilemmas" article (Delpit, 1986) to read and discuss, and wrote that her students really understood and identified with what I was saying. To quote her letter:

> One young man said that he had dropped out of high school because he failed the exit exam. He noted that he had then passed the GED without a problem after three weeks of prep. He said that his high school English teacher claimed to use a process approach, but what she really did was hide behind fancy words to give herself permission to do nothing in the classroom.

The students I have spoken of seem to be saying that the teacher has denied them access to herself as the source of knowledge necessary to learn the forms they need to succeed. Again, I tentatively attribute the problem to teachers' resistance to exhibiting power in the classroom. Somehow, to exhibit one's personal power as expert source is viewed as disempowering one's students.

Two qualifiers are necessary, however. The teacher cannot be the only expert in the classroom. To deny students their own expert knowledge is to disempower them. Amanda Branscombe, when she was working with Black high school students classified as "slow learners," had the students analyze RAP songs to discover their underlying patterns. The students became the experts in explaining to the teacher the rules for creating a new RAP song. The teacher then used the patterns the students identified as a base to begin an explanation of the structure of grammar, and then of Shakespeare's plays. Both student and teacher are expert at what they know best.

The second qualifier is that merely adopting direct instruction is not the answer. Actual writing for real audiences and real purposes is a vital element in helping students to understand that they have an important voice in their own learning processes. Siddle (1988) examines the results of various kinds of interventions in a primarily process-oriented writing class for Black students. Based on readers' blind assessments, she found that the intervention that produced the most positive changes in the students' writing was a "mini-lesson" consisting of direct instruction about some standard writing convention. But what produced the *second* highest number of positive changes was a subsequent student-centered conference with the teacher. (Peer conferencing in this group of Black students who were not members of the culture of power produced the least number of changes in students' writing. However, the classroom teacher maintained—and I concur—that such activities are necessary to introduce the elements of "real audience" into the task, along with more teacher-directed strategies.)

> "It's really a shame but she (that Black teacher upstairs) seems to be so authoritarian, so focused on skills and so teacher directed. Those poor kids never seem to be allowed to really express their creativity. (And she even yells at them.)"

This statement directly concerns the display of power and authority in the classroom. One way to understand the difference in perspective between Black teachers and their progressive colleagues on this issue is to explore culturally influenced oral interactions.

In *Ways With Words*, Shirley Brice Heath (1983) quotes the verbal directives given by the middle-class "townspeople" teachers (p. 280):

—"Is this where the scissors belong?"

—"You want to do your best work today."

By contrast, many Black teachers are more likely to say:

—"Put those scissors on that shelf."

—"Put your name on the papers and make sure to get the right answer for each question."

Is one oral style more authoritarian than another?

Other researchers have identified differences in middle-class and working-class speech to children.

Snow et al. (1976), for example, report that working-class mothers use more directives to their children than do middle- and upper-class parents. Middle-class parents are likely to give the directive to a child to take his bath as, "Isn't it time for your bath?" Even though the utterance is couched as a question, both child and adult understand it as a directive. The child may respond with "Aw Mom, can't I wait until . . ." but whether or not negotiation is attempted, both conversants understand the intent of the utterance.

By contrast, a Black mother, in whose house I was recently a guest, said to her eight-year-old son, "Boy, get your rusty behind in that bathtub." Now I happen to know that this woman loves her son as much as any mother, but she would never have posed the directive to her son to take a bath in the form of a question. Were she to ask, "Would you like to take your bath now?" she would not have been issuing a directive but offering a true alternative. Consequently, as Heath suggests, upon entering school the child from such a family may not understand the indirect statement of the teacher as a direct command. Both White and Black working-class children in the communities Heath studied "had difficulty interpreting these indirect requests for adherence to an unstated set of rules" (p. 280).

But those veiled commands are commands nonetheless, representing true power, and with true consequences for disobedience. If veiled commands are ignored, the child will be labeled a behavior problem and possibly officially classified as behavior disordered. In other words, the attempt by the teacher to reduce an exhibition of power by expressing herself in indirect terms may remove the very explicitness that the child needs to understand the rules of the new classroom culture.

A Black elementary school principal in Fairbanks, Alaska, reported to me that she has a lot of difficulty with Black children who are placed in some White teachers' classrooms. The teachers often send the children to the office for disobeying teacher directives. Their parents are frequently called in for conferences. The parents' response to the teacher is usually the same: "They do what I say; if you just *tell* them what to do, they'll do it. I tell them at home that they have to listen to what you say." And so, does not the power still exist? Its veiled nature only makes it more difficult for some children to respond appropriately, but that in no way mitigates its existence.

I don't mean to imply, however, that the only time the Black child disobeys the teacher is when he or she misunderstands the request for certain behavior. There are other factors that may produce such behavior. Black children expect an authority figure to act with authority. When the teacher instead acts as a "chum," the message sent is that this adult has no authority, and the children react accordingly. One reason this is so is that Black people often view issues of power and authority differently than people from mainstream middle-class backgrounds.[3] Many people of color expect authority to be earned by personal efforts and exhibited by personal characteristics. In other words, "the authoritative person gets to be a teacher because she is authoritative." Some members of middle-class cultures, by contrast, expect one to achieve authority by the acquisition of an authoritative role. That is, "the teacher is the authority because she is the teacher."

In the first instance, because authority is earned, the teacher must consistently prove the characteristics that give her authority. These characteristics may vary across cultures, but in the Black community they tend to cluster around several abilities. The authoritative teacher can control the class through exhibition of personal power; establishes meaningful interpersonal relationships that garner student respect; exhibits a strong belief that all students can learn; establishes a standard of achievement and "pushes" the students to achieve that standard; and holds the attention of the students by incorporating interactional features of Black communicative style in his or her teaching.

By contrast, the teacher whose authority is vested in the role has *many* more options of behavior at her disposal. For instance, she does not need to express any sense of personal power because her authority does not come from anything she herself does or says. Hence, the power she actually holds may be veiled in such questions/commands as "Would you like to sit down now?" If the children in her class understand authority as she does, it is mutually agreed upon that they are to obey her no matter how indirect, softspoken, or unassuming she may be. Her indirectness and soft-spokenness may indeed be, as I suggested earlier, an attempt to reduce the implication of overt power in order to establish a more egalitarian and nonauthoritarian classroom atmosphere.

If the children operate under another notion of authority, however, then there is trouble. The Black child may perceive the middle-class teacher as weak, ineffectual, and incapable of taking on the role of being the teacher; therefore, there is no need to follow her directives. In her dissertation, Michelle Foster (1987) quotes one young Black man describing such a teacher:

---

[3]I would like to thank Michelle Foster, who is presently planning a more in-depth treatment of the subject, for her astute clarification of the idea.

She is boring, bo::ing. She could do something creative. Instead she just stands there. She can't control the class, doesn't know how to control the class. She asked me what she was doing wrong. I told her she just stands there like she's meditating. I told her she could be meditating for all I know. She says that we're supposed to know what to do. I told her I don't know nothing unless she tells me. She just can't control the class. I hope we don't have her next semester. (pp. 67–68)*

*Editor's Note: The colons [::] refer to elongated vowels.

But of course the teacher may not view the problem as residing in herself but in the student, and the child may once again become the behavior-disordered Black boy in special education.

What characteristics do Black students attribute to the good teacher? Again, Foster's dissertation provides a quotation that supports my experience with Black students. A young Black man is discussing a former teacher with a group of friends:

We had fu::n in her class, but she was mean. I can remember she used to say, "Tell me what's in the story, Wayne." She pushed, she used to get on me and push me to know. She made us learn. We had to get in the books. There was this tall guy and he tried to take her on, but she was in charge of that class and she didn't let anyone run her. I still have this book we used in her class. It's a bunch of stories in it. I just read one on Coca-Cola again the other day (p. 68).*

*Editor's Note: The colons [::] refer to elongated vowels.

To clarify, this student was *proud* of the teacher's "meanness," an attribute he seemed to describe as the ability to run the class and pushing and expecting students to learn. Now, does the liberal perspective of the negatively authoritarian Black teacher really hold up? I suggest that although all "explicit" Black teachers are not also good teachers, there are different attitudes in different cultural groups about which characteristics make for a good teacher. Thus, it is impossible to create a model for the good teacher without taking issues of culture and community context into account.

And now to the final comment I present for examination:

Children have the right to their own language, their own culture. We must fight cultural hegemony and fight the system by insisting that children be allowed to express themselves in their own language style. It is not they, the children, who must change, but the schools. To push children to do anything else is repressive and reactionary.

A statement such as this originally inspired me to write the "Skills and Other Dilemmas" article. It was first written as a letter to a colleague in response to a situation that had developed in our department. I was teaching a senior-level teacher education course. Students were asked to prepare a written autobiographical document for the class that would also be shared with their placement school prior to their student teaching.

One student, a talented young Native American woman, submitted a paper in which the ideas were lost because of technical problems—from spelling to sentence structure to paragraph structure. Removing her name, I duplicated the paper for a discussion with some faculty members. I had hoped to initiate a discussion about what we could do to ensure that our students did not reach the senior level without getting assistance in technical writing skills when they needed them.

I was amazed at the response. Some faculty implied that the student should never have been allowed into the teacher education program. Others, some of the more progressive minded, suggested that I was attempting to function as gate-keeper by raising the issue and had internalized repressive and disempowering forces of the power elite to suggest that something was wrong with a Native American student just because she had another style of writing. With few exceptions, I found myself alone in arguing against both camps.

No, this student should not have been denied entry to the program. To deny her entry under the notion of upholding standards is to blame the victim for the crime. We cannot justifiably enlist exclusionary standards when the reason this student lacked the skills demanded was poor teaching at best and institutionalized racism at worst.

However, to bring this student into the program and pass her through without attending to obvious deficits in the codes needed for her to function effectively as a teacher is equally criminal—for though we may assuage our own consciences for not participating in victim blaming, she will surely be accused and convicted as soon as she leaves the university. As Native Alaskans were quick to tell me, and as I understood through my own experience in the Black community, not only would she not be hired as a teacher, but those who did not hire her would make the (false) assumption that the university was putting out only incompetent Natives and that they should stop looking seriously at any Native applicants. A White applicant who exhibits problems is an individual with problems. A person of color who exhibits problems immediately becomes a representative of her cultural group.

No, either stance is criminal. The answer is to *accept* students but also to take responsibility to *teach* them. I decided to talk to the student and found out she had recognized that she needed some assistance in the technical aspects of writing soon after she entered the university as a freshman. She had gone to various members of the education faculty and received the same two kinds of responses I met with four years later: faculty members told her either that she should not even attempt to be a teacher, or that it didn't matter and that she shouldn't worry about such trivial issues. In her desperation, she had found a helpful professor in the English Department, but he left the university when she was in her sophomore year.

We sat down together, worked out a plan for attending to specific areas of writing competence, and set up regular meetings. I stressed to her the need to use her own learning process as insight into how best to teach her future students those "skills" that her own schooling had failed to teach her. I gave her some explicit rules to follow in some areas; for others, we devised various kinds of journals that, along with readings about the structure of the language, allowed her to find her own insights into how the language worked. All that happened two years ago, and the young woman is now successfully teaching. What the experience led me to understand is that pretending that gatekeeping points don't exist is to ensure that many students will not pass through them.

Now you may have inferred that I believe that because there is a culture of power, everyone should learn the codes to participate in it, and that is how the world should be. Actually, nothing could be further from the truth. I believe in a diversity of style, and I believe the world will be diminished if cultural diversity is ever obliterated. Further, I believe strongly, as do my liberal colleagues, that each cultural group should have the right to maintain its own language style. When I speak, therefore, of the culture of power, I don't speak of how I wish things to be but of how they are.

I further believe that to act as if power does not exist is to ensure that the power status quo remains the same. To imply to children or adults (but of course the adults won't believe you anyway) that it doesn't matter how you talk or how you write is to ensure their ultimate failure. I prefer to be honest with my students. Tell them that their language and cultural style is unique and wonderful but that there is a political power game that is also being played, and if they want to be in on that game there are certain games that they too must play.

But don't think that I let the onus of change rest entirely with the students. I am also involved in political work both inside and outside of the educational system, and that political work demands that I place myself to influence as many gate-keeping points as possible. And it is there that I agitate for change—pushing gate-keepers to open their doors to a variety of styles and codes. What I'm saying, however, is that I do not believe that political change toward diversity can be effected from the bottom up, as do some of my colleagues. They seem to believe that if we accept and encourage diversity within classrooms of children, then diversity will automatically be accepted at gatekeeping points.

I believe that will never happen. What will happen is that the students who reach the gatekeeping points—like Amanda Branscombe's student who dropped out of high school because he failed his exit exam—will understand that they have been lied to and will react accordingly. No, I am certain that if we are truly to effect societal change, we cannot do so from the bottom up, but we must push and agitate from the top down. And in the meantime, we must take the responsibility to *teach,* to provide for students who do not already possess them, the additional codes of power.[4]

But I also do not believe that we should teach students to passively adopt an alternate code. They must be encouraged to understand the value of the code they already possess as well as to understand the power realities in this country. Otherwise they will be unable to work to change these realities. And how does one do that?

Martha Demientieff, a masterly Native Alaskan teacher of Athabaskan Indian students, tells me that her students, who live in a small, isolated, rural village of less than two hundred people, are not aware that there are different codes of English. She takes their writing and analyzes it for features of what has been referred to by Alaskan linguists as "Village English," and then covers half a bulletin board with words or phrases from the students' writing, which she labels "Our Heritage Language." On the other half of the bulletin board she puts the equivalent statements in "standard" English, which she labels "Formal English."

She and the students spend a long time on the "Heritage English" section, savoring the words, discussing the nuances. She tells the students, "That's the way we say things. Doesn't it feel good? Isn't it the absolute best way of getting that idea across?" Then she turns to the other side of the board. She tells the students that there are people, not like those in their village, who judge others by the way they talk or write.

> We listen to the way people talk, not to judge them, but to tell what part of the river they come from. These other people are not like that. They think everybody needs to talk like them. Unlike us, they have a hard time hearing what people say if they don't talk exactly like them. Their way of talking and writing is called "Formal English."
>
> We have to feel a little sorry for them because they have only one way to talk. We're going to learn two ways to say things. Isn't that better? One way will be our Heritage way. The other will be Formal English. Then, when we go

---

[4]Bernstein (1975) makes a similar point when he proposes that different educational frames cannot be successfully institutionalized in the lower levels of education until there are fundamental changes at the post-secondary levels.

to get jobs, we'll be able to talk like those people who only know and can only really listen to one way. Maybe after we get the jobs we can help them to learn how it feels to have another language, like ours, that feels so good. We'll talk like them when we have to, but we'll always know our way is best.

Martha then does all sorts of activities with the notions of Formal and Heritage or informal English. She tells the students,

In the village, everyone speaks informally most of the time unless there's a pot-latch or something. You don't think about it, you don't worry about following any rules—it's sort of like how you eat food at a picnic—nobody pays attention to whether you use your fingers or a fork, and it feels so good. Now, Formal English is more like a formal dinner. There are rules to follow about where the knife and fork belong, about where people sit, about how you eat. That can be really nice, too, because it's nice to dress up sometimes.

The students then prepare a formal dinner in the class, for which they dress up and set a big table with fancy tablecloths, china, and silverware. They speak only Formal English at this meal. Then they prepare a picnic where only informal English is allowed.

She also contrasts the "wordy" academic way of saying things with the metaphoric style of Athabaskan. The students discuss how book language always uses more words, but in Heritage language, the shorter way of saying something is always better. Students then write papers in the academic way, discussing with Martha and with each other whether they believe they've said enough to sound like a book. Next, they take those papers and try to reduce the meaning to a few sentences. Finally, students further reduce the message to a "saying" brief enough to go on the front of a T-shirt, and the sayings are put on little paper T-shirts that the students cut out and hang throughout the room. Sometimes the students reduce other authors' wordy texts to their essential meanings as well.

The following transcript provides another example. It is from a conversation between a Black teacher and a Southern Black high school student named Joey, who is a speaker of Black English. The teacher believes it very important to discuss openly and honestly the issues of language diversity and power. She has begun the discussion by giving the student a children's book written in Black English to read.

Teacher: What do you think about that book?

Joey: I think it's nice.

Teacher: Why?

Joey: I don't know. It just told about a Black family, that's all.

Teacher: Was it difficult to read?

Joey: No.

Teacher: Was the text different from what you have seen in other books?

Joey: Yeah. The writing was.

Teacher: How?

Joey: It use more of a southern-like accent in this book.

Teacher: Uhm-hmm. Do you think that's good or bad?

Joey: Well, uh, I don't think it's good for people down this a way, cause that's the way they grow up talking anyway. They ought to get the right way to talk.

Teacher: Oh. So you think it's wrong to talk like that?

Joey: Well . . . [Laughs]

Teacher: Hard question, huh?

Joey: Uhm-hmm, that's a hard question. But I think they shouldn't make books like that.

Teacher: *Why?*

Joey: Because they not using the right way to talk and in school they take off for that and li'l chirren grow up talking like that and reading like that so they might think that's right and all the time they getting bad grades in school, talking like that and writing like that.

Teacher: Do you think they should be getting bad grades for talking like that?

Joey: [Pauses, answers very slowly] No . . . No.

Teacher: So you don't think that it matters whether you talk one way or another?

Joey: No, not long as you understood.

Teacher: Uhm-hmm. Well, that's a hard question for me to answer, too. It's, ah, that's a question that's come up in a lot of schools now as to whether they should correct children who speak the way we speak all the time. Cause when we're talking to each other we talk like that even though we might not talk like that when we get into other situations, and who's to say whether it's—

Joey: *[Interrupting)* Right or wrong.

Teacher: Yeah.

Joey: Maybe they ought to come *up* with another kind of . . . maybe Black English or something. A course in Black English. Maybe Black folks would be good in that cause people talk, I mean Black people talk like that, so . . . but I guess there's a right way and wrong way to talk, you know, not regarding what race. I don't know.

Teacher: But who decided what's right or wrong?

Joey: Well that's true . . . I guess White people did.

[Laughter. End of tape.]

Notice how throughout the conversation Joey's consciousness has been raised by thinking about codes of language. This teacher further advocates having students interview various personnel officers in actual workplaces about their attitudes toward divergent styles in oral and written language. Students begin to understand how arbitrary language standards are, but also how politically charged they are. They compare various pieces written in different styles, discuss the impact of different styles on the message by making translations and back translations across styles, and discuss the history, apparent purpose, and contextual appropriateness of each of the technical writing rules presented by their teacher. *And* they practice writing different forms to different audiences based on rules appropriate for each audience. Such a program not only "teaches" standard linguistic forms, but also explores aspects of power as exhibited through linguistic forms.

Tony Burgess, in a study of secondary writing in England by Britton, Burgess, Martin, McLeod, and Rosen (1975/1977), suggests that we should not teach "iron conventions . . . imposed without rationale or grounding in communicative intent," . . . but "critical and ultimately cultural awarenesses" (p. 54). Courtney Cazden (1987) calls for a two-pronged approach:

1. Continuous opportunities for writers to participate in some authentic bit of the unending conversation . . . thereby becoming part of a vital community of talkers and writers in a particular domain, and

2. Periodic, temporary focus on conventions of form, taught as cultural conventions expected in a particular community. (p. 20)

Just so that there is no confusion about what Cazden means by a focus on conventions of form, or about what I mean by "skills," let me stress that neither of us is speaking of page after page of "skill sheets" creating compound words or identifying nouns and adverbs, but rather about helping students gain a useful knowledge of the conventions of print while engaging in real and useful communicative activities. Kay Rowe Grubis, a junior high school teacher in a multicultural school, makes lists of certain technical rules for her eighth graders' review and then gives them papers from a third grade to "correct." The students not only have to correct other students' work, but also tell them why they have changed or questioned aspects of the writing.

A village teacher, Howard Cloud, teaches his high school students the conventions of formal letter writing and the formulation of careful questions in the context of issues surrounding the amendment of the Alaska Land Claims Settlement Act. Native Alaskan leaders hold differing views on this issue, critical to the future of local sovereignty and land rights. The students compose letters to leaders who reside in different areas of the state seeking their perspectives, set up audioconference calls for interview/debate sessions, and, finally, develop a videotape to present the differing views.

To summarize, I suggest that students must be *taught* the codes needed to participate fully in the mainstream of American life, not by being forced to attend to hollow, inane, decontextualized subskills, but rather within the context of meaningful communicative endeavors; that they must be allowed the resource of the teacher's expert knowledge, while being helped to acknowledge their own "expertness" as well; and that even while students are assisted in learning the culture of power, they must also be helped to learn about the arbitrariness of those codes and about the power relationships they represent.

I am also suggesting that appropriate education for poor children and children of color can only be devised in consultation with adults who share their culture. Black parents, teachers of color, and members of poor communities must be allowed to participate fully in the discussion of what kind of instruction is in their children's best interest. Good liberal intentions are not enough. In an insightful study entitled "Racism without Racists: Institutional Racism in Urban Schools," Massey, Scott, and Dornbusch (1975) found that under the pressures of teaching, and with all intentions of "being nice," teachers had essentially stopped attempting to teach Black children. In their words: "We have shown that oppression can arise out of warmth, friendliness, and concern. Paternalism and a lack of challenging standards are creating a distorted system of evaluation in the schools" (p. 10). Educators must open themselves to, and allow themselves to be affected by, these alternative voices.

In conclusion, I am proposing a resolution for the skills/process debate. In short, the debate is fallacious; the dichotomy is false. The issue is really an illusion created initially not by teachers but by academics whose world view demands the creation of categorical divisions—not for the purpose of better teaching, but for the goal of easier analysis. As I have been reminded by many teachers since the publication of my article, those who are most skillful at educating Black and poor children do not allow themselves to be placed in "skills" or "process" boxes. They understand the need for both approaches, the need to help students to establish their own voices, but to coach those voices to produce notes that will be heard clearly in the larger society.

The dilemma is not really in the debate over instructional methodology, but rather in communicating across cultures and in addressing the more fundamental issue of power, of whose voice gets to be heard in determining what is best for poor children and children of color. Will Black teachers and parents continue to be silenced by the very forces that claim to "give voice" to our children? Such an outcome would be tragic, for both groups truly have something to say to one another. As a result of careful listening to alternative points of view, I have myself come to a viable synthesis of perspectives. But both sides do need to be able to listen, and I contend that it is those with the most power, those in the majority, who must take the greater responsibility for initiating the process.

To do so takes a very special kind of listening, listening that requires not only open eyes and ears, but open hearts and minds. We do not really see through our eyes or hear through our ears, but through our beliefs. To put our beliefs on hold is to cease to exist as ourselves for a moment—and that is not easy. It is painful as well, because it means turning yourself inside out, giving up your own sense of who you are, and being willing to see yourself in the unflattering light of another's angry gaze. It is not easy, but it is the only way to learn what it might feel like to be someone else and the only way to start the dialogue.

There are several guidelines. We must keep the perspective that people are experts on their own lives. There are certainly aspects of the outside world of which they may not be aware, but they can be the only authentic chroniclers of their own experience. We must not be too quick to deny their interpretations, or accuse them of "false consciousness." We must believe that people are rational beings, and therefore always act rationally. We may not understand their rationales, but that in no way militates against the existence of these rationales or reduces our responsibility to attempt to apprehend them. And finally, we must learn to be vulnerable enough to allow our world to turn upside down in order to allow the realities of others to edge themselves into our consciousness. In other words, we must become ethnographers in the true sense.

Teachers are in an ideal position to play this role, to attempt to get all of the issues on the table in order to initiate true dialogue. This can only be done, however, by seeking out those whose perspectives may differ most, by learning to give their words complete attention, by understanding one's own power, even if that power stems merely from being in the majority, by being unafraid to raise questions about discrimination and voicelessness with people of color, and to listen, no, to *hear* what they say. I suggest that the results of such interactions may be the most powerful and empowering coalescence yet seen in the educational realm—for *all* teachers and for *all* the students they teach.

References

Apple, M. W. (1979). *Ideology and curriculum.* Boston: Routledge & Kegan Paul.

Bernstein, B. (1975). Class and pedagogies: Visible and invisible. In B. Bernstein, *Class, codes, and control (Vol. 3).* Boston: Routledge & Kegan Paul.

Britton, J., Burgess, T., Martin, N., McLeod, A., & Rosen, H. (1975/1977). *The development of writing abilities.* London: Macmillan Education for the Schools Council, and Urbana, IL: National Council of Teachers of English.

Cazden, C. (1987, January). *The myth of autonomous text.* Paper presented at the Third International Conference on Thinking, Hawaii.

Delpit, L. D. (1986). Skills and other dilemmas of a progressive Black educator. *Harvard Educational Review, 56*(4), 379–385.

Foster, M. (1987). *It's cookin' now: An ethnographic study of the teaching style of a successful Black teacher in an urban community college.* Unpublished doctoral dissertation, Harvard University.

Gwaltney, J. (1980). *Drylongso.* New York: Vintage Books.

Heath, S. B. (1983). *Ways with words.* Cambridge: Cambridge University Press.

Massey, G. C., Scott, M. V., & Dornbusch, S. M. (1975). Racism without racists: Institutional racism in urban schools. *The Black Scholar, 7*(3), 2–11.

Siddle, E. V. (1986). *A critical assessment of the natural process approach to teaching writing.* Unpublished qualifying paper, Harvard University.

Siddle E. V. (1988). *The effect of intervention strategies on the revisions ninth graders make in a narrative essay.* Unpublished doctoral dissertation, Harvard University.

Snow, C. E., Ariman-Rup, A., Hassing, Y., Josbe, J., Joosten, J., & Vorster, J. (1976). Mother's speech in three social classes. *Journal of Psycholinguistic Research, 5,* 1–20.

10

White Privilege and Male Privilege

A Personal Account of Coming to See Correspondences Through Work in Women's Studies

Peggy McIntosh

In this groundbreaking paper, Peggy McIntosh (1988), the Associate Director of the Center for Research on Women at Wellesley College, explores the ways in which, as a White woman, she experiences unearned advantages because of her race. She then draws the parallel between this notion and the advantage that men have in American society because of their gender. Included in her essay are 46 instances when being White represents an unearned advantage. In addition to race as a source of privilege in American culture, she lists eight areas in which being heterosexual is a similar, unearned social asset.

NOTE: Copyright 1988 by Peggy McIntosh. Working Paper #189, Wellesley Colelge Center fro Research on Women, Wellesley, MA. Permission to reprint must be obtained by the author: Peggy McIntosh, Wellesley Centers for Women, Wellesley, MA 02481, mmcintosh@wellesley.edu, 781-283-2520.

As you read McIntosh's work consider the following questions:

1. What are some of the ways that you are advantaged or disadvantaged in your daily life by race? How does your list compare with McIntosh's?

2. What are some of the ways that you are advantaged or disadvantaged in your daily life by class? How does your list compare with McIntosh's?

3. What are some of the ways that you are advantaged or disadvantaged in your daily life by gender? How does your list compare with McIntosh's?

4. How does privilege potentially function in school settings to the advantage or the disadvantage of certain students or groups over others?

Through work to bring materials and perspectives from Women's Studies into the rest of the curriculum, I have often noticed men's unwillingness to grant that they are overprivileged in the curriculum, even though they may grant that women are disadvantaged. Denials that amount to taboos surround the subject of advantages that men gain from women's disadvantages. These denials protect male privilege from being fully recognized, acknowledged, lessened, or ended.

Thinking through unacknowledged male privilege as a phenomenon with a life of its own, I realized that since hierarchies in our society are interlocking, there was most likely a phenomenon of white privilege that was similarly denied and protected, but alive and real in its effects. As a white person, I realized I had been taught about racism as something that puts others at a disadvantage, but had been taught not to see one of its corollary aspects, white privilege, which puts me at an advantage.

I think whites are carefully taught not to recognize white privilege, as males are taught not to recognize male privilege. So I have begun in an untutored way to ask what it is like to have white privilege. This paper is a partial record of my personal observations and not a scholarly analysis. It is based on my daily experiences within my particular circumstances.

I have come to see white privilege as an invisible package of unearned assets that I can count on cashing in each day, but about which I was "meant" to remain oblivious. White privilege is like an invisible weightless knapsack of special provisions, assurances, tools, maps, guides, code-books, passports, visas, clothes, compass, emergency gear, and blank checks.

Since I have had trouble facing white privilege, and describing its results in my life, I saw parallels here with men's reluctance to acknowledge male privilege. Only rarely will a man go beyond acknowledging that women are disadvantaged to acknowledging that men have unearned advantage, or that unearned privilege has not been good for men's development as human beings, or for society's development, or that privilege systems might ever be challenged and *changed*.

I will review here several types or layers of denial that I see at work protecting, and preventing awareness about, entrenched male privilege. Then I will draw parallels, from my own experience, with the denials that veil the facts of white privilege. Finally, I will list forty-six ordinary and daily ways in which I experience having white privilege, by contrast with my African American colleagues in the same building. This list is not intended to be generalizable. Others can make their own lists from within their own life circumstances.

Writing this paper has been difficult, despite warm receptions for the talks on which it is based. For describing white privilege makes one newly accountable. As we in Women's Studies work reveal male privilege and ask men to give up some of their power, so one who writes about having white privilege must ask, "Having described it, what will I do to lessen or end it?"

The denial of men's overprivileged state takes many forms in discussions of curriculum change work. Some claim that men must be central in the curriculum because they have done most of what is important or distinctive in life or in civilization. Some recognize sexism in the curriculum but deny that it makes male students seem unduly important in life. Others agree that certain *individual* thinkers are male oriented but deny that there is any *systemic* tendency in disciplinary frameworks or epistemology to overempower men as a group. Those men who do grant that male privilege takes institutionalized and embedded forms are still likely to deny that male hegemony has opened doors for them personally. Virtually all men deny that male overreward alone can explain men's centrality in all the inner sanctums of our most powerful institutions. Moreover, those few who will acknowledge that male privilege systems have overempowered them usually end up doubting that we could dismantle these privilege systems. They may say they will work to improve women's status, in the society or in the university, but they can't or won't support the idea of lessening men's. In curricular terms, this is the point at which they say that they regret they cannot use any of the interesting new scholarship on women because the syllabus is full. When the talk turns to giving men less cultural room, even the most thoughtful and fair-minded of the men I know will tend to reflect, or fall back on, conservative assumptions about the inevitability of present gender relations and distributions of power, calling on precedent or sociobiology and psychobiology to demonstrate that male domination is natural and follows inevitably from evolutionary pressures. Others resort to arguments from "experience" or religion or social responsibility or wishing and dreaming.

After I realized, through faculty development work in Women's Studies, the extent to which men work from a base of unacknowledged privilege, I understood that much of their oppressiveness was unconscious. Then I remembered the frequent charges from women of color that white women whom they encounter are oppressive. I began to understand why we are justly seen as oppressive, even when we don't see ourselves that way. At the very least, obliviousness of one's privileged state can make a person or group irritating to be with. I began to count the ways in which I enjoy unearned skin privilege and have been conditioned into oblivion about its existence, unable to see that it put me "ahead" in any way, or put my people ahead, overrewarding us and yet also paradoxically damaging us, or that it could or should be changed.

My schooling gave me no training in seeing myself as an oppressor, as an unfairly advantaged person, or as a participant in a damaged culture, I was taught to see myself as an individual whose moral state depended on her individual moral will. At school, we were not taught about slavery in any depth; we were not taught to see slave-holders as damaged people. Slaves were seen as the only group at risk of being dehumanized. My schooling followed the pattern which Elizabeth Minnich has pointed out: whites are taught to think of their lives as morally neutral, normative, and average, and also ideal, so that when we work to benefit others, this is seen as work that will allow "them" to be more like "us." I think many of us know how obnoxious this attitude can be in men.

After frustration with men who would not recognize male privilege, I decided to try to work on myself at least by identifying some of the daily effects of white privilege in my life. It is crude work, at this stage, but I will give here a list of special circumstances and conditions I experience that I did not earn but that I have been made to feel are mine by birth, by citizenship, and by virtue of being a conscientious law-abiding "normal" person of goodwill. I have chosen those conditions that I think in my case attach somewhat more to skin-color privilege than to class, religion, ethnic status, or geographical location, though these other privileging factors are intricately intertwined. As far as I can see, my Afro-American co-workers, friends, and acquaintances with whom I come into daily or frequent contact in this particular time, place, and line of work cannot count on most of these conditions.

1. I can, if I wish, arrange to be in the company of people of my race most of the time.

2. I can avoid spending time with people whom I was trained to mistrust and who have learned to mistrust my kind or me.

3. If I should need to move, I can be pretty sure of renting or purchasing housing in an area which I can afford and in which I would want to live.

4. I can be reasonably sure that my neighbors in such a location will be neutral or pleasant to me.

5. I can go shopping alone most of the time, fairly well assured that I will not be followed or harassed by store detectives.

6. I can turn on the television or open to the front page of the paper and see people of my race widely and positively represented.

7. When I am told about our national heritage or about "civilization," I am shown that people of my color made it what it is.

8. I can be sure that my children will be given curricular materials that testify to the existence of their race.

9. If I want to, I can be pretty sure of finding a publisher for this piece on white privilege.

10. I can be fairly sure of having my voice heard in a group in which I am the only member of my race.

11. I can be casual about whether or not to listen to another woman's voice in a group in which she is the only member of her race.

12. I can go into a book shop and count on finding the writing of my race represented, into a supermarket and find the staple foods that fit with my cultural traditions, into a hairdresser's shop and find someone who can deal with my hair.

13. Whether I use checks, credit cards, or cash, I can count on my skin color not to work against the appearance that I am financially reliable.

14. I could arrange to protect our young children most of the time from people who might not like them.

15. I did not have to educate our children to be aware of systemic racism for their own daily physical protection.

16. I can be pretty sure that my children's teachers and employers will tolerate them if they fit school and workplace norms; my chief worries about them do not concern others' attitudes toward their race.

17. I can talk with my mouth full and not have people put this down to my color.

18. I can swear, or dress in secondhand clothes, or not answer letters, without having people attribute these choices to the bad morals, the poverty, or the illiteracy of my race.

19. I can speak in public to a powerful male group without putting my race on trial.

20. I can do well in a challenging situation without being called a credit to my race.

21. I am never asked to speak for all the people of my racial group.

22. I can remain oblivious to the language and customs of persons of color who constitute the world's majority without feeling in my culture any penalty for such oblivion.

23. I can criticize our government and talk about how much I fear its policies and behavior without being seen as a cultural outsider.

24. I can be reasonably sure that if I ask to talk to "the person in charge," I will be facing a person of my race.

25. If a traffic cop pulls me over or if the IRS audits my tax return, I can be sure I haven't been singled out because of my race.

26. I can easily buy posters, postcards, picture books, greeting cards, dolls, toys, and children's magazines featuring people of my race.

27. I can go home from most meetings of organizations I belong to feeling somewhat tied in, rather than isolated, out of place, outnumbered, unheard, held at a distance, or feared.

28. I can be pretty sure that an argument with a colleague of another race is more likely to jeopardize her chances for advancement than to jeopardize mine.

29. I can be fairly sure that if I argue for the promotion of a person of another race, or a program centering on race, this is not likely to cost me heavily within my present setting, even if my colleagues disagree with me.

30. If I declare there is a racial issue at hand, or there isn't a racial issue at hand, my race will lend me more credibility for either position than a person of color will have.

31. I can choose to ignore developments in minority writing and minority activist programs, or disparage them, or learn from them, but in any case, I can find ways to be more or less protected from negative consequences of any of these choices.

32. My culture gives me little fear about ignoring the perspectives and powers of people of other races.

33. I am not made acutely aware that my shape, bearing, or body odor will be taken as a reflection on my race.

34. I can worry about racism without being seen as self-interested or self-seeking.

35. I can take a job with an affirmative action employer without having my coworkers on the job suspect that I got it because of my race.

36. If my day, week, or year is going badly, I need not ask of each negative episode or situation whether it has racial overtones.

37. I can be pretty sure of finding people who would be willing to talk with me and advise me about my next steps, professionally.

38. I can think over many options, social, political, imaginative, or professional, without asking whether a person of my race would be accepted or allowed to do what I want to do.

39. I can be late to a meeting without having the lateness reflect on my race.

40. I can choose public accommodation without fearing that people of my race cannot get in or will be mistreated in the places I have chosen.

41. I can be sure that if I need legal or medical help, my race will not work against me.

42. I can arrange my activities so that I will never have to experience feelings of rejection owing to my race.

43. If I have low credibility as a leader, I can be sure that my race is not the problem.

44. I can easily find academic courses and institutions that give attention only to people of my race.

45. I can expect figurative language and imagery in all of the arts to testify to experiences of my race.

46. I can choose blemish cover or bandages in "flesh" color and have them more or less match my skin.

I repeatedly forgot each of the realizations on this list until I wrote it down. For me, white privilege has turned out to be an elusive and fugitive subject. The pressure to avoid it is great, for in facing it I must give up the myth of meritocracy. If these things are true, this is not such a free country; one's life is not what one makes it; many doors open for certain people through no virtues of their own. These perceptions mean also that my moral condition is not what I had been led to believe. The appearance of being a good citizen rather than a troublemaker comes in large part from having all sorts of doors open automatically because of my color.

A further paralysis of nerve comes from literary silence protecting privilege. My clearest memories of finding such analysis are in Lillian Smith's unparalleled *Killers of the Dream* and Margaret Andersen's review of Karen and Mamie Fields' *Lemon Swamp*. Smith, for example, wrote about walking toward black children on the street and knowing they would step into the gutter; Andersen contrasted the pleasure that she, as a white child, took on summer driving trips to the south with Karen Fields' memories of driving in a closed car stocked with all necessities lest, in stopping, her black family should suffer "insult, or worse." Adrienne

Rich also recognizes and writes about daily experiences of privilege, but in my observation, white women's writing in this area is far more often on systemic racism than on our daily lives as light-skinned women. In unpacking this invisible knapsack of white privilege, I have listed conditions of daily experience that I once took for granted, as neutral, normal, and universally available to everybody, just as I once thought of a male-focused curriculum as the neutral or accurate account that can speak for all. Nor did I think of any of these perquisites as bad for the holder. I now think that we need a more finely differentiated taxonomy of privilege, for some of these varieties are only what one would want for everyone in a just society, and others give license to be ignorant, oblivious, arrogant, and destructive. Before proposing some more finely tuned categorization, I will make some observations about the general effects of these conditions on my life and expectations.

In this potpourri of examples, some privileges make me feel at home in the world. Others allow me to escape penalties or dangers that others suffer. Through some, I escape fear, anxiety, insult, injury, or a sense of not being welcome, not being real. Some keep me from having to hide, to be in disguise, to feel sick or crazy, to negotiate each transaction from the position of being an outsider or, within my group, a person who is suspected of having too close links with a dominant culture. Most keep me from having to be angry.

I see a pattern running through the matrix of white privilege, a pattern of assumptions that were passed on to me as a white person. There was one main piece of cultural turf; it was my own turf and I was among those who could control the turf. I could measure up to the cultural standards and take advantage of the many options I saw around me to make what the culture would call a success of my life. *My skin color was an asset for any move I was educated to want to make.* I could think of myself as "belonging" in major ways and of making social systems work for me. I could freely disparage, fear, neglect, or be oblivious to anything outside of the dominant cultural forms. Being of the main culture, I could also criticize it fairly freely. My life was reflected back to me frequently enough so that I felt, with regard to my race, if not to my sex, like one of the real people. Whether through the curriculum or in the newspaper, the television, the economic system, or the general look of people in the streets, I received daily signals and indications that my people counted and that others *either didn't exist or must be trying not very successfully, to be like people of my race.* I was given cultural permission not to hear voices of people of other races or a tepid cultural tolerance for hearing or acting on such voices. I was also raised not to suffer seriously from anything that darker-skinned people might say about my group, "protected," though perhaps I should more accurately say *pro-hibited* through the habits of my economic class and social group, from living in racially mixed groups or being reflective about interactions between people of differing races.

In proportion as my racial group was being made confident, comfort-able, and oblivious, other groups were likely being made unconfident, uncomfortable, and alienated. Whiteness protected me from many kinds of hostility, distress, and violence, which I was being subtly trained to visit in turn upon people of color.

For this reason, the word "privilege" now seems to me misleading. Its connotations are too positive to fit the conditions and behaviors which "privilege systems" produce. We usually think of privilege as being a favored state, whether earned, or conferred by birth or luck. School grad-uates are reminded they are privileged and urged to use their (enviable) assets well. The word "privilege" carries the connotation of being some-thing everyone must want. Yet some of the conditions I have described here work to systemically over-empower certain groups. Such privilege simply *confers dominance,* gives permission to control, because of one's race or sex. The kind of privilege that gives license to some people to be, at best, thoughtless and, at worst, murderous should not continue to be referred to as a desirable attribute. Such "privilege" may be widely desired without being in any way beneficial to the whole society.

Moreover; though "privilege" may confer power, it does not confer moral strength. Those who do not depend on conferred dominance have traits and qualities that may never develop in those who do. Just as Women's Studies courses indicate that women survive their political cir-cumstances to lead lives that hold the human race together, so "underpriv-ileged" people of color who are the world's majority have survived their oppression and lived survivors' lives from which the white global minority can and must learn. In some groups, those dominated have actually become strong through *not* having all of these unearned advantages, and this gives them a great deal to teach the others. Members of so-called privileged groups can seem foolish, ridiculous, infantile, or dangerous by contrast.

I want, then, to distinguish between earned strength and unearned power conferred systemically. Power from unearned privilege can look like strength when it is, in fact, permission to escape or to dominate. But not all of the privileges on my list are inevitably damaging. Some, like the expectation that neighbors will be decent to you, or that your race will not count against you in court, should be the norm in a just society and should be considered as the entitlement of everyone. Others, like the privilege not to listen to less powerful people, distort the humanity of the holders as well as the ignored groups. Still others, like finding one's staple foods everywhere, may be a function of being a member of a numerical majority in the population. Others have to do with not having to labor under pervasive negative stereotyping and mythology.

We might at least start by distinguishing between positive advantages that we can work to spread, to the point where they are not advantages at all but simply part of the normal civic and social fabric, and negative types of advantage that unless rejected will always reinforce our present hierarchies. For example, the positive "privilege" of belonging, the feeling that one belongs within the human circle, as Native Americans say, fosters development and should not be seen as privilege for a few. It is, let us say, an entitlement that none of us should have to earn; ideally it is an *unearned entitlement*. At present, since only a few have it, it is an *unearned advantage* for them. The negative "privilege" that gave me cultural permission not to take darker-skinned Others seriously can be seen as arbitrarily conferred dominance and should not be desirable for anyone. This paper results from a process of coming to see that some of the power that I originally saw as attendant on being a human being in the United States consisted in *unearned advantage* and *conferred dominance,* as well as other kinds of special circumstance not universally taken for granted.

In writing this paper I have also realized that white identity and status (as well as class identity and status) give me considerable power to choose whether to broach this subject and its trouble. I can pretty well decide whether to disappear and avoid and not listen and escape the dislike I may engender in other people through this essay, or interrupt, answer, interpret, preach, correct, criticize, and control to some extent what goes on in reaction to it. Being white, I am given considerable power to escape many kinds of danger or penalty as well as to choose which risks I want to take.

There is an analogy here, once again, with Women's Studies. Our male colleagues do not have a great deal to lose in supporting Women's Studies, but they do not have a great deal to lose if they oppose it either. They simply have the power to decide whether to commit themselves to more equitable distributions of power. They will probably feel few penalties whatever choice they make; they do not seem, in any obvious short-term sense, the ones at risk, though they and we are all at risk because of the behaviors that have been rewarded in them.

Through Women's Studies work I have met very few men who are truly distressed about systemic, unearned male advantage and conferred domi-nance. And so one question for me and others like me is whether we will be like them, or whether we will get truly distressed, even outraged, about unearned race advantage and conferred dominance and if so, what we will do to lessen them. In any case, we need to do more work in identifying how they actually affect our daily lives. We need more down-to-earth writing by people about these taboo subjects. We need more understanding of the ways in which white "privilege" damages white people, for these are not the same ways in which it damages the victimized. Skewed white psyches are an inseparable part of the picture, though I do not want to confuse the kinds of damage done to the holders of special assets and to those who suffer the deficits. Many, perhaps most, of our white students in the United States think that racism doesn't affect them because they are not people of color; they do not see "whiteness" as a racial identity. Many men likewise think that Women's Studies does not bear on their own existences because they are not female; they do not see themselves as having gendered identities. Insisting on the universal "effects" of "privilege" systems, then, becomes one of our chief tasks, and being more explicit about the particular effects in particular contexts in another. Men need to join us in this work.

In addition, since race and sex are not the only advantaging systems at work, we need to similarly examine the daily experience of having age advantage, or ethnic advantage, or physical ability, or advantage related to nationality, religion, or sexual orientation. Professor Marnie Evans suggested to me that in many ways the list I made also applies directly to heterosexual privilege. This is a still more taboo subject than race privilege: the daily ways in which heterosexual privilege makes some persons comfortable or powerful, providing supports, assets, approvals, and rewards to those who live or expect to live in heterosexual pairs. Unpacking that content is still more difficult, owing to the deeper imbeddedness of heterosexual advantage and dominance and stricter taboos surrounding these.

But to start such an analysis I would put this observation from my own experience: The fact that I live under the same roof with a man triggers all kinds of societal assumptions about my worth, politics, life, and values and triggers a host of unearned advantages and powers. After recasting many elements from the original list I would add further observations like these:

1. My children do not have to answer questions about why I live with my partner (my husband).

2. I have no difficulty finding neighborhoods where people approve of our household.

3. Our children are given texts and classes that implicitly support our kind of family unit and do not turn them against my choice of domestic partnership.

4. I can travel alone or with my husband without expecting embarrassment or hostility in those who deal with us.

5. Most people I meet will see my marital arrangements as an asset to my life or as a favorable comment on my likeability, my competence, or my mental health.

6. I can talk about the social events of a weekend without fearing most listeners' reactions.

7. I will feel welcomed and "normal" in the usual walks of public life, institutional and social.

8. In many contexts, I am seen as "all right" in daily work on women because I do not live chiefly with women.

Difficulties and dangers surrounding the task of finding parallels are many. Since racism, sexism, and heterosexism are not the same, the advantages associated with them should not be seen as the same. In addition, it is hard to isolate aspects of unearned advantage that derive chiefly from social class, economic class, race, religion, region, sex, or ethnic identity. The oppressions are both distinct and interlocking, as the Combahee River Collective statement of 1977 continues to remind us eloquently.

One factor seems clear about all of the interlocking oppressions. They take both active forms that we can see and embedded forms that members of the dominant group are taught not to see. In my class and place, I did not see myself as racist because I was taught to recognize racism only in individual acts of meanness by members of my group, never in invisible systems conferring racial dominance on my group from birth. Likewise, we are taught to think that sexism or heterosexism is carried on only through intentional, individual acts of discrimination, meanness, or cruelty, rather than in invisible systems conferring unsought dominance on certain groups. Disapproving of the systems won't be enough to change them. I was taught to think that racism could end if white individuals changed their attitudes; many men think sexism can be ended by individual changes in daily behavior toward women. But a man's sex provides advantage for him whether or not he approves of the way in which dominance has been conferred on his group. A "white" skin in the United States opens many doors for whites whether or not we approve of the way dominance has been conferred on us. Individual acts can palliate, but cannot end, these problems. To redesign social systems, we need first to acknowledge their colossal unseen dimensions. The silences and denials surrounding privilege are the key political tool here. They keep the thinking about equality or equity incomplete, protecting unearned advantage and conferred dominance by making these taboo subjects. Most talk by whites about equal opportunity seems to me now to be about equal opportunity to try to get into a position of dominance while denying that *systems* of dominance exist.

Obliviousness about white advantage, like obliviousness about male advantage, is kept strongly inculturated in the United States so as to maintain the myth of meritocracy, the myth that democratic choice is equally available to all. Keeping most people unaware that freedom of confident action is there for just a small number of people props up those in power and serves to keep power in the hands of the same groups that have most of it already. Though systemic change takes many decades, there are pressing questions for me and I imagine for some others like me if we raise our daily consciousness on the perquisites of being light-skinned. What will we do with such knowledge? As we know from watching men, it is an open question whether we will choose to use unearned advantage to weaken invisible privilege systems and whether we will use any of our arbitrarily awarded power to try to reconstruct power systems on a broader base.

11

Teaching Themes of Care

Nel Noddings

In the following article, the feminist and educational theorist Nel Noddings (1995) calls for a complete reorganization of the traditional school curriculum. In doing so, she focuses on themes of care—caring for others, caring for self, caring for the natural world, and so on. Noddings believes that the current curriculum found in American public education, with its emphasis on standards and test scores, is impoverished. She believes that much is to be gained with the development and implementation of a curriculum focused around issues of care. Including issues of care has the potential to expand the meaning of the curriculum and the cultural literacy and knowledge of our students. In addition, the inclusion of care connects the standard curriculum to the different subjects included in the curriculum and larger questions about who and what we are as human beings and how we should live. A curriculum focusing on care also helps us understand that we are not alone in the world and that we can transcend the frequent tragedies found in human life through love. Finally, care also involves a search for competence—that is, doing the very best for the objects and things we care about.

As you read Noddings's essay, consider the following questions:

1. Is there time for a curriculum of care in a world where we need to educate people to deal with new technologies and increasing challenges in terms of the demands of work?

NOTE: Used with personal permission of the author.

2. What are the consequences of not investing in children in terms of their emotional and physical needs?

3. What is the role of teaching students to be critical thinkers?

4. Which role should or do teachers need to play in the emotional lives of their students?

5. How should we train teachers to work in more "caring" environments?

Some educators today—and I include myself among them—would like to see a complete reorganization of the school curriculum. We would like to give a central place to the questions and issues that lie at the core of human existence. One possibility would be to organize the curriculum around themes of care—caring for self, for intimate others, for strangers and global others, for the natural world and its nonhuman creatures, for the human-made world, and for ideas.[1]

A realistic assessment of schooling in the present political climate makes it clear that such a plan is not likely to be implemented. However, we can use the rich vocabulary of care in educational planning and introduce themes of care into regular subject-matter classes. In this article, I will first give a brief rationale for teaching themes of care; second, I will suggest ways of choosing and organizing such themes; and, finally, I'll say a bit about the structures required to support such teaching.

Why Teach Caring?

In an age when violence among schoolchildren is at an unprecedented level, when children are bearing children with little knowledge of how to care for them, when the society and even the schools often concentrate on materialistic messages, it may be unnecessary to argue that we should care more genuinely for our children and teach them to care. However, many otherwise reasonable people seem to believe that our educational problems consist largely of low scores on achievement tests. My contention is, first, that we should want more from our educational efforts than adequate academic achievement and, second, that we will not achieve even that meager success

---

[1]For the theoretical argument, see Nel Noddings, *The Challenge to Care in Schools* (New York: Teachers College Press, 1992); for a practical example and rich documentation, see Sharon Quint, *Schooling Homeless Children* (New York: Teachers College Press, 1994).

unless our children believe that they themselves are cared for and learn to care for others.

There is much to be gained, both academically and humanly, by including themes of care in our curriculum. First, such inclusion may well expand our students' cultural literacy. For example, as we discuss in math classes the attempts of great mathematicians to prove the existence of God or to reconcile a God who is all good with the reality of evil in the world, students will hear names, ideas, and words that are not part of the standard curriculum. Although such incidental learning cannot replace the systematic and sequential learning required by those who plan careers in mathematically oriented fields, it can be powerful in expanding students' cultural horizons and in inspiring further study.

Second, themes of care help us to connect the standard subjects. The use of literature in mathematics classes, of history in science classes, and of art and music in all classes can give students a feeling of the wholeness in their education. After all, why should they seriously study five different subjects if their teachers, who are educated people, only seem to know and appreciate one?

Third, themes of care connect our students and our subjects to great existential questions. What is the meaning of life? Are there gods? How should I live?

Fourth, sharing such themes can connect us person-to-person. When teachers discuss themes of care, they may become real persons to their students and so enable them to construct new knowledge. Martin Buber put it this way:

> Trust, trust in the world, because this human being exists—that is the most inward achievement of the relation in education. Because this human being exists, meaninglessness, however hard pressed you are by it, cannot be the real truth. Because this human being exists, in the darkness the light lies hidden, in fear salvation, and in the callousness of one's fellow-man the great love.[2]

Finally, I should emphasize that caring is not just a warm, fuzzy feeling that makes people kind and likable. Caring implies a continuous search for competence. When we care, we want to do our very best for the objects of our care. To have as our educational goal the production of caring, competent, loving, and lovable people is not anti-intellectual. Rather, it demonstrates respect for the full range of human talents. Not all human beings are good at or interested in mathematics, science, or British literature. But all

---

[2]Martin Buber, *Between Man and Man* (New York: Macmillan, 1965), p. 98.

humans can be helped to lead lives of deep concern for others, for the natural world and its creatures, and for the preservation of the human-made world. They can be led to develop the skills and knowledge necessary to make positive contributions, regardless of the occupation they may choose.

Choosing and Organizing Themes of Care

Care is conveyed in many ways. At the institutional level, schools can be organized to provide continuity and support for relationships of care and trust.[3] At the individual level, parents and teachers show their caring through characteristic forms of attention: by cooperating in children's activities, by sharing their own dreams and doubts, and by providing carefully for the steady growth of the children in their charge. Personal manifestations of care are probably more important in children's lives than any particular curriculum or pattern of pedagogy.

However, curriculum can be selected with caring in mind. That is, educators can manifest their care in the choice of curriculum, and appropriately chosen curriculum can contribute to the growth of children as carers. Within each large domain of care, many topics are suitable for thematic units: in the domain of "caring for self," for example, we might consider life stages, spiritual growth, and what it means to develop an admirable character; in exploring the topic of caring for intimate others, we might include units on love, friendship, and parenting; under the theme of caring for strangers and global others, we might study war, poverty, and tolerance; in addressing the idea of caring for the human-made world, we might encourage competence with the machines that surround us and a real appreciation for the marvels of technology. Many other examples exist. Furthermore, there are at least two different ways to approach the development of such themes: units can be constructed by interdisciplinary teams, or themes can be identified by individual teachers and addressed periodically throughout a year's or semester's work.

The interdisciplinary approach is familiar in core programs, and such programs are becoming more and more popular at the middle school level. One key to a successful interdisciplinary unit is the degree of genuinely enthusiastic support it receives from the teachers involved. Too often, arbitrary or artificial groupings are formed, and teachers are forced to make contributions that they themselves do not value highly. For example, math and science teachers are sometimes automatically lumped together, and rich

---

[3]Noddings, chap. 12.

humanistic possibilities may be lost. If I, as a math teacher, want to include historical, biographical, and literary topics in my math lessons, I might prefer to work with English and social studies teachers. Thus it is important to involve teachers in the initial selection of broad areas for themes, as well as in their implementation.

Such interdisciplinary arrangements also work well at the college level. I recently received a copy of the syllabus for a college course titled "The Search for Meaning," which was co-taught by an economist, a university chaplain, and a psychiatrist.[4] The course is interdisciplinary, intellectually rich, and aimed squarely at the central questions of life.

At the high school level, where students desperately need to engage in the study and practice of caring, it is harder to form interdisciplinary teams. A conflict arises as teachers acknowledge the intensity of the subject-matter preparation their students need for further education. Good teachers often wish there were time in the day to co-teach unconventional topics of great importance, and they even admit that their students are not getting what they need for full personal development. But they feel constrained by the requirements of a highly competitive world and the structures of schooling established by that world.

Is there a way out of this conflict? Imaginative, like-minded teachers might agree to emphasize a particular theme in their separate classes. Such themes as war, poverty, crime, racism, or sexism can be addressed in almost every subject area. The teachers should agree on some core ideas related to caring that will be discussed in all classes, but beyond the central commitment to address themes of care, the topics can be handled in whatever way seems suitable in a given subject.

Consider, for example, what a mathematics class might contribute to a unit on crime. Statistical information might be gathered on the location and number of crimes, on rates for various kinds of crime, on the ages of offenders, and on the cost to society; graphs and charts could be constructed. Data on changes in crime rates could be assembled. Intriguing questions could be asked: Were property crime rates lower when penalties were more severe—when, for example, even children were hanged as thieves? What does an average criminal case cost by way of lawyers' fees, police investigation, and court processing? Does it cost more to house a youth in a detention center or in an elite private school?

None of this would have to occupy a full period every day. The regular sequential work of the math class could go on at a slightly reduced rate

---

[4]See Thomas H. Naylor, William H. Willimon, and Magdalena R. Naylor, *The Search for Meaning* (Nashville, Tenn.: Abingdon Press, 1994).

(e.g., fewer textbook exercises as homework), and the work on crime could proceed in the form of interdisciplinary projects over a considerable period of time. Most important would be the continual reminder in all classes that the topic is part of a larger theme of caring for strangers and fellow citizens. It takes only a few minutes to talk about what it means to live in safety, to trust one's neighbors, to feel secure in greeting strangers. Students should be told that metal detectors and security guards were not part of their parents' school lives, and they should be encouraged to hope for a safer and more open future. Notice the words I've used in this paragraph: caring, trust, safety, strangers, hope. Each could be used as an organizing theme for another unit of study.

English and social studies teachers would obviously have much to contribute to a unit on crime. For example, students might read *Oliver Twist*, and they might also study and discuss the social conditions that seemed to promote crime in 19th-century England. Do similar conditions exist in our country today? The selection of materials could include both classic works and modern stories and films. Students might even be introduced to some of the mystery stories that adults read so avidly on airplanes and beaches, and teachers should be engaged in lively discussion about the comparative value of the various stories.

Science teachers might find that a unit on crime would enrich their teaching of evolution. They could bring up the topic of social Darwinism, which played such a strong role in social policy during the late 19th and early 20th centuries. To what degree are criminal tendencies inherited? Should children be tested for the genetic defects that are suspected of predisposing some people to crime? Are females less competent than males in moral reasoning? (Why did some scientists and philosophers think this was true?) Why do males commit so many more violent acts than females?

Teachers of the arts can also be involved. A unit on crime might provide a wonderful opportunity to critique "gangsta rap" and other currently popular forms of music. Students might profitably learn how the control of art contributed to national criminality during the Nazi era. These are ideas that pop into my mind. Far more various and far richer ideas will come from teachers who specialize in these subjects.

There are risks, of course, in undertaking any unit of study that focuses on matters of controversy or deep existential concern, and teachers should anticipate these risks. What if students want to compare the incomes of teachers and cocaine dealers? What if they point to contemporary personalities from politics, entertainment, business, or sports who seem to escape the law and profit from what seems to be criminal behavior? My own

inclination would be to allow free discussion of these cases
pared to counteract them with powerful stories of hones'
moderation, and charity.

An even more difficult problem may arise. Suppose a student disc.
his or her own criminal activities? Fear of this sort of occurrence may send
teachers scurrying for safer topics. But, in fact, any instructional method
that uses narrative forms or encourages personal expression runs this risk.
For example, students of English as a second language who write proudly
about their own hard lives and new hopes may disclose that their parents
are illegal immigrants. A girl may write passages that lead her teacher to
suspect sexual abuse. A boy may brag about objects he has "ripped off."
Clearly, as we use these powerful methods that encourage students to initiate discussion and share their experiences, we must reflect on the ethical
issues involved, consider appropriate responses to such issues, and prepare
teachers to handle them responsibly.

Caring teachers must help students make wise decisions about what
information they will share about themselves. On the one hand, teachers
want their students to express themselves, and they want their students to
trust in and consult them. On the other hand, teachers have an obligation
to protect immature students from making disclosures that they might later
regret. There is a deep ethical problem here. Too often educators assume
that only religious fundamentalists and right-wing extremists object to the
discussion of emotionally and morally charged issues. In reality, there is a
real danger of intrusiveness and lack of respect in methods that fail to recognize the vulnerability of students. Therefore, as teachers plan units and
lessons on moral issues, they should anticipate the tough problems that may
arise. I am arguing here that it is morally irresponsible to simply ignore existential questions and themes of care; we must attend to them. But it is
equally irresponsible to approach these deep concerns without caution and
careful preparation.

So far I have discussed two ways of organizing interdisciplinary units on
themes of care. In one, teachers actually teach together in teams; in the
other, teachers agree on a theme and a central focus on care, but they do
what they can, when they can, in their own classrooms. A variation on this
second way—which is also open to teachers who have to work alone—is to
choose several themes and weave them into regular course material over an
entire semester or year. The particular themes will depend on the interests
and preparation of each teacher.

For example, if I were teaching high school mathematics today, I would
use religious/existential questions as a pervasive theme because the
biographies of mathematicians are filled with accounts of their speculations

on matters of God, other dimensions, and the infinite—and because these topics fascinate me. There are so many wonderful stories to be told: Descartes' proof of the existence of God, Pascal's famous wager, Plato's world of forms, Newton's attempt to verify Biblical chronology, Leibniz' detailed theodicy, current attempts to describe a divine domain in terms of metasystems, and mystical speculations on the infinite.[5] Some of these stories can be told as rich "asides" in five minutes or less. Others might occupy the better part of several class periods.

Other mathematics teachers might use an interest in architecture and design, art, music, or machinery as continuing themes in the domain of "caring for the human-made world." Still others might introduce the mathematics of living things. The possibilities are endless. In choosing and pursuing these themes, teachers should be aware that they are both helping their students learn to care and demonstrating their own caring by sharing interests that go well beyond the demands of textbook pedagogy.

Still another way to introduce themes of care into regular classrooms is to be prepared to respond spontaneously to events that occur in the school or in the neighborhood. Older teachers have one advantage in this area: they probably have a greater store of experience and stories on which to draw. However, younger teachers have the advantage of being closer to their students' lives and experiences; they are more likely to be familiar with the music, films, and sports figures that interest their students.

All teachers should be prepared to respond to the needs of students who are suffering from the death of friends, conflicts between groups of students, pressure to use drugs or to engage in sex, and other troubles so rampant in the lives of today's children. Too often schools rely on experts—"grief counselors" and the like—when what children really need is the continuing compassion and presence of adults who represent constancy and care in their lives. Artificially separating the emotional, academic, and moral care of children into tasks for specially designated experts contributes to the fragmentation of life in schools.

Of course, I do not mean to imply that experts are unnecessary, nor do I mean to suggest that some matters should not be reserved for parents or psychologists. But our society has gone too far in compartmentalizing the care of its children. When we ask whose job it is to teach children how to care, an appropriate initial response is "Everyone's." Having accepted universal responsibility, we can then ask about the special contributions and limitations of various individuals and groups.

---

[5]For many more examples, see Nel Noddings, *Educating for Intelligent Belief and Unbelief* (New York: Teachers College Press, 1993).

Supporting Structures

What kind of schools and teacher preparation are required, if themes of care are to be taught effectively? First, and most important, care must be taken seriously as a major purpose of schools; that is, educators must recognize that caring for students is fundamental in teaching and that developing people with a strong capacity for care is a major objective of responsible education. Schools properly pursue many other objectives—developing artistic talent, promoting multicultural understanding, diversifying curriculum to meet the academic and vocational needs of all students, forging connections with community agencies and parents, and so on. Schools cannot be single-purpose institutions. Indeed, many of us would argue that it is logically and practically impossible to achieve that single academic purpose if other purposes are not recognized and accepted. This contention is confirmed in the success stories of several inner-city schools.[6]

Once it is recognized that school is a place in which students are cared for and learn to care, that recognition should be powerful in guiding policy. In the late 1950s, schools in the U.S., under the guidance of James Conant and others, placed the curriculum at the top of the educational priority list. Because the nation's leaders wanted schools to provide high-powered courses in mathematics and science, it was recommended that small high schools be replaced by efficient larger structures complete with sophisticated laboratories and specialist teachers. Economies of scale were anticipated, but the main argument for consolidation and regionalization centered on the curriculum. All over the country, small schools were closed, and students were herded into larger facilities with "more offerings." We did not think carefully about schools as communities and about what might be lost as we pursued a curriculum-driven ideal.

Today many educators are calling for smaller schools and more family-like groupings. These are good proposals, but teachers, parents, and students should be engaged in continuing discussion about what they are trying to achieve through the new arrangements. For example, if test scores do not immediately rise, participants should be courageous in explaining that test scores were not the main object of the changes. Most of us who argue for caring in schools are intuitively quite sure that children in such settings will in fact become more competent learners. But, if they cannot prove their academic competence in a prescribed period of time, should we give up on

---

[6]See Deborah Meier, "How Our Schools Could Be," *Phi Delta Kappan*, January 1995, pp. 369–73; and Quint, op. cit.

caring and on teaching them to care? That would be foolish. There is more to life and learning than the academic proficiency demonstrated by test scores.

In addition to steadfastness of purpose, schools must consider continuity of people and place. If we are concerned with caring and community, then we must make it possible for students and teachers to stay together for several years so that mutual trust can develop and students can feel a sense of belonging in their "schoolhome."[7]

More than one scheme of organization can satisfy the need for continuity. Elementary school children can stay with the same teacher for several years, or they can work with a stable team of specialist teachers for several years. In the latter arrangement, there may be program advantages; that is, children taught by subject-matter experts who get to know them well over an extended period of time may learn more about the particular subjects. At the high school level, the same specialist teachers might work with students throughout their years in high school. Or, as Theodore Sizer has suggested, one teacher might teach two subjects to a group of 30 students rather than one subject to 60 students, thereby reducing the number of different adults with whom students interact each day.[8] In all the suggested arrangements, placements should be made by mutual consent whenever possible. Teachers and students who hate or distrust one another should not be forced to stay together.

A policy of keeping students and teachers together for several years supports caring in two essential ways: it provides time for the development of caring relations, and it makes teaching themes of care more feasible. When trust has been established, teacher and students can discuss matters that would be hard for a group of strangers to approach, and classmates learn to support one another in sensitive situations.

The structural changes suggested here are not expensive. If a high school teacher must teach five classes a day, it costs no more for three of these classes to be composed of continuing students than for all five classes to comprise new students—i.e., strangers. The recommended changes come directly out of a clear-headed assessment of our major aims and purposes. We failed to suggest them earlier because we had other, too limited, goals in mind.

I have made one set of structural changes sound easy, and I do believe that they are easily made. But the curricular and pedagogical changes that

---

[7] See Jane Roland Martin, *The Schoolhome: Rethinking Schools for Changing Families* (Cambridge, Mass.: Harvard University Press, 1992).

[8] Theodore Sizer, *Horace's Compromise: The Dilemma of the American High School* (Boston: Houghton Mifflin, 1984).

are required may be more difficult. High school textbooks rarely contain the kinds of supplementary material I have described, and teachers are not formally prepared to incorporate such material. Too often, even the people we regard as strongly prepared in a liberal arts major are unprepared to discuss the history of their subject, its relation to other subjects, the biographies of its great figures, its connections to the great existential questions, and the ethical responsibilities of those who work in that discipline. To teach themes of care in an academically effective way, teachers will have to engage in projects of self-education.

At present, neither liberal arts departments nor schools of education pay much attention to connecting academic subjects with themes of care. For example, biology students may learn something of the anatomy and physiology of mammals but nothing at all about the care of living animals; they may never be asked to consider the moral issues involved in the annual euthanasia of millions of pets. Mathematics students may learn to solve quadratic equations but never study what it means to live in a mathematicized world. In enlightened history classes, students may learn something about the problems of racism and colonialism but never hear anything about the evolution of childhood, the contributions of women in both domestic and public caregiving, or the connection between the feminization of caregiving and public policy. A liberal education that neglects matters that are central to a fully human life hardly warrants the name,[9] and a professional education that confines itself to technique does nothing to close the gaps in liberal education.

The greatest structural obstacle, however, may simply be legitimizing the inclusion of themes of care in the curriculum. Teachers in the early grades have long included such themes as a regular part of their work, and middle school educators are becoming more sensitive to developmental needs involving care. But secondary schools—where violence, apathy, and alienation are most evident—do little to develop the capacity to care. Today, even elementary teachers complain that the pressure to produce high test scores inhibits the work they regard as central to their mission: the development of caring and competent people. Therefore, it would seem that the most fundamental change required is one of attitude. Teachers can be very special people in the lives of children, and it should be legitimate for them to spend time developing relations of trust, talking with students about problems that are central to their lives, and guiding them toward greater sensitivity and competence across all the domains of care.

---

[9]See Bruce Wilshire, *The Moral Collapse of the University* (Albany: State University of New York Press, 1990).

PART V

Teaching as Work

12. Prologue From *Horace's Compromise*
    Theodore R. Sizer

13. Selection From *My Posse Don't Do Homework*
    LouAnne Johnson

14. "What Teachers Make"
    Taylor Mali

Deciding to be a teacher involves a commitment to a certain type of life—one that has both social and ethical implications. Several of Lortie's (1975) attractors to teaching come to mind in this context. You shouldn't teach if you aren't interested in people as individuals (the *interpersonal theme*) and providing meaning in their lives (the *service theme*). Teaching is good middle-class work. But if you have a need for luxuries and the means to buy a lot of things, don't become a teacher unless you have other sources of income (the *material benefits theme*).

Who you are and how you represent yourself in your work are key elements in being a teacher. Many teachers often forget this fact.

In the selection from *Horace's Compromise,* Theodore Sizer (1984) describes the day-to-day life of an Advanced Placement high school English teacher. It is followed by LouAnne Johnson's (1992) description of working with minority and diverse secondary students in her novel *My Posse Don't Do Homework,* which was the basis for the 1995 movie *Dangerous Minds* starring Michelle Pfeiffer. The chapter concludes with Taylor Mali's (1999) poem "What Teachers Make."

Further Readings: An extremely interesting recent book dealing with the experience of teaching is Leslie Baldacci's *Inside Mrs. B's Classroom: Courage, Hope and Learning on Chicago's South Side* (McGraw-Hill, 2004). It describes the day-to-day challenges of teaching in an inner-city school in Chicago. Michele Foster provides personal accounts from African American teachers in her book *Black Teachers on Teaching* (New Press, 1977). Another interesting novel dealing with a life in teaching is *The Girls in the Back of the Class* (St. Martin's, 1996).

Linking to Popular Culture: There are numerous movies that describe the lives of teachers and their work. Among the best known and most interesting is *Goodbye, Mr. Chips* (1939), in which a retired English schoolmaster thinks back on his career. The movie is based on James Hilton's 1934 novel of the same title. A remake of the movie was made in 1969 starring Petula Clark and Peter O'Toole. *Good Morning, Miss Dove* (1956) is about a spinster schoolteacher and her effect on her students and the small town in which she lives. *Teachers* is a 1984 comedy starring Nick Nolte and JoBeth Williams. The film centers around Alex Jurel (played by Nolte), a disaffected social studies teacher who nonetheless is able to connect with his students. In *The Man Without a Face* (1993), a disfigured teacher and a fatherless boy work with one another, and each grows as a result of the experience. In *Mr. Holland's Opus* (1995), a frustrated composer turns to teaching to support himself and, despite problems, finds a meaningful life. In *Freedom Writers* (2007), a young lawyer becomes a teacher and helps students find their lives through writing.

On YouTube, there are many interesting films depicting the work of teachers. The French 2002 film *Être et Avoir (To Be and to Have)* is a beautiful documentary film about a year in the classroom life of a gifted rural French schoolteacher named Georges Lopez. If your French is not good, look for the subtitled versions. Taylor Mali's slam poetry recitals on YouTube are wonderful. Particularly make a point of viewing "What Teachers Make," a live performance of the poem included as the third reading in this section. Also highly recommended on YouTube is Mali's "Miracle Workers," which describes what teachers do in their work.

References

Johnson, L. (1992). *My posse don't do homework*. New York: St. Martin's.

Lortie, D. C. (1975). *Schoolteacher: A sociological study*. Chicago: University of Chicago Press.

Mali, T. (1999). What teachers make, or Objection overruled, or If things don't work out, you can always go to law school. Retrieved from http://taylormali.com/index.cfm?webid=13

Sizer, T. (1984). *Horace's compromise*. Boston: Houghton Mifflin.

12

Prologue From
Horace's Compromise

Theodore R. Sizer

In this classic analysis of American secondary education, Ted Sizer (1984), the former Dean of Education at Harvard and the founder of the Coalition for Essential Schools, looks at what goes on in high schools and whether it really makes sense. Sizer calls for a number of reforms, including voluntary high school attendance and emphasizing the personal interests and needs of students. In the prologue to the book, Sizer describes the life of an Advanced Placement teacher. Consider the following questions as you read Sizer's prologue:

1. Is teaching a rewarding job for Horace? If yes, why? If not, why not?

2. What types of things do you think Horace needs to make teaching a better job for him?

3. Why is there the discrepancy between what university and college teachers do, in terms of their work, and what a high school teacher like Horace does?

4. Are there ways Horace could lobby or negotiate for better working conditions? What should be the role of a teachers' union in this context? What should be the role of the local school administration and school board?

Here is an English teacher, Horace Smith. He's fifty-three, a twenty-eight-year veteran of high school classrooms, what one calls an old pro. He's proud, respected, and committed to his practice. He'd do nothing else. Teaching is too much fun, too rewarding, to yield to another line of work.

Horace has been at Franklin High in a suburb of a big city for nineteen years. He served for eight years as English department chairman, but turned the job over to a colleague, because he felt that even the minimal administrative chores of that post interfered with the teaching he loved best.

He arises at 5:45 A.M., careful not to awaken either his wife or grown daughter. He likes to be at school by 7:00, and the drive there from his home takes forty minutes. He wishes he owned a home near the school, but he can't afford it. Only a few of his colleagues live in the school's town, and they are the wives of executives whose salaries can handle the mortgages. His wife's job at the liquor store that she, he, and her brother own doesn't start until 10:00 A.M., and their daughter, a new associate in a law firm in the city, likes to sleep until the last possible minute and skip breakfast. He washes and dresses on tiptoe.

Horace prepares the coffee, makes some toast, and leaves the house at 6:20. He's not the first at school. The custodians and other, usually older, teachers are already there, "puttering around," one of the teachers says.

The teachers' room is large, really two rooms. The inner portion, windowless, is arranged in a honeycomb of carrels, one for each older teacher. Younger or newer teachers share carrels. Each has a built-in desk and a chair. Most have file cabinets. The walls on three sides, five feet high, are festooned with posters, photographs, lists, little sayings, notes from colleagues on issues long past. Horace: Call home. Horace: The following students in the chorus are excused from your Period 7 class: Adelson, Cartwright, Donato. . . .

Horace goes to his carrel, puts down his briefcase, picks up his mug, and walks to the coffee pot at the corner of the outer portion of the teachers' room, a space well lit by wide windows and fitted with a clutter of tables, vinyl-covered sofas, and chairs. The space is a familiar, comfortable jumble, fragrant with the smell of cigarettes smoked hours before. Horace lights up a fresh one, almost involuntarily, as a way perhaps to counteract yesterday's dead vapors. After pouring himself some coffee, he chats with some colleagues, mostly other English teachers.

The warning bell rings at 7:20. Horace smothers his cigarette, takes his still partly filled cup back to his carrel and adds it to the shuffle on his desk, collects some books and papers, and, with his briefcase, carries them down the hall to his classroom. Students are already clattering in, friendly, noisy, most of them ignoring him completely—not thoughtlessly, but without thinking. Horace often thinks of the importance of this semantic difference. Many adults are thoughtless about us teachers. Most students, however, just don't know we're here at all, people to think about. Innocents, he concludes.

7:30, and its bell. There are seventeen students here; there should be twenty-two. Bill Adams is ill; Horace has been told that by the office. Joyce Lezcowitz is at her grandmother's funeral; Horace hasn't been officially told that, but he knows it to be true. He marks Joyce "Ex Ab"—excused absence—on his attendance list. Looking up from the list, he sees two more students arrive, hustling to seats. You're late. Sorry . . . Sorry . . . The bus. . . . Horace ignores the apologies and excuses and checks the two off on his list. One name is yet unaccounted for. Where is Jimmy Tibbetts? Silence. Tibbetts gets an "Abs" after his name.

Horace gets the class's attention by making some announcements about next week's test and about the method by which copies of the next play being read will be shared. This inordinately concerns some students and holds no interest for others. Mr. Smith, how can I finish the play when both Rosalie and I have to work after school? Mr. Smith, Sandy and I are on different buses. Can we switch partners? All these sorts of queries are from girls. There is whispering among some students. You got it? Horace asks, abruptly. Silence, signaling affirmation. Horace knows it is an illusion. Some character will come up two days later and guiltlessly assert that he has no play book, doesn't know how to get one, and has never heard of the plans to share the limited copies. Horace makes a mental note to inform Adams, Lezcowitz, and Tibbetts of the text-sharing plan.

This is a class of juniors, mostly seventeen. The department syllabus calls for Shakespeare during this marking period, and *Romeo and Juliet* is the choice this year. The students have been assigned to read Act IV for this week, and Horace and his colleagues all get them to read the play out loud. The previous class had been memorable: Juliet's suicide had provoked much mirth. Romeo. I come! The kids thought it funny, clumsily melodramatic. Several, sniggering, saw a sexual meaning. Horace knew this to be inevitable; he had taught the play many times before.

We'll start at Scene Four. A rustle of books. Two kids looking helplessly around. They had forgotten their books, even though reading had been a daily exercise for three weeks. Mr. Smith, I forgot my book. You've got to remember, Alice . . . remember! All this with a smile as well as honest exasperation. Share with George. Alice gets up and moves her desk next to that of George. They solemnly peer into George's book while two girls across the classroom giggle.

Gloria, you're Lady Capulet. Mary, the Nurse. George, you're old man Capulet. Gloria starts, reading without punctuation: Hold take these keys and fetch more spices Nurse. Horace: Gloria. Those commas. They mean something. Use them. Now, again. Hold. Take these keys. And fetch more spices. Nurse. Horace swallows. Better . . . Go on, Mary. They call for dates and quinces in the pastry. What's a quince? a voice asks. Someone answers, It's a fruit, Fruit! Horace ignores this digression but is reminded how he doesn't like this group of kids. Individually, they're nice, but the chemistry of them together doesn't work. Classes are too much a game for them. Go on . . . George?

Come. Stir! Stir! Stir! The second cock hath crow'd. Horace knows that reference to "cock" will give an opening to some jokester, and he squelches it before it can begin, by being sure he is looking at the class and not at his book as the words are read.

The curfew bell hath rung. 'Tis three o'clock. Look to the bak'd meats, good Angelica. George reads accurately, but with little accentuation.

Mary: Go. You cot-quean. Go. Horace interrupts, and explains "cot-quean," a touch of contempt by the Nurse for the meddling Capulet. Horace does not go into the word's etymology, although he knows it. He feels that such a digression would be lost on this group, if not on his third-period class. He'll tell them. And so he returns: George, you're still Capulet. Reply to that cheeky Nurse.

The reading goes on for about forty minutes, to 8:15. The play's repartee among the musicians and Peter was a struggle, and Horace cut off the reading-out-loud before the end of the fifth scene. He assigns Act V for the next period and explains what will be on the *Romeo and Juliet* test. Mr. Smith, Ms. Viola isn't giving a test to her class. The statement is, of course, an accusing question. Well, we are. Ms. Viola's class will get something else, don't you worry. The bell rings.

The students rush out as the next class tries to push in. The newcomers are freshmen and give way to the eleventh-graders. They get into their seats expectantly, without quite the swagger of the older kids. Even though this is March, some of these students are still overwhelmed by the size of the high school.

There should be thirty students in this class, but twenty-seven are present. He marks three absences on his sheet. The students watch him; there is no chatter, but a good deal of squirming. These kids have the wriggles, Horace has often said. The bell rings: 8:24.

Horace tells the students to open their textbooks to page 104 and read the paragraph at its top. Two students have no textbook. Horace tells them to share with their neighbors. Always bring your textbook to class. We never know when we'll need them. The severity in his voice causes quiet. The students read.

Horace asks: Betty, which of the words in the first sentence is an adverb? Silence. Betty stares at her book. More silence. Betty, what is an adverb? Silence. Bill, help Betty. It's sort of a verb that tells you about things. Horace pauses: Not quite, Bill, but close. Phil, you try. Phil: An adverb modifies a verb. Horace: OK, Phil, but what does "modify" mean? Silence. A voice: "Darkly." Who said that? Horace asks. The sentence was "Heathcliff was a darkly brooding character." I did, Taffy says. O.K., Horace follows, you're correct, Taffy, but tell us why "darkly" is an adverb. Taffy: It modifies "character." No, Taffy, try again. Heathcliff? No. Brooding? Yes, now why? Is "brooding" a verb? Silence.

Horace goes to the board, writes the sentence with chalk. He underlines *darkly*. Betty writes a note to her neighbor.

The class proceeds with this slow trudge through a paragraph from the textbook, searching for adverbs. Horace presses ahead patiently, almost dumbly at times. He is so familiar with the mistakes that ninth-graders make that he can sense them coming even before their utterance. Adverbs are always tougher to teach than adjectives. What frustrates him most are the partly correct answers; Horace worries that if he signals that a reply is somewhat accurate, all the students will think it is entirely accurate. At the same time, if he takes some minutes to sort out the truth from the falsity, the entire train of thought will be lost. He can never pursue any one student's errors to completion without losing all the others. Teaching grammar to classes like this is slow business, Horace feels. The bell rings. The students rush out, now more boisterous.

This is an Assembly Day, Horace remembers with pleasure. He leaves his papers on his desk, turns off the lights, shuts the door, and returns to the teachers' room. He can avoid assemblies; only the deans have to go. It's some student concert, in any event.

The teachers' room is full. Horace takes pleasure in it and wonders how his colleagues in schools in the city make do without such a sanctuary. Having a personal carrel is a luxury, he knows. He'd lose his here, he also knows, if enrollments went up again. The teachers' room was one happy consequence of the "baby bust."

The card game is going, set up on a square coffee table surrounded by a sofa and chairs. The kibitzers outnumber the players; all have coffee, some are smoking. The chatter is incessant, joshingly insulting. The staff members like one another.

Horace takes his mug, empties the cold leavings into the drain of the water fountain, and refills it. He puts a quarter in the large Maxwell House can supplied for that purpose, an honor system. He never pays for his early cup; Horace feels that if you come early, you get one on the house. He moves toward a clutch of fellow English and social studies teachers, and they gossip, mostly about a bit of trouble at the previous night's basketball game. No one was injured—that rarely happens at this high school—but indecorous words had been shouted back and forth, and Coke cans rolled on the gym floor. Someone could have been hurt. No teacher is much exercised about the incident. The talk is about things of more immediate importance to people: personal lives, essences even more transitory, Horace knows, than the odors of their collective cigarettes.

Horace looks about for Ms. Viola to find out whether it's true that she's not going to give a test on *Romeo and Juliet*. She isn't in sight, and Horace remembers why: she is a nonsmoker and is offended by smoke. He leaves his group and goes to Viola's carrel, where he finds her. She is put off by his query. Of course she is giving a test. Horace's lame explanation that a student told him differently doesn't help.

9:53. The third-period class of juniors. *Romeo and Juliet* again. Announcements over the public address system fill the first portion of the period, but Horace and a bunch of kids who call themselves "theater jocks" ignore them and talk about how to read Shakespeare well. They have to speak loudly to overpower the PA. The rest of the class chatter among themselves. The readings from the play are lively, and Horace is able to exhibit his etymological talents with a disquisition on "cot-quean." The students are well engaged by the scene involving the musicians and Peter until the class is interrupted by a proctor from the principal's office, collecting absence slips for the first-class periods. Nonetheless, the lesson ends with a widespread sense of good feeling. Horace never gets around to giving out the assignment, talking about the upcoming test, or arranging for play books to be shared.

10:47. The Advanced Placement class. They are reading *Ulysses*, a novel with which Horace himself had trouble. Its circumlocutions more precious than clever, he thinks, but he can't let on. Joyce is likely to be on the AP Exam, which will put him on a pedestal. There are eighteen seniors in this class, but only five arrive. Horace remembers: This is United Nations Week at the local college, and a group of the high school's seniors is taking part, representing places like Mauritius and Libya. Many of the students in the UN Club are also those in Advanced Placement classes. Horace welcomes this remnant of five and suggests they use the hour to read. Although he is annoyed at losing several teaching days with this class, he is still quietly grateful for the respite this morning.

11:36. Lunch. Horace buys a salad on the cafeteria line—as a teacher he can jump ahead of students—and he takes it to the dining room. He nods to the assistant principal on duty as he passes by. He takes a place at an empty table and is almost immediately joined by three physical education teachers, all of them coaches of varsity teams, who are noisily wrangling about the previous night's basketball game controversy. Horace listens, entertained. The coaches are having a good time, arguing with heat because they know the issue is really inconsequential and thus their disagreement will not mean much. Lunch is relaxing for Horace.

12:17. A free period. Horace checks with a colleague in the book store-room about copies of a text soon to be used by the ninth-graders. Can he get more copies? His specific allotment is settled after some minutes' discussion. Horace returns to the teachers' room, to his carrel. He finds a note to call a Mrs. Altschuler, who turns out to be the stepmother of a former student. She asks, on behalf of her stepson, whether Horace will write a character reference for the young man to use in his search for a job. Horace agrees. Horace also finds a note to call the office. Was Tibbetts in your Period One class? No, Horace tells the assistant principal; that's why I marked him absent on the attendance sheet. The assistant principal overlooks this sarcasm.

Well, he says, Tibbetts wasn't marked absent at any other class. Horace replies, That's someone else's problem. He was not in my class. The assistant principal: You're sure? Horace: Of course I'm sure.

The minutes of the free period remaining are spent in organizing a set of papers that is to be returned to Horace's third junior English class. Horace sometimes alternates weeks when he collects homework so as not totally to bury himself. He feels guilty about this. The sixth-period class had its turn this week. Horace had skimmed these exercises—a series of questions on Shakespeare's life—and hastily graded them, but using only a plus, check, or minus. He hadn't had time enough to do more.

1:11. More *Romeo and Juliet*. This section is less rambunctious than the first-period group and less interesting than that of the third period. The students are actually rather dull, perhaps because the class meets at the end of the day. Everyone is ready to leave; there is little energy for Montagues and Capulets. However, as with other sections, the kids are responsive when spoken to individually. It is their blandness when they are in a group that Horace finds trying. At least they aren't hellraisers, the way some last-period-of-the-day sections can be. The final bell rings at 2:00.

Horace has learned to stay in his classroom at the day's end so that students who want to consult with him can always find him there. Several appear today. One wants Horace to speak on his behalf to a prospective employer. Another needs to get an assignment. A couple of other students come by actually just to come by. They have no special errand, but seem to like to check in and chat. These youngsters puzzle Horace. They always seem to need reassurance.

Three students from the Theater Club arrive with questions about scenery for the upcoming play. (Horace is the faculty adviser to the stage crew.) Their shared construction work on sets behind the scenes gives Horace great pleasure. He knows these kids and likes their company.

By the time Horace finishes in his classroom, it is 2:30. He drops his papers and books at his carrel, selecting some—papers given him by his Advanced Placement students two days previously that he has yet to find time to read—to put in his briefcase. He does not check in on the card game, now winding down, in the outer section of the teachers' room but, rather, goes briefly to the auditorium to watch the Theater Club actors starting their rehearsals.

The play is Wilder's *Our Town*. Horace is both grateful and wistful that the production requires virtually no set to be constructed. The challenge for his stage crew, Horace knows, will be in the lighting.

Horace drives directly to his liquor store, arriving shortly after 4:00. He gives his brother-in-law some help in the stockroom and helps at the counter during the usual 4:30–6:30 surge of customers. His wife had earlier left for home and has supper ready for them both and their daughter at 7:45.

After dinner, Horace works for an hour on the papers he has brought home and on the Joyce classes he knows are ahead of him once the UN Mock Assembly is over. He has two telephone calls from students, one who has been ill and wants an assignment and another who wants to talk about the lighting for *Our Town*. The latter, an eager but shy boy, calls Horace often.

Horace turns in at 10:45, can't sleep, and watches the 11:00 news while his wife sleeps. He finally drifts off just before midnight.

Horace has high standards. Almost above all, he believes in the importance of writing, having his students learn to use language well. He believes in having his students write and be criticized, often. Horace has his five classes of fewer than thirty students each, a total of 120. (He is lucky; his colleagues in inner cities like New York, San Diego, Detroit, and St. Louis have a school board-union negotiated "load" base of 175 students.) Horace believes that each student should write something for criticism at least twice a week—but he is realistic. As a rule, his students write once a week.

Most of Horace's students are juniors and seniors, young people who should be beyond sentence and paragraph exercises and who should be working on short essays, written arguments with moderately complex sequencing and, if not grace exactly, at least clarity.

A page or two would be a minimum—but Horace is realistic. He assigns but one or two paragraphs.

Being a veteran teacher, Horace takes only fifteen to twenty minutes to check over each student's daily homework, to read the week's theme, and to write an analysis of it. (The "good" papers take a shorter time, usually, and the work of inept or demoralized students takes much longer.) Horace wonders how his inner-city colleagues, who usually have a far greater percentage of demoralized students, manage. Horace is realistic: even in his accommodating suburban school, fifteen minutes is too much to spend. He compromises, averaging five minutes for each student's work by cutting all but the most essential corners (the reading of the paragraphs in the themes takes but a few seconds; it is the thoughtful criticizing, in red ball point pen in the margins and elsewhere, that takes the minutes).

So, to check homework and to read and criticize one paragraph per week per student with the maximum feasible corner-cutting takes six hundred minutes or ten hours, assuming no coffee breaks or flagging attention (which is some assumption, considering how enervating is most students' forced and misspelled prose).

Horace's fifty-some-minute classes consume about twenty-three hours per week. Administrative chores chew up another hour and a half. Horace cares about his teaching and feels that he should take a half-hour to prepare for each class meeting, particularly for his classes with older students, who are swiftly moving over quite abstract and unfamiliar material, and his class of ninth-graders, which requires teaching that is highly individualized. However, he is realistic. He will compromise by spending no more than ten minutes' preparation time, on average, per class. (In effect, he concentrates his prep time on the Advanced Placement class, and teaches the others from old notes.) Three of his sections are ostensibly of the same course, but because the students are different in each case, he knows that he cannot satisfactorily clone each lesson plan twice and teach to his satisfaction. (Horace is uneasy with this compromise but feels he can live with it.) Horace's class preparation time per week: four hours.

Horace loves the theater, and when the principal begged him to help out with the afternoon drama program, he agreed. He is paid $800 extra per year to help the student stage crews prepare sets. This takes him in all about four hours per week, save for the ten days before the shows, when he and his crew happily work for hours on end.

Of course, Horace would like time to work on the curriculum with his colleagues. He would like to visit their classes and to work with them on the English department program. He would like to meet his students' parents, to read in his field, and, most important for him, to counsel students as they need such counseling one on one. Being a popular teacher, he is asked to write over fifty recommendations for college admissions offices each year, a Christmas vacation task that usually takes three full days. (He knows he is good at it now. When he was less experienced, the reference writing used to take him a full week. He can now quickly crank out the expected felicitous verbiage.) Yet Horace feels uneasy writing the crucial references for students with whom he has rarely exchanged ten consecutive sentences of private conversation. However, one does what one can and hopes that one is not sending the colleges too many lies.

And so before Horace assigns his one or two paragraphs per week, he is committed for over thirty-two hours of teaching, administration, class preparation, and extracurricular drama work. Collecting one short piece of writing per week from students and spending a bare five minutes per week on each student's weekly work adds ten hours, yielding a forty hour work week. Lunch periods, supervisory duties frequently, if irregularly, assigned, coffee breaks, travel to and from school, and time for the courtesies, civilities, and biological necessities of life are all in addition.

For this, Horace, a twenty-eight-year veteran, is paid $27,000, a good salary for a teacher in his district. He works at the liquor store and earns another $8,000 there, given a good year. The district adds 7 percent of his base salary to an invested pension account, and Horace tries to put away something more each month in an IRA. Fortunately, his wife also works at the store, and their one child went to the state university and its law school. She just received her JD. Her starting salary in the law firm is $32,000.

Horace is a gentle man. He reads the frequent criticism of his profession in the press with compassion. Johnny can't read. Teachers have low Graduate Record Examination scores. We must vary our teaching to the learning styles of our pupils. We must relate to the community. We must be scholarly, keeping up with our fields. English teachers should be practicing, published writers. If they aren't all these things, it is obvious that they don't care. Horace is a trooper; he hides his bitterness. Nothing can be gained by showing it. The critics do not really want to hear him or to face facts. He will go with the flow. What alternative is there?

A prestigious college near Franklin High School assigns its full-time freshman expository writing instructors a maximum of two sections, totaling forty students. Horace thinks about his 120. Like these college freshmen, at least they show up, most of them turn in what homework he assigns, and they give him little hassle. The teachers in the city have 175 kids, almost half of whom may be absent on any given day but all of whom remain the teacher's responsibility. And those kids are a resentful, wary, often troublesome lot. Horace is relieved that he is where he is. He wonders whether any of those college teachers ever read any of the recommendations he writes each Christmas vacation.

Most jobs in the real world have a gap between what would be nice and what is possible. One adjusts. The tragedy for many high school teachers is that the gap is a chasm, not crossed by reasonable and judicious adjustments. Even after adroit accommodations and devastating compromises—only five minutes per week of attention on the written work of each student and an average of ten minutes of planning for each fifty-odd-minute class—the task is already crushing, in reality a sixty-hour work week. For this, Horace is paid a wage enjoyed by age-mates in semiskilled and low-pressure blue-collar jobs and by novices, twenty-five years his junior, in some other white-collar professions. Furthermore, none of these sixty-plus hours is spent in replenishing his own academic capital. That has to be done in addition, perhaps during the summer. However, he needs to earn more money then, and there is no pay for upgrading his teacher's skills. He has to take on tutoring work or increase his involvement at the liquor store.

Fortunately (from one point of view), few people seem to care whether he simply does not assign that paragraph per week, or whether he farms its criticism out to other students. ("Exchange papers, class, and take ten minutes to grade your neighbor's essay.") He is a colorful teacher, and he knows that he can do a good job of lecturing, some of which can, in theory at least, replace the coaching that Horace knows is the heart of high school teaching. By using an overhead projector he can publicly analyze the paragraphs of six of his students. But he will have assigned writing to all of them. As long as he does not let on which six papers he will at the last minute "pull" to analyze, he will have given real practice to all. There are tricks like this to use.

His classes are quiet and orderly, and he has the reputation in the community of being a good teacher. Accordingly, he gets his administrators' blessings. If he were to complain about the extent of his overload, he would find no seriously empathetic audience. Reducing teacher load is, when all the negotiating is over, a low agenda item for the unions and school boards. The administration will arrange for in-service days on "teacher burnout" (more time away from grading paragraphs) run by moonlighting education professors who will get more pay for giving a few "professional workshops" than Horace gets for a year's worth of set construction in the theater.

No one blames the system; everyone blames him. Relax, the consultants advise. Here are some exercises to help you get some perspective. Morphine, Horace thinks. It dulls my pain. Come now, he mutters to himself. Don't get cynical. Don't keep insisting that these "experts" should try my job for a week. They assure me that they understand me, only they say, "We hear you, Horace." I wonder who their English teachers were.

Horace's students will get into college, their parents may remember to thank him for the references he wrote for their offspring (unlikely), and the better colleges will teach the kids to write. The students who do not get the coaching in college, or who do not go to college, do not complain. No one seems upset. Just let it all continue, a conspiracy, a toleration of a chasm between the necessary and the provided and acceptance of big rhetoric and little reality. Horace dares not express his bitterness to the visitor conducting a study of high schools, because he fears he will be portrayed as a whining hypocrite.

13

Selection From *My Posse Don't Do Homework*

LouAnne Johnson

LouAnne Johnson is a former Marine Corps officer and high school teacher. Her 1992 novel *My Posse Don't Do Homework* became the basis for the 1995 movie *Dangerous Minds* starring Michelle Pfieffer. After serving 9 years in the Marines, Johnson began teaching reading and writing to non-English speakers while working as an intern at a high school in California. Two years later, she became the head of a special program for at-risk teens. Much of her fiction is based on her experience in the classroom. More recently, she has written another autobiographical work, *The Girls in the Back of the Class,* an account of students overcoming challenges in the classroom, as well as several practical books, including *The Queen of Education* and a collection of essays titled *Teaching Outside of the Box.*

As you read the following selection from *My Posse Don't Do Homework,* consider the following questions:

1. How does one deal with students who are being rude and who are challenging you in the classroom (as in the case of Adam Stone and Johnson) before one has even begun to teach?

2. How does Johnson use humor to get her students under control and to engage them?

3. Which role does grading play in Johnson's control of her classroom and teaching?

4. What is it that makes it possible for Johnson to start reaching her students and to actually begin to teach them?

Hal Gray only gave me a couple of weeks to catch my breath after taking over Miss Sheppard's class before he sent me into the arena to face his seventh period accelerated English class. After I'd observed his class, the idea of teaching those students held zero appeal. Hal's class was a zoo.

"Well?" Hal locked his hands behind his head and leaned back in his squeaky swivel chair. "What do you think?"

I resisted the urge to express my honest opinion, which was that Hal was either deaf and blind or simply dumb. From my vantage point in the back of the room, it appeared that only two of the students in his class had even the faintest idea of what had transpired during the first act of *Julius Caesar*. The other students were too busy braiding their hair, reading *Motorhead* magazines, copying each other's math homework, or passing personal notes to concern themselves with Caesar's dilemma. Two boys, Nader and Brandon, often brought a deck of cards and played poker in the far corner, making no effort to hide the cards from view.

Hal was an intelligent, perceptive person, so I knew there had to be a reason why he didn't reprimand the students, but the reason escaped me. At first, I thought perhaps he was so caught up in his presentation of the Shakespearean drama that he didn't notice the students' behavior, but he was far too bright, and the students were much too blatant in their indifference, for that to have been true. Maybe he graded students solely on the basis of their exam scores, I speculated. But the entire class would flunk, which would certainly call the matter to the attention of the district office, and I knew Hal had no desire to chat with the superintendent. Maybe he just didn't care. Immediately ashamed, I shook my head to clear it of such disloyal thoughts, but I wasn't fast enough. Hal sat upright in his chair and rubbed his palm over his silver-gray crewcut.

"I bet you think I let the kids get away with murder, don't you?" he asked.

"Well, I did notice that quite a few of them seem to be off track," I said, hoping to soften the truth with tact. Hal exhaled, blowing the tact off my response as easily as he flicked a speck of dust off his tattered green desk blotter. He leaned forward, crossed his arms on his desktop, and looked me straight in the eye, his expression solemn.

"This is an ACL class, Miss Johnson. Accelerated. That means headed for college. These kids are fifteen, sixteen years old—old enough to start being responsible for themselves. I give them the information. If they don't get it, screw 'em."

My jaw dropped about six inches, which obviously amused Hal. His tanned face crinkled into a broad smile and his eyes flashed like two small blue suns, with rays of wrinkles etched into his leathery skin. "Ah, don't mind me," he said, "I'm a crusty old fart and I'm going to retire next year. Say good-bye gracefully and sail out to sea. Thirty years is long enough, maybe too long. Teachers should retire before they get stale."

"I don't think you're stale," I lied.

"Oh, yes, you do," he responded. "And you're right. You're also young. You're fresh, energetic, creative. That's what we need—new teachers with new ideas. Young blood."

Suddenly, I felt guilty for being younger than Hal. "I'm not as young as most new teachers," I pointed out.

"Don't apologize," he said. "I used to be like you. I wanted to mold young minds, stretch their imaginations, introduce them to the exciting world of words. Make the English language and literature come alive for them. Right?"

"Exactly," I agreed.

"You'll get over it," he said, abruptly.

"How long do you think that will take?" I asked. "Before I get over it?" Even as I asked, I was silently thinking that if and when that unlikely day came, I would leave the classroom immediately. But I truly didn't believe such a day would come. Hal cleared his desk and stuffed his green gradebook into a worn leather shoulder bag as, once again, he read my mind.

"You don't believe it will ever happen to you. No one does," he said. "Maybe it won't. Maybe you'll be one of the lucky teachers who hangs on to the enthusiasm in spite of the system. It happens sometimes, to the ones with fire in their hearts." He motioned me out the door and snapped off the lights.

"Do you think you have fire?" Hal asked as we reached the front gate of the school.

"At least a spark," I said, modestly.

"I think so, too," he agreed. "So you might as well take over the class tomorrow. Act two. No sense in waiting any longer."

"Tomorrow?" I echoed, stunned.

"Tomorrow," Hal repeated. Before I could think of an argument, Hal was half a block away, his battered leather shoulder bag swaying in rhythm with his jaunty step.

That night, I read and reread Act II. At midnight, satisfied that I knew my stuff, I finally closed the cover on *Julius Caesar*. Lying in bed, I reviewed the past two years of studies in preparation for my teaching credential: curriculum development, reading and phonics, adolescent psychology, models of teaching. I had my finger on the pulse of today's youth; I knew what was happening. The kids wouldn't be off track when I was teaching, I vowed to myself. I was going to do it right.

The students' built-in radar told them something was up the second they walked into B-9. Unnaturally quiet, they took their seats and stared at me as Hal explained that I would be taking over the class and he expected them to treat me with the same courtesy and respect that they showed to him. He wrote my name on the chalkboard, gave me a thumbs-up, and left the room. My first mistake was to ask if the class had any questions. Adam Stone, a pale blond boy with a beautiful baby face, raised his hand.

"Miss Johnson?" he said, smiling sweetly. "

Yes?" I returned his smile.

"Where do you get off barging in here and trying to act like a real teacher?"

My initial impulse was to grab Adam's skinny neck and squeeze until his pimply adolescent face turned blue, but that was not recommended in any of my methods courses, so I took a deep breath and forced a calm smile as I explained that I wanted to be a teacher in order to share my love of language and literature with teenagers. It was the absolute truth, but it sounded phony, even to my ears, as I said it. It didn't matter what I said, because none of the students listened. They followed Hal's instructions to the letter. They acted exactly as they did when he was in the room—absolutely oblivious to the teacher.

The next day I went to class prepared. Muscle had worked well with my regular P class, so I planned to flex for the ACL kids. I had a worksheet with questions about the play. I had a firm attitude. I had a seating chart. And, for a few brief moments, I had the students' attention.

"Aw! Come on! A seating chart! You're kidding!" They moaned and groaned as they slumped into their assigned seats and slammed their books on their desks.

"Why do we have to have a seating chart?" one of the girls whined.

"Because I don't want you sitting in the back of the room combing your hair and scratching your armpits during class," I explained.

"Ee-uu! Gross!" the kids complained.

"Hey, it could be worse," I pointed out. "I could have said I didn't want you to pick your noses and wipe it under the desktops." In unison, everyone in class crinkled their noses and pressed themselves backward, as far away from the desks as they could.

"I don't want to sit by Ryan," Adam said.

"You don't have to marry him," I retorted. "You don't have to hold his hand or kiss him. You don't even have to like him. All you have to do is sit beside him for fifty minutes once a day. I don't think you'll die from it and if you do, I'll take full responsibility for your death."

I distributed the worksheets, which were designed to stimulate classroom discussion by bringing out the kids' own ideas about the play. "Let's look at the first question on the sheet," I said. "Which character do you like the best in this play and why?" No one answered.

"Nader, which one do you like best?" I crossed my fingers behind my back and hoped he would answer. Nader was a handsome kid and a natural leader—intelligent, congenial, and born with a built-in B.S. meter. If he decided to play school, I was in. No such luck. He shrugged his shoulders.

"I don't know."

"Brandon?"

"Uh-uh."

"Diana?"

Diana didn't answer, either, but at least she looked at me. She was a nice kid, with a strong need to be liked by everyone. After my first day of teaching the class, she had stopped to wish me good luck and advised me not to take Adam's insults personally. I asked her again, although her eyes begged me not to. Her face contorted in agony. She was clearly torn between her desire to earn a good grade and be liked by her teacher and the necessity of maintaining the respect and approval of her friends. I turned to Callie West, who was always willing to say what was on her mind.

"Come on, Callie. Which character do you like the best?"

"Caesar's wife," Callie said. As soon as she spoke, several of the boys started coughing loudly, protesting her participation.

"Why?" I asked. More coughs. Every time Callie started to speak, the boys coughed en masse. She flicked her hands near her head, as though waving away a swarm of pesky gnats.

"I don't know," she said, giving up.

"Okay," I said. "I'll write the names of the characters on the board so we can all see the choices." Tactical error. The moment I turned my back, someone coughed. Wham! Wham! Wham! Three books slammed against desktops. I spun around. Twenty blank faces. Forty hands folded quietly in their owners' laps. I turned back to the board. No one coughed this time but after a few seconds, a chair leg scraped the floor. Wham! Wham! Wham! Wham! Wham! I recalled Hal's earlier advice: When they test you, which they will, hit them fast right where it hurts-in the gradebook.

"With a regular class," he said, "there are always a few who don't care if they pass. Flunking them doesn't faze them. But in an accelerated class, most of the kids are college bound and all of them want good grades. If you have to, use that for leverage."

Calmly, I placed the chalk on the tray beneath the chalkboard and wiped the dust from my hands. I walked to the desk and opened the gradebook. Pencil poised, I glanced about the room.

"This entire worksheet is due at the end of the class period. It is worth one hundred points, which means that if you don't do it, it will have a significant effect on your grade. Any questions?"

A hostile silence descended on the classroom as the students attacked their worksheets. When the bell rang, the kids stalked to the front of the room, holding their completed worksheets gingerly between thumbs and index fingers to avoid further contamination, and flicked the papers into the basket on my desk. No one looked at me.

The following day, I read some of their answers out loud, providing constructive criticism of their responses. As I discussed their answers, they rolled their eyes to the ceiling, and when I handed back their graded worksheets, they rolled them into tight, crumpled balls. Each day, I gave them another worksheet and each day they quietly completed it, providing perfunctory answers. When I asked for volunteers to read, no one responded, so I assigned roles and they dutifully read them in barely audible voices, devoid of expression. During the class discussions, students responded only when called upon and even then they offered curt, uninspired answers. The message was clear. You can lead the class to the lesson, Teacher, but you can't make us learn.

After a week, the tension had built to an intolerable level. One afternoon, I lost it. Someone—I couldn't tell who—had been whistling softly at a very high pitch for thirty minutes without a break. Callie West grew so irritated that she stomped out of class. The remaining students shuffled their papers loudly every time I turned my back. I felt like screaming, so I did. I stopped dead and bellowed at top volume. It felt great, so I flailed my arms and shook my head wildly, letting my lips blubber loosely. It felt so good that I kept it up until I ran out of breath. When I stopped screaming and flopped into my chair, the kids were wide-eyed and dumbstruck.

"Anybody here see *Rain Man?*" I asked. A few kids nodded their heads, but nobody spoke.

"Remember that scene where Dustin Hoffman is in the airport and Tom Cruise is trying to make him get on a plane and he doesn't want to go, so he pitches a fit?"

Again the kids nodded silently.

"I know exactly how he felt," I said. No one responded, so we sat staring silently at each other until the bell rang. I ignored the bell. The kids waited for a few minutes until they realized I wasn't going to dismiss them. Nader quietly picked up his books and tiptoed gingerly past my desk, as though afraid any sudden movement or sound might trigger another tantrum. The rest of the class followed.

Wild screaming didn't appeal to me as a viable teaching technique, so I asked Hal to observe the class in action to see if he could identify my mistakes and offer some suggestions. They weren't angels when he taught, but at least they didn't hate him. With their official teacher in the back of the room, the students stopped throwing books for a day, but their lack of interest and unwillingness to participate remained the same. As soon as the bell rang and the kids disappeared, Hal moved forward and sat down in one of the student's desks in the front row. He raised his hand and said, "Miss Johnson?"

"Yes?" I smiled, playing my role. Hal didn't return my smile. Instead, his face wore the same closed expression I saw on twenty faces for an hour every afternoon.

"You don't like us, Miss Johnson. You're very clever and witty and educated and you can verbally demolish us whenever you want to because you're older than we are and you know a lot more, but that isn't fair. It isn't very nice. And it isn't teaching."

My knees buckled and I sat down hard. My chair rolled backward and crashed into the chalkboard with a jolt.

"You're right. I'm not teaching. Now what am I going to do?"

"Forget all that B.S. they taught you in college," Hal said. "You can't learn how to teach by sitting in a classroom listening to lectures. You learn how to teach by teaching. You can't hide behind your desk or your authority or your education. Just trust your instincts. If you're wrong, the kids will tell you, loud and clear."

"That's a pretty tough assignment, Hal," I said.

He smiled. "About as tough as understanding Shakespeare when you're only fifteen years old."

Glumly, I gazed out the window at the rolling California hills and wondered whatever had possessed me to believe I could teach teenagers. A wad of paper sailed through the air, expertly launched, and landed in the trash can next to my desk, breaking my reverie.

"Hey!" Hal said softly. "Think about it. If teaching were easy, they wouldn't have to pay us such exorbitant salaries, would they?"

"I have a confession to make," I told the ACL English class. For the first time, genuine interest shone in the eyes of the students. Even Adam glanced at me over the top of the sunglasses that he had started wearing to class every day, claiming that the fluorescent lights made his eyes burn. I didn't believe him for a second, but I did believe Hal's theory that Adam was having trouble accepting his parents' recent divorce and the sunglasses gave him the illusion that his tender feelings were less exposed. "I haven't been very nice to you," I continued. "I'm sorry. But you haven't been very nice to me, either. You put me on the defensive the very first day and I never got over it. Well, I'm over it now. The reason I made a seating chart was not to punish you or make you miserable. I made it because I want to help you be the most effective students you can be, so you can learn. Because I like you. If I didn't like you, I would let you sit in the back of the room and play cards instead of reading Shakespeare. See this little note?"

I held up a sheet of paper from a yellow sticky pad. BE NICE was printed in bold black letters on the paper.

"This is my reminder to be nice to you. And I'd appreciate it if you would do the same. What do you think?"

For a few seconds, I was afraid that my new, improved, humanistic approach wasn't going to work any better than the old dictatorial one. I held my breath while the students looked around the room, checking each other's responses. I knew most of the kids would follow Nader's example.

"Nader?" I said.

"Miss Johnson?" he responded quickly, mimicking my questioning tone exactly. He didn't smile, but there was a sparkle in his dark eyes.

"Pretty please?" I smiled at him and gave a thumbs-up. He returned my thumbs-up and the class breathed a collective sigh of relief. It was hard work fighting the teacher and refusing to learn, especially for a group of intelligent students.

"Now, let's take a look at where we are in *Julius Caesar*," I said. "Does anybody have any questions about the first two acts?" Although my question was sincere, I didn't expect an answer. Brandon raised his hand.

"Yes?"

"Can I ask a real question, Miss Johnson?" he asked.

"That's what we're here for."

He took off his A's baseball cap and put it backward, and drew a deep breath, as though preparing for a dangerous dive. "What's going on? I can't tell the names apart and the words don't make any sense. It looks like English, but it isn't really. It's just a bunch of bullshit."

I was tempted to point out that during the days on which I observed the class, Brandon never had his book open to follow along as Mr. Gray discussed the play. Most of the time, he had been playing poker with Nader, and he had been reading *Hotrod* magazine when Mr. Gray showed a film

of the first act. But I controlled myself. Brandon knew he
attention, but maybe he didn't pay attention because he didn'
Or maybe he thought I was a sucker. Either way, I had promi
and nice I would be or die trying.

"Can somebody give a brief summary of what's happened so far?" I
asked the class. "Just describe the plot in your own words?" No one
responded.

"Come on, boys and girls," I said. "I thought we just agreed that we'd
all be nice. Somebody must know what's going on. Why were the citizens
celebrating at the opening of the play?"

Diana cleared her throat. "It was a celebration for the ides of March?"

"What an airhead!" Adam mumbled and sighed loudly.

"Not nice!" I pointed at Adam.

"Caesar made a bunch of enemies in the war," Nader suggested. "They're
following him around, trying to kill him or something. But they all have the
same name almost. Everybody's name begins with a C. Not very smart."

"Yeah," Ryan said. Several other heads nodded.

"I admit that it isn't an easy play to read, but the story is simple," I said.
"Julius Caesar is a powerful politician and whenever someone has power,
somebody else wants to take the power away. In this case, the people who
want to take the power happen to be Caesar's closest friends. That's what
makes the play so dramatic. Imagine how you would feel if all your best
friends had secret meetings and ganged up on you and eventually beat you
up or killed you just because you were more popular than they were or
because you got better grades."

"I would say it sucked," Adam whispered, glancing over the rims of his
sunglasses, obviously testing our newly established truce.

"And Caesar would have said, 'Methinks this sucketh,'" I said.

We ended up reading the entire second act over again, this time with more
enthusiasm. At the end of each scene, we stopped to discuss what had happened. It was an exhilarating, natural give and take between teacher and
teachee. After the final bell, I sat at my desk, enjoying the sweet sound of
students discussing the play. As they collected their books, they actually
argued with each other about which of Shakespeare's characters was more
believable. For an hour, I had been a teacher. And it was good.

14

"What Teachers Make, or Objection Overruled, or If things don't work out, you can always go to law school"

Taylor Mali

Taylor Mali has his B.A. in English from Bowdoin College and his M.A. in English and Creative Writing from Kansas State University. A talented writer and slam poetry performer, he taught for many years at the Browning School on the Upper East Side of Manhattan and at the Cape Cod Academy. In 2001, he developed a one-man show titled *Teacher! Teacher!* He is passionate in his belief that teachers do not get the respect they deserve, and is actively involved in recruiting 1,000 new teachers into the profession through his poetry.

As you read Mali's (1999) poem, "What Teachers Make," consider the following questions:

1. Why do you think a job that is as important as teaching is looked down on when compared to other professions such as law or medicine?

NOTE: Used with personal permission of the author.

2. The Irish playwright George Bernard Shaw (1856–1950) is famous for his quote, "Those who can, do, those who can't, teach." Is it a fair or accurate statement? Why do you think it is frequently cited?

3. Mali's poem is widely quoted by teachers. Why do you think it is so popular?

4. Do you think is it important for teachers to express themselves as artists? Should teachers be political and/or social critics?

5. Do you think Mali's poem is inspiring? If yes, why?

He says the problem with teachers is, "What's a kid going to learn from someone who decided his best option in life was to become a teacher?"
He reminds the other dinner guests that it's true what they say about teachers:
Those who can, do; those who can't, teach.
I decide to bite my tongue instead of his
and resist the temptation to remind the other dinner guests
that it's also true what they say about lawyers.

Because we're eating, after all, and this is polite company.

"I mean, you're a teacher, Taylor," he says.
"Be honest. What do you make?"

And I wish he hadn't done that
(asked me to be honest)
because, you see, I have a policy
about honesty and ass-kicking:
if you ask for it, I have to let you have it.

You want to know what I make?

I make kids work harder than they ever thought they could.
I can make a C+ feel like a Congressional medal of honor
and an A– feel like a slap in the face.
How dare you waste my time with anything less than your very best.

I make kids sit through 40 minutes of study hall
in absolute silence. No, you may not work in groups.
No, you may not ask a question.
Why won't I let you get a drink of water?
Because you're not thirsty, you're bored, that's why.

I make parents tremble in fear when I call home:
I hope I haven't called at a bad time,
I just wanted to talk to you about something Billy said today.
Billy said, "Leave the kid alone. I still cry sometimes, don't you?"
And it was the noblest act of courage I have ever seen.

I make parents see their children for who they are
and what they can be.

You want to know what I make?

I make kids wonder,
I make them question.
I make them criticize.
I make them apologize and mean it.
I make them write, write, write.
And then I make them read.
I make them spell definitely beautiful, definitely beautiful, definitely
beautiful
over and over and over again until they will never misspell
either one of those words again.
I make them show all their work in math.
And hide it on their final drafts in English.
I make them understand that if you got this (brains)
then you follow this (heart) and if someone ever tries to judge you
by what you make, you give them this (the finger).

Let me break it down for you, so you know what I say is true:
I make a goddamn difference! What about you?

PART VI

Teaching as Social Activism

15. Selection From *Death at an Early Age: The Destruction of the Hearts and Minds of Negro Children in the Boston Public Schools*
    Jonathan Kozol

16. Should the Teacher Always Be Neutral?
    George S. Counts

17. Selection From *Roll of Thunder, Hear My Cry*
    Mildred D. Taylor

There has been a constant tension in the teaching profession, going back to the beginning of the 20th century and the organizing of teacher unions, as to whether teachers should be political and social activists. In 1932, George S. Counts, a professor at Teachers College, Columbia University, asked in his short pamphlet, "Dare the Schools Build a New Social Order?" Counts was writing in the depths of the American Great Depression. He believed that teachers should take an active role in reforming the society. He felt that they should do this not only by being politically active in their private lives but also by shaping the political and social consciousness of the students they taught.

The idea of teachers acting as agents for change and social justice is an important issue in education. If schools function primarily as means of reproducing the existing social system (what is called a functionalist model), then having teachers who are activists may be highly problematic. In fact, a conservative social and educational system will prefer teachers who are passive and accepting of the status quo. Activism implies the idea that there is a need to criticize and change things. This is a process that challenges authority and ultimately the system.

In a nation that was founded on the basis of revolution and espouses democratic values, activism and political engagement are supposed to be highly valued. The reality is that challenging the system may be seen as problematic and threatening to those in authority. This is certainly the case in the first reading included in this chapter, in which Jonathan Kozol (1967) describes his experience teaching fourth grade in a Boston inner-city school during the mid-1960s. The selection by George S. Counts (1969) raises the question of whether teachers should be neutral in their work or consciously take social and political positions. Finally, Mildred Taylor's (1976) fictional account of a black teacher quietly protesting the discrimination practiced by White society against her students in a rural Mississippi school in the mid-1930s, being dealt with as separate and unequal, suggests the ways in which individual teachers can quietly make their voices heard to protest injustice and discrimination.

Further Readings: In addition to the "Letter to a Young Teacher" written by Joseph Featherstone included in this book, an excellent similar work is Jonathan Kozol's *Letters to a Young Teacher* (Crown, 2007). Also of interest is Sonia Nieto's *Why We Teach* (Teachers College Press, 2005).

Linking to Popular Culture: There are a number of films that portray the teacher as activist. The 1983 film *Teachers,* starring Nick Nolte, tells the story of a disenchanted teacher who defies the system to defend the rights of his students. A similar theme is found in the 1988 film *Stand and Deliver,* which describes how Jaime Escalante helped students at an inner-city high school in Los Angeles achieve academic excellence in mathematics.

References

Counts, G. S. (1932). *Dare the schools build a new social order?* New York: John Day.

Counts, G. S. (1969). Should the teacher always be neutral? *Phi Delta Kappan, 51*(4), 186–189.

Kozol, J. (1967). *Death at an early age: The destruction of the hearts and minds of Negro children in the Boston public schools.* Boston: Houghton-Mifflin.

Taylor, M. D. (1976). *Roll of thunder, hear my cry.* New York: Bantam.

15

Selection From
Death at an Early Age

The Destruction of the Hearts and Minds of Negro Children in the Boston Public Schools

Jonathan Kozol

To be vulnerable is to be open to either physical or emotional harm. Teachers can be vulnerable in the workplace for a number of reasons. They can be physically threatened by students, or they can be fearful of censure and criticism. Handling the complex emotional stew of 25 or 30 students in a classroom can make anyone feel somewhat vulnerable. Teachers, in their work, make dozens of decisions in an hour: "Does Joe really need to go to the bathroom, or can I have him wait?" "Is this the right way to teach this material?" "How should I approach my principal concerning a problem?"

Vulnerability in social settings such as schools is closely related to issues of power—who has it and who doesn't have it and who gets to maintain it.

NOTE: Kozol, J. (1967). *Death at an early age: The destruction of the hearts and minds of Negro children in the Boston public schools.* Boston: Houghton-Mifflin.

Jonathan Kozol's (1967) account of his experience as a beginning teacher in an inner-city fourth-grade classroom in Boston during the mid-1960s makes clear how beginning teachers can be made vulnerable and how this is often done to maintain the status quo in the society. *Death at an Early Age* documents a period when public school busing had not yet been mandated in Boston. Tensions concerning issues of integration and the fair distribution of resources, however, can still be felt powerfully in Kozol's book.

Jonathan Kozol has spent his career writing about homelessness, inadequate public education, and other injustices experienced by poor people in America. The product of a privileged education himself, including a B.A. from Harvard and a Rhodes Scholarship stint at Oxford, Kozol chose public school teaching in the inner city over other occupations that were open to him. His many nonfiction works recount his experiences teaching elementary-age children, running a free school, and working in adult illiteracy programs. *Death at an Early Age* received the National Book Award in 1968. His most recent writing, including *Savage Inequalities: Children in America's Schools* (1991), revisited the themes of his earlier works. It received the New England Book Award and other citations.

As you read this selection, consider the following questions:

1. As a beginning teacher, can Kozol be expected to protest against the discrimination that his students face?

2. Do you think that the schools in wealthier neighborhoods in Boston had the same problems, such as windows falling in on students, as Kozol's classroom did? If not, why do you think Kozol's students were being treated unequally?

3. How important for his students was it for Kozol to present an alternative curriculum in the form of poetry and, more specifically, the work of Langston Hughes?

4. Do you feel that the school's administration had the right to terminate Kozol's employment because he was not strictly following the assigned curriculum?

5. Was Kozol's teaching of Langston Hughes's poetry an act of social consciousness or simply an English lesson with materials that were not included in the traditional curriculum?

The room in which I taught my Fourth Grade was not a room at all, but the corner of an auditorium. The first time I approached that corner, I noticed only a huge torn stage curtain, a couple of broken windows, a badly listing blackboard and about thirty-five bewildered-looking children, most of whom were Negro. White was overcome in black among them, but white and black together were overcome in chaos. They had desks and a teacher, but they did not really have a class. What they had was about one quarter of the auditorium. Three or four blackboards, two of them broken, made them seem a little bit set apart. Over at the other end of the auditorium there was another Fourth Grade class. Not much was happening at the other side at that minute so that for the moment the noise did not seem so bad. But it became a real nightmare of conflicting noises a little later on. Generally it was not until ten o'clock that the bad crossfire started. By ten-thirty it would have attained such a crescendo that the children in the back rows of my section often couldn't hear my questions and I could not hear their answers. There were no carpetings or sound-absorbers of any kind. The room, being large, and echoing, and wooden, added resonance to every sound. Sometimes the other teacher and I would stagger the lessons in which our classes would have to speak aloud, but this was a makeshift method and it also meant that our classes had to be induced to maintain an unnatural and otherwise unnecessary rule of silence during the rest of the time. We couldn't always do it anyway, and usually the only way out was to try to outshout each other so that both of us often left school hoarse or wheezing. While her class was reciting in unison you could not hear very much in mine. When she was talking alone I could be heard above her but the trouble then was that little bits of her talk got overheard by my class. Suddenly in the middle of our geography you could hear her saying:

"AFTER YOU COMPARE, YOU HAVE GOT TO BRING DOWN."
Or "PLEASE GIVE THAT PENCIL BACK TO HENRIETTA!!!"

Neither my class nor I could help but be distracted for a moment of sudden curiosity about exactly what was going on. Hours were lost in this way. Yet that was not the worst. More troublesome still was the fact that we did not ever feel apart. We were tucked in the corner and anybody who wanted could peek in or walk in or walk past. I never minded an intruder or observer, but to notice and to stare at any casual passer-by grew to be an irresistible temptation for the class. On repeated occasions I had to say to the children: "The class is still going. Let them have their discussion. Let them walk by if they have to. You should still be paying attention over here."

Soon after I came into that auditorium, I discovered that it was not only our two Fourth Grades that were going to have their classes here. We were to share the space also with the glee club, with play rehearsals, special reading, special arithmetic, and also at certain times a Third or Fourth Grade phonics class. I began to make head-counts of numbers of pupils and I started jotting them down:

Seventy children from the two regular Fourth Grades before the invasion.
Then ninety one days with the glee club and remedial arithmetic.
One hundred and seven with the play rehearsal.

One day the sewing class came in with their sewing machines and then that seemed to become a regular practice in the hall. Once I counted one hundred and twenty people. All in the one room. All talking, singing, yelling, laughing, reciting—and all at the same time. Before the Christmas break it became apocalyptic. Not more than one half of the classroom lessons I had planned took place throughout that time.

"Mr. Kozol, I can't hear you."

"Mr. Kozol, what's going on out there?"

"Mr. Kozol, couldn't we sing with them?"

One day something happened to dramatize to me, even more powerfully than anything yet, just what a desperate situation we were really in. What happened was that a window whose frame had rotted was blown right out of its sashes by a strong gust of wind and began to fall into the auditorium, just above my children's heads. I had noticed that window several times before and I had seen that its frame was rotting, but there were so many other things equally rotted or broken in the school building that it didn't occur to me to say anything about it. The feeling I had was that the Principal and custodians and Reading Teacher and other people had been in that building for a long time before me and they must have seen the condition of the windows. If anything could be done, if there were any way to get it corrected, I assumed they would have done it by this time. Thus, by not complaining and by not pointing it out to anyone, in a sense I went along with the rest of them and accepted it as something inevitable. One of the most grim things about teaching in such a school and such a system is that you do not like to be an incessant barb and irritation to everybody else, so you come under a rather strong compulsion to keep quiet. But after you have been quiet for a while there is an equally strong temptation to begin to accept the conditions of your work or of the children's plight as natural. This, in a sense, is what had happened to me during that period and that, I suppose, is why I didn't say anything about the rotting window. Now one day it caved in.

First there was a cracking sound, then a burst of icy air. The next thing I knew, a child was saying: "Mr. Kozol—look at the window! I turned and looked and saw that it was starting to fall in. It was maybe four or five feet tall and it came straight inward out of its sashes toward the heads of the children. I was standing, by coincidence, only about four or five feet off and was able to catch it with my hand. But the wind was so strong that it nearly blew right out of my hands. A couple of seconds of good luck—for it was a matter of chance that I was standing there—kept glass from the desks of six or seven children and very possibly preserved the original shape of half a dozen of their heads. The ones who had been under the glass were terrified but the thing that I noticed with most wonder was that they tried very hard to hide their fear in order to help me get over my own sense of embarrassment and guilt. I soon realized I was not going to be able to hold the thing up by myself and I was obliged to ask one of the stronger boys in the class to come over and give me a hand. Meanwhile, as the children beneath us shivered with the icy wind and as the two of us now shivered also since it was a day when the mercury was hovering all morning close to freezing, I asked one of the children in the front row to run down and fetch the janitor.

When he asked me what he should tell him, I said: "Tell him the house is falling in." The children laughed. It was the first time I had ever come out and said anything like that when the children could hear me. I am sure my reluctance to speak out like that more often must seem odd to many readers, for at this perspective it seems odd to me as well. Certainly there were plenty of things wrong within that school building and there was enough we could have joked about. The truth, however, is that I did not often talk like that, nor did many of the other teachers, and there was a practical reason for this. Unless you were ready to buck the system utterly, it would become far too difficult to teach in an atmosphere of that kind of honesty. It generally seemed a great deal easier to pretend as well as you could that everything was normal and okay. Some teachers carried out this posture with so much eagerness, in fact, that their defense of the school ended up as something like a hymn of praise and adoration. "You children should thank God and feel blessed with good luck for all you've got. There are so many little children in the world who have been given so much less." The books are junk, the paint peels, the cellar stinks, the teachers call you nigger, and the windows fall in on your heads. "Thank God that you don't live in Russia or Africa! Thank God for all the blessings that you've got!" Once, finally, the day after the window blew in, I said to a friend of mine in the evening after school: "I guess that the building I teach in is not in very good condition." But to state a condition of dilapidation and ugliness and physical danger in words as mild and indirect as those is almost worse than not saying anything at all. I had a hard time with that problem—the problem of being honest and of confronting openly the extent to which I was compromised by going along with things that were abhorrent and by accepting as moderately reasonable or unavoidably troublesome things which, if they were inflicted on children of my own, I would have condemned savagely.

After the window blew in on us that time, the janitor finally came up and hammered it shut with nails so that it would not fall in again but also so that it could not open. It was a month before anything was done about the large gap left by a missing pane. Children shivered a few feet away from it.

The Principal walked by frequently and saw us. So did supervisors from the School Department. So of course did the various lady experts who traveled all day from room to room within our school. No one can say that dozens of people did not know that children were sitting within the range of freezing air. At last one day the janitor came up with a piece of cardboard or pasteboard and covered over about a quarter of that lower window so that there was no more wind coming in but just that much less sunshine too. I remember wondering what a piece of glass could cost in Boston and I had the idea of going out and buying some and trying to put it in myself. That rectangle of cardboard over our nailed-shut window was not removed for a quarter of the year. When it was removed, it was only because a television station was going to come and visit in the building and the School Department wanted to make the room look more attractive. But it was winter when the window broke, and the repairs did not take place until the middle of the spring.

In case a reader imagines that my school may have been unusual and that some of the other schools in Roxbury must have been in better shape, I think it's worthwhile to point out that the exact opposite seems to have been the case. The conditions in my school were said by many people to be considerably better than those in several of the other ghetto schools.

Perhaps a reader would like to know what it is like to go into a new classroom in the same way that I did and to see before you suddenly, and in terms you cannot avoid recognizing, the dreadful consequences of a year's wastage of real lives.

You walk into a narrow and old wood-smelling classroom and you see before you thirty-five curious, cautious and untrusting children, aged eight to thirteen, of whom about two-thirds are Negro. Three of the children are designated to you as special students. Thirty per cent of the class is reading at the Second grade level in a year and in a month in which they should be reading at the height of Fourth Grade performance or at the beginning of the Fifth. Seven children out of the class are up to par. Ten substitutes or teacher changes. Or twelve changes. Or eight. Or eleven. Nobody seems to know how many teachers they have had. Seven of their lifetime records are missing: symptomatic and emblematic at once of the chaos that has been with them all year long. Many more lives than just seven have already been wasted but the seven missing records become an embittering symbol of the lives behind them which, equally, have been lost or mislaid. (You have to spend the first three nights staying up until dawn trying to reconstruct these records out of notes and scraps.) On the first math test you give, the class average comes out to 36. The children tell you with embarrassment that it has been like that since fall.

You check around the classroom. Of forty desks, five have tops with no hinges. You lift a desk-top to fetch a paper and you find that the top has fallen off. There are three windows. One cannot be opened. A sign on it written in the messy scribble of a hurried teacher or some custodial person warns you: DO NOT UNLOCK THIS WINDOW IT IS BROKEN. The general look of the room is as of a bleak-light photograph of a mental hospital. Above the one poor blackboard, gray rather than really black, and hard to write on, hangs from one tack, lopsided, a motto attributed to Benjamin Franklin: "*Well begun is half done.*" Everything, or almost everything like that, seems a mockery of itself.

Into this grim scenario, drawing on your own pleasures and memories, you do what you can to bring some kind of life. You bring in some cheerful and colorful paintings by Joan Miro and Paul Klee. While the Miro do not arouse much interest, the ones by Klee become an instantaneous success. One picture in particular, a watercolor titled "Bird Garden," catches the fascination of the entire class. You slip it out of the book and tack it up on the wall beside the doorway and it creates a traffic jam every time the children have to file in or file out. You discuss with your students some of the reasons why Klee may have painted the way he did and you talk about the things that can be accomplished in a painting which could not be accomplished in a photograph. None of this seems to be above the children's heads. Despite this, you are advised flatly by the Art Teacher that your naïveté has gotten the best of you and that the children cannot possibly appreciate this. Klee is too difficult. Children will not enjoy it. You are unable to escape the idea that the Art Teacher means herself instead.

For poetry, in place of the recommended memory gems, going back again into your own college days, you make up your mind to introduce a poem of William Butler Yeats. It is about a lake isle called Innisfree, about birds that have the funny name of "linnets" and about a "bee-loud glade." The children do not all go crazy about it but a number of them seem to like it as much as you do and you tell them how once, three years before, you were living in England and you helped a man in the country to make his home from wattles and clay. The children become intrigued. They pay good attention and many of them grow more curious about the poem than they appeared at first. Here again, however, you are advised by older teachers that you are making a mistake: Yeats is too difficult for children. They can't enjoy it, won't appreciate it, wouldn't like it. You are aiming way above their heads. . . . Another idea comes to mind and you decide to try out an easy and rather well-known and not very complicated poem of Robert Frost. The poem is called "Stopping By Woods on a Snowy Evening." This time, your supervisor happens to drop in from the School Department. He looks over the mimeograph, agrees with you that it's a nice poem, then points out to you—tolerantly, but strictly—that you have made another mistake. "Stopping By Woods" is scheduled for Sixth Grade. It is not "a Fourth Grade poem," and it is not to be read or looked at during the Fourth Grade. Bewildered as you are by what appears to be a kind of idiocy, you still feel reproved and criticized and muted and set back and you feel that you have been caught in the commission of a serious mistake.

On a series of other occasions, the situation is repeated. The children are offered something new and something lively. They respond to it energetically and they are attentive and their attention does not waver. For the first time in a long while perhaps there is actually some real excitement and some growing and some thinking going on within that one small room. In each case, however, you are advised sooner or later that you are making a mistake. Your mistake, in fact, is to have impinged upon the standardized condescension on which the entire administration of the school is based. To hand Paul Klee's pictures to the children of this classroom, and particularly in a twenty-dollar volume, constitutes a threat to the school system. It is not different from sending a little girl from the Negro ghetto into an art class near Harvard Yard. Transcending the field of familiarity of the administration, you are endangering its authority and casting a blow at its self-confidence. The way the threat is handled is by a continual and standardized underrating of the children: They can't do it, couldn't do it, wouldn't like it, don't deserve it. . . . In such a manner, many children are tragically and unjustifiably held back from a great many of the good things that they might come to like or admire and are pinned down instead to books the teacher knows and to easy tastes that she can handle. This includes, above all, of course, the kind of material that is contained in the Course of Study.

Try to imagine, for a child, how great the gap between the outside world and the world conveyed within this kind of school must seem: A little girl, maybe Negro, comes in from a street that is lined with car-carcasses. Old purple Hudsons and one-wheel-missing Cadillacs represent her horizon and mark the edges of her dreams. In the kitchen of her house roaches creep and large rats crawl. On the way to school a wino totters. Some teenage white boys slow down their car to insult her, and speed on. At school, she stands frozen for fifteen minutes in a yard of cracked cement that overlooks a hillside on which trash has been unloaded and at the bottom of which the New York, New Haven and Hartford Railroad rumbles past. In the basement, she sits upon broken or splintery seats in filthy toilets and she is yelled at in the halls. Upstairs, when something has been stolen, she is told that she is the one who stole it and is called a liar and forced abjectly to apologize before a teacher who has not the slightest idea in the world of who the culprit truly was. The same teacher, behind the child's back, ponders audibly with imagined compassion: "What can you do with this kind of material? How can you begin to teach this kind of child?"

Gradually going crazy, the child is sent after two years of misery to a pupil adjustment counselor who arranges for her to have some tests and considers the entire situation and discusses it with the teacher and finally files a long report. She is, some months later, put onto a waiting-list some place for once-a-week therapy but another year passes before she has gotten anywhere near to the front of a long line. By now she is fourteen, has lost whatever innocence she still had in the back seat of the old Cadillac and, within two additional years, she will be ready and eager for dropping out of school.

Once at school, when she was eight or nine, she drew a picture of a rich-looking lady in an evening gown with a handsome man bowing before her but she was told by an insensate and wild-eyed teacher that what she had done was junk and garbage and the picture was torn up and thrown away before her eyes. The rock and roll music that she hears on the Negro station is considered "primitive" by her teachers but she prefers its insistent rhythms to the dreary monotony of school. Once, in Fourth Grade, she got excited at school about some writing she had never heard about before. A handsome green book, brand new, was held up before her and then put into her hands. Out of this book her teacher read a poem. The poem was about a Negro— a woman who was a maid in the house of a white person—and she liked it. It remained in her memory. Somehow without meaning to, she found that she had done the impossible for her: she had memorized that poem. Perhaps, horribly, in the heart of her already she was aware that it was telling about her future: fifty dollars a week to scrub floors and bathe little white babies in the suburbs after an hour's street-car ride. The poem made her want to cry. The white lady, the lady for whom the maid was working, told the maid she loved her. But the maid in the poem wasn't going to tell any lies in return. She knew she didn't feel any love for the white lady and she told the lady so. The poem was shocking to her, but it seemed bitter, strong and true. Another poem in the same green book was about a little boy on a merry-go-round. She laughed with the class at the question he asked about a Jim Crow section on a merry-go-round, but she also was old enough to know that it was not a funny poem really and it made her, valuably, sad. She wanted to know how she could get hold of that poem, and maybe that whole book. The poems were moving to her. . . .

This was a child in my class. Details are changed somewhat but it is essentially one child. The girl was one of the three unplaced special students in that Fourth Grade room. She was not an easy girl to teach and it was hard even to keep her at her seat on many mornings, but I do not remember that there was any difficulty at all in gaining and holding onto her attention on the day that I brought in that green book of Langston Hughes.

Of all the poems of Langston Hughes that I read to my Fourth Graders, the one that the children liked most was a poem that has the title "Ballad of the Landlord." This poem may not satisfy the taste of every critic, and I am not making any claims to immortality for a poem just because I happen to like it a great deal. But the reason this poem did have so much value and meaning for me and, I believe, for many of my students, is that it not only seems moving in an obvious and immediate human way but that it finds its emotion in something ordinary. It is a poem which really does allow both heroism and pathos to poor people, sees strength in awkwardness and attributes to a poor person standing on the stoop of his slum house every bit as much significance as William Wordsworth saw in daffodils, waterfalls and clouds. At the request of the children later on I mimeographed that poem and, although nobody in the classroom was asked to do this, several of the children took it home and memorized it on their own. I did not assign it for memory, because I do not think memorizing a poem has any special value. Some of the children just came in and asked if they could recite it. Before long, almost every child in the room had asked to have a turn.

All of the poems that you read to Negro children obviously are not going to be by or about Negro people. Nor would anyone expect that all poems which are read to a class of poor children ought to be grim or gloomy or heart-breaking or sad. But when, among the works of many different authors, you do have the will to read children a poem by a man so highly renowned as Langston Hughes, then I think it is important not to try to pick a poem that is innocuous, being like any other poet's kind of poem, but I think you ought to choose a poem that is genuinely representative and then try to make it real to the children in front of you in the way that I tried. I also think it ought to be taken seriously by a teacher when a group of young children come in to him one morning and announce that they have liked something so much that they have memorized it voluntarily. It surprised me and impressed me when that happened. It was all I needed to know to confirm for me the value of reading that poem and the value of reading many other poems to children which will build upon and not attempt to break down the most important observation and very deepest foundations of their lives.

Boston Public Schools
School Committee
15 Beacon Street, Boston 8, Massachusetts

Attorney

Thomas S. Eisenstadt

Member

A careful investigation of the facts pertaining to the discharge of Mr. Jonathan Kozol reveal that the administration of the Boston Public Schools were fully justified in terminating his service.

Contrary to publicized reports, I have found that the poem incident was not the sole reason for Mr. Kozol's discharge. Rather, this particular incident was merely the climax to a series of incidents involving this teacher. On numerous occasions during his six months of service.... Mr. Kozol was advised and counseled by his Principal, Miss _____, and his Supervisor, Mr. _____, to restrict his reading and reference materials to the list of approved publications. These admonitions were brought about by Mr. Kozol's continual deviation from the 4th grade course of study.

It has been established as a fact that Mr. Kozol taught the poem, "Ballad of the Landlord" to his class and later distributed mimeographed copies of it to his pupils for home memorization. It is also true that a parent of one of his pupils registered a strong objection to the poem to the school principal. Miss _____, properly carrying out her responsibility to all of the pupils and to their parents, admonished the neophyte teacher for his persistent deviation from the course of study. She further suggested that the poem "Ballad of the Landlord" was unsuitable for 4th graders since it could be interpreted as advocating defiance of authority. At this point Mr. Kozol became rude and told Miss _____ that he was a better judge of good literature than she.

The confirmation of the above facts is adequate justification for the discharge of a temporary teacher hired on a day-to-day trial basis. It has been stated quite adequately that the curriculum of this particular school, which is saturated with compensatory programs in an effort to specially assist disadvantaged pupils, does allow for innovation and creative teaching. However, this flexibility does not and should not allow for a teacher to implant in the minds of young children any and all ideas. Obviously, a measure of control over the course of study is essential to protect the 94,000 Boston school children from ideologies and concepts not

(Continued)

(Continued)

acceptable to our way of life. Without any restrictions, what guarantees would parents have that their children were not being taught that Adolf Hitler and Nazism were right for Germany and beneficial to mankind?

It should be understood that the fact of the poem's author [sic] happened to be a Negro had no bearing on this matter whatsoever. As a matter of fact, Mr. Kozol was asked by the school principal why other works of Langston Hughes, non-controversial in nature, were not selected for study. In fact, a reference source suggested in the course of study recommends use of the book entitled, "Time for Poetry," published by Foresman which contains six of Langston Hughes' poems; and the Administrative Library contains the book, "More Silver Pennies," by MacMillian [sic] which includes more of Langston Hughes' poems, and also poems by the Negro poet Countee Cullen.

When Miss _____ reported the incident to Deputy Superintendent Sullivan and requested Mr. Kozol's removal from the teaching staff of the _____ School, it climaxed a series of complaints made to Miss Sullivan's office concerning this particular teacher. Superintendent Ohrenberger's decision after carefully weighing the facts of the case was to relieve Mr. Kozol from further service in the Boston Public Schools.

It should be understood that many temporary teachers are released from service every year by the administration of the Boston Public Schools. They are released for a variety of reasons. The overwhelming majority of such cases are discharged because in the opinion of the administrators and supervisors the certain temporary teachers are found unsuitable in training, personality, or character. Mr. Kozol, or anyone else who lacks the personal discipline to abide by rules and regulations, as we all must in our civilized society, is obviously unsuited for the highly responsible profession of teaching.

In conclusion, I must add that Mr. Kozol did bring to his pupils an enthusiastic spirit, a high degree of initiative, and other fine qualities found in the best teachers. It is my hope that Mr. Kozol will develop his latent talents and concomitantly develop an understanding and respect for the value of working within the acceptable codes of behavior.

16

"Should the Teacher Always Be Neutral?"

George S. Counts

George S. Counts (1884–1974) was among the most important figures in educational theory during the mid-20th century. He was a committed social activist who believed that teachers, whether at the university level or the elementary and secondary levels, had an obligation to dare to "build a new social order." According to Counts (1969), teachers were obligated to help in the creation of a more just and democratic society. Counts's ideas were part of what came to be known as the social reconstructivist movement in education. Besides being an editor for the radical education magazine *The Social Frontier,* which was published between 1934 and 1943, Counts headed the teachers' union in New York City and continued to write books and scholarly articles until the end of his life.

In the following article on whether the teacher should always be neutral, consider these questions:

1. Does teaching, as Counts suggests, involve an inevitable degree of indoctrination? Is this necessarily a bad thing?

2. Education involves inheriting a cultural heritage and tradition. What if that tradition is discriminatory or unfair?

NOTE: Counts, G. S. (1969). Should the teacher always be neutral? *Phi Delta Kappan, 51*(4), 186–189. Used with the permission of Mary Counts.

3. Can education be value free or neutral?

4. What values should we impose on the child?

"A foolish consistency is the hobgoblin of little minds."

—Ralph Waldo Emerson

In my later years (I am 80 this month) I always warn my students at the first meeting of a class by quoting an old English proverb: "Old men and far travelers may lie by authority." Since I am both, having visited 17 countries, I tell them to put a question mark after everything that I tell them. An old man can say that he remembers something very well, that it happened when he was in high school. Also, if a question is raised about some other country, he can say that he traveled all over that country in his own Ford automobile. To illustrate, I tell them that the only time I ever saw Abraham Lincoln on the television screen was when he read the Emancipation Proclamation and that I can still recall the image of that tall and lean man dressed in a long black coat and wearing the sideburns and beard of the "common man"! I am reminded here of an observation made by Oscar Wilde: "To give an accurate description of what has never occurred is not merely the proper occupation of the historian, but the inalienable privilege of any man of parts and culture."

This article is supposed to be a "response" to the very interesting and challenging essay by Joe Junell.[1] However, I shall merely attempt to write a few words relative to the subject of indoctrination and imposition in the educative process. My involvement in this issue emerged full-blown in a debate with John Dewey at a meeting of educators in February 1932. I defended the thesis that a measure of indoctrination is inevitable, although I rejected the proposition that anything should be taught as absolutely fixed and final and rather defended the idea of "imposition" as a basic and inescapable aspect of the process of rearing the young in any society. Of course I emphasized the point that I was not using the term in a pejorative sense but in its original meaning derived from the Latin verb, *imponere,* "to place on." A few weeks later I gave an address at a meeting of teachers in New York City. Present in the rear of the auditorium was John Dewey. When the time came for questions and remarks from the floor, the great philosopher stood up and said

---

[1]Joseph S. Junell, "Do Teachers Have the Right to Indoctrinate?" Phi Delta Kappan, December 1969, pp. 182–185. We must realize, however, that no two individuals are identical and that every individual responds to his culture in terms of his own unique character.

that he had checked the meaning of the word "indoctrination" in Webster's dictionary and discovered that it meant "teaching."

It is impossible to discuss the question under consideration without an understanding of the role of culture in the life of man. First of all, we must realize that every human being is born helpless, but with infinite potential in all directions. If left alone, he would quickly perish. But being born in a society with its cultural heritage he may rise above the angels or sink below the level of the brute. We can see this demonstrated throughout the ages and obviously in this twentieth century. Although every individual is unique, he is molded by his culture and thus becomes a human being. Quotations from two very distinguished anthropologists are most appropriate here. Graham Wallas in his *Our Social Heritage,* published in 1921, wrote that "we have become, one may say, biologically parasitic upon our social heritage." Bronislaw Malinowski in the last of his great works, *Freedom and Civilization,* published after his death in 1944, said approximately the same thing in these words: "This brief outline of the cultural background of our problem in evolutionary perspective was given to show first and foremost that not a single human act, relevant to the science of man, occurs outside the context of culture." A distinguished British mathematician, H. Levy, in his *The Universe of Science* (1932) places the capstone on the argument: "It [our culture] has inherited us." Consequently, the nature of the human being is dependent on the culture which inherits him. Here is the supreme imposition.

Since the origin of *Homo sapiens,* education, in both its informal and its formal aspects, has embraced the total process of inducting the young into a given society with its culture, its ways of acting, feeling, and thinking, its language, its tools, its institutions, its ethical and aesthetic values, its basic ideas, religious doctrines, and philosophical presuppositions. It is therefore not an autonomous process governed by its own laws and everywhere the same. This process begins at birth and continues on through the years. And we are beginning to realize that the preschool years, the period of infancy and early childhood, are by far the most important years in the development of the talents and the molding of the character of the individual. During my first trip to the Soviet Union in 1927 I became acquainted with the Commissar of Education, Anatole Lunacharsky. One day when we were discussing the Soviet program of preschool education he repeated an old Russian proverb: "We can mold a child of 5 to 6 years into anything we wish; at the age of 8 to 9 we have to bend him; at the age of 16 or 17 we must break him; and thereafter one may well say, 'only the grave can correct a hunchback!'"

Without this imposition of the culture, as all of this makes clear, man would not be man, except in a biological sense—if he could survive. But the fact should be emphasized that cultures are extremely diverse. Consequently, a human being born and reared in one culture may differ greatly from one born and reared in another culture. I have often told my students that a person doesn't see with his eyes or hear with his ears, but with what is behind his eyes or behind his ears. And this depends on his native culture and his experience therein. This principle applies even to physical objects, such as the sun, the moon, and the stars. Obviously, the moon will never again be what it was before the flight of Apollo 11.

The language that is imposed on the child from the moment of his birth may well be regarded as symbolic of the culture. Lewis Mumford in his *The Myth of the Machine* (1968) demonstrates very clearly that in the evolution of man language has played a much greater role than the machine. Indeed, without language man would not be man. And of course we all know that there are many different languages. But the truth is not sufficiently emphasized that languages differ, not only in forms and sounds but also in values. One may well say that every language, in a sense, constitutes a world apart from others. The translation of one language into another is often difficult because the "same" word will differ in meaning from one language to another. A dictionary will be of some assistance but it will not solve all the problems. The basic idea in these observations is well documented in a great book entitled The Poetry of Freedom (1945), edited by William Rose Bent and Norman Cousins, which is a collection of poems from the major languages of the world. More than two-thirds of the volume, 554 of the 806 pages, is devoted to poems from the English-speaking peoples. And I know that the editors did everything they could to find appropriate poems from other languages. If they had chosen some other theme, such as worship of nature or military valor or romantic love, I am certain that the proportions would have been different. It is clear therefore that language constitutes a tremendous imposition on the individual. I have often told my students that, if we do not want to impose anything on the individual, we should not allow him to learn a language until he becomes 21 years of age and then let him choose the language he prefers.

A given society is always a bearer of a particular culture, and societies vary as their cultures vary. Consequently, an education that would be appropriate for one society might destroy another. After the first Sputnik soared into outer space in October 1957, the question was asked over and over again: Is Soviet education superior to ours? The answer, of course, is that the question makes no sense because the two societies are so profoundly different. However, if the question were presented in this form the answer would be different: "Does Soviet education serve the purposes of Soviet society better than our education serves the purposes of our society?" In this case the answer might be in the affirmative, since education for a democracy is far more difficult than education for a dictatorship.

This truth has been recognized through the ages. More than two centuries ago Montesquieu in his great classic, *On the Spirit of the Laws,* wrote that "it is in a republican [democratic] government that the whole power of education is required." The reason for this resides in the fact that such a government must rest on "virtue," which involves "self-renunciation" and is "ever arduous and painful." Also, it "requires a constant preference of public to private interest," and "to inspire such love ought to be the principal business of education." Thomas Jefferson, the father of our democracy, agreed with Montesquieu. In 1824, the year before he died, he wrote in a letter to a friend: "The qualifications for self-government are not innate. They are the result of habit and long training." Horace Mann, father of our common school, saw clearly the relation of education to social and political systems. In his Ninth Annual Report (1845), he warned the citizens of Massachusetts: "If there are not two things wider asunder than freedom and slavery, then must the course of training which fits children for these opposite conditions of life be as diverse as the points to which they lead." Finally, Herbert Spencer, in his *The Americans* (1892), issued the following challenge to our education: "The republican form of government is the highest form of government; but because of this it requires the highest form of human nature—a type nowhere at present existing." In spite of the unprecedented expansion of our schools in this century, we have obviously failed to develop the "form of human nature required." To have done so would have required a revolutionary form of imposition. Political liberty, with all of its demands on human nature, if it is to endure, is certainly one of the most extraordinary impositions on the mind and character of man in the entire history of *Homo sapiens.*

We must realize also that we are living not only in a very special kind of society but also in an age of revolution as wide as the planet. Henry Steele Commager, in his *The American Mind* (1950), warned us that "the decade of the Nineties [was] the watershed of American history"—a watershed between an "America predominantly agricultural" and an "America predominantly urban and industrial." And Carl Bridenbaugh stated without equivocation in his inaugural address as president of the American Historical Association in 1963, "It is my conviction that the greatest turning point in all human history, of which we have any record, has occurred within the twentieth century." Thus, in view of the swiftness of social change, we may say that an education that may be appropriate for one generation may not be appropriate for another. We are consequently confronted today with William F. Ogburn's "cultural lag" and Alfred North Whitehead's generation gap. The fact is that since crossing the great watershed we have never sat down and considered seriously how our children and youth should spend their years in our urbanized and industrialized society. Also, with the reduction of the earth to the dimensions of a neighborhood, we have failed to sense that the age of tribalism and nationalism is closing and that a new age of internationalism is well over the horizon. The nature of the imposition must be radically altered.

A few words in closing about the school. We must realize that, whenever choices are made in the launching of a program, values are involved. This is obviously true in the shaping of the curriculum, the selection of text-books, the giving of grades, the organization of social activities, the con-struction of a school building, the hanging of pictures and paintings on the walls of a schoolroom, and in the selection of a teacher. I have often told my students that, if we want to avoid imposing anything on our children, we should alter the architectural style of the building every day. Also, I call their attention to the fact that our arithmetic textbooks transmit to the younger generation countless social, political, and moral ideas—for the most part a white middle-class culture. And we know that our history text-books, until very recently, practically excluded the Negro.

The need for developing the independent and critical mind in the members of the younger generation is implicit in much that I have written and is clearly a form of imposition. However, something more must be said. The student should not be encouraged to engage in criticism just for the sake of criticism. The truly critical mind is one of the most precious resources of a free society. At the same time such a mind should be highly disciplined. We should never disregard the basic thesis of Carl Becker in his *Freedom and Responsibility in the American Way of Life* (1945), one of the most insightful books in the liter-ature of our democracy. That thesis is that with every right or freedom there goes a responsibility. The alternative is chaos and anarchy. The critical mind should be armed with knowledge and understanding, and perhaps with a mod-icum of humility and wisdom. Even a scientist must undergo and practice a severe discipline. He must practice the intellectual virtues of accuracy, precision, truthfulness, open-mindedness, and absolute integrity. The limits of freedom in the rearing of the child are thus expressed by Bronislaw Malinowski in his *Freedom and Civilization:* "We see quite clearly why the freedom of the child, in the sense of letting him do what he wishes and as he likes, is unreal. In the interest of his own organism he has constantly to be trammeled in education from acts which are biologically dangerous or are culturally useless." And Judge Learned Hand, one of our foremost students of jurisprudence, warned us: "A society in which men recognize no check upon their freedom soon becomes a society where freedom is a possession of only a savage few."

The big question, therefore, is not whether we should impose anything on the child in the process of education but what we should impose. In the swiftly changing world of the twentieth century we must certainly examine our cultural heritage critically in the light of the great and inescapable realities of the present age and the trends toward tomorrow. What this means, in my opinion, is to present to the younger generation a vision of the possibility of finally fulfilling the great promise of America expressed in the Declaration of Independence: "We hold these truths to be self-evident, that all men are created equal, that they are endowed by their Creator with certain unalienable Rights, that among these are Life, Liberty, and the pursuit of Happiness." Clearly, if science and technology can show us how to fly to the moon and circumnavigate the planets, we should be able to employ these powerful forces for bringing our practices into harmony with our historic professions.

A final illustration of the critical importance of the question of imposition in the rearing of the young in our democracy is clearly revealed in our treatment of the Negro down through the generations. Gunnar Myrdal, a renowned Swedish social scientist, in his great two-volume work, *An American Dilemma* (1944), issues a challenge that we can disregard only at our peril. In his first chapter, entitled "American Ideals and the American Conscience," he states: "America, compared to every other country in Western civilization, large or small, has the most explicitly expressed system of general ideals in reference to human interrelations." These ideals embrace "the essential dignity of the individual human being, of the fundamental equality of all men, and of certain inalienable rights to freedom, justice, and a fair opportunity." Our dilemma is the consequence of the great gap between our professed ideals and our practices. He adds, therefore, that "the treatment of the Negro is America's greatest and most conspicuous scandal. . . . America's greatest failure." And then he relates this condition to the subject of my article in the following generalization: "The simple fact is that an educational offensive against racial intolerance, going deeper than the reiteration of the 'glittering generalities' in the nation's political creed, has never seriously been attempted in America." Certainly a major problem confronting our program of education is the resolution of this dilemma in the shortest possible period of time. But to achieve this goal the teacher cannot be neutral and the essence of the traditional pattern of imposition in our culture must be reversed.

Selection From *Roll of Thunder, Hear My Cry*

Mildred D. Taylor

Mildred Delois Taylor is an African American writer whose books explore the historical struggle faced by Black families in the Deep South. Taylor originally came from Jackson, Mississippi, and then moved north to Toledo, Ohio, where she spent most of her childhood. Four of her novels chronicle the experiences of the Logan family during the 1930s and 1940s. The most well known of these works is *Roll of Thunder, Hear My Cry*, which won the 1977 Newberry Medal from the American Library Association for best children's novel of the year.

In the following selection from *Roll of Thunder, Hear My Cry*, Taylor (1976) describes an incident in which Black students in a rural school district in Mississippi are given books that have been discarded by the White local school district. Several of the students, along with one of the teachers, Mary Logan, take a defiant stand against the overt discrimination of being given cast-off materials to work with as though they are new.

As you read the following selection, consider these questions:

1. Why is the lead African American teacher, Miss Crocker, not as upset by getting the worn-out textbooks as Little Man or Cassie's mother Mary is?

---

did Cassie's mother risk by pasting blank white pages into the fronts of the
;?

ild Cassie's mother, like Little Man, simply have refused to accept the books?

4. What is the significance of this selection in terms of the 1954 *Brown v. Topeka* decision that led to the desegregation of American schools?

5. What does a selection like this suggest about the meaning of privilege?

By ten o'clock, Miss Crocker had rearranged our seating and written our names on her seating chart. I was still sitting beside Gracey and Alma but we had been moved from the third to the first row in front of a small pot-bellied stove. Although being eyeball to eyeball with Miss Crocker was nothing to look forward to, the prospect of being warm once the cold weather set in was nothing to be sneezed at either, so I resolved to make the best of my rather dubious position.

Now Miss Crocker made a startling announcement: This year we would all have books.

Everyone gasped, for most of the students had never handled a book at all besides the family Bible. I admit that even I was somewhat excited. Although Marna had several books, I had never had one of my very own.

"Now we're very fortunate to get these readers," Miss Crocker explained while we eagerly awaited the unveiling. "The county superintendent of schools himself brought these books down here for our use and we must take extra-good care of them." She moved toward her desk. "So let's all promise that well take the best care possible of these new books." She stared down, expecting our response. "All right, all together, let's repeat, 'We promise to take good care of our new books.'" She looked sharply at me as she spoke.

"WE PROMISE TO TAKE GOOD CARE OF OUR NEW BOOKS!"

"Fine," Miss Crocker beamed, then proudly threw back the tarpaulin.

Sitting so close to the desk, I could see that the covers of the books, a motley red, were badly worn and that the gray edges of the pages had been marred by pencils, crayons, and ink. My anticipation at having my own book ebbed to a sinking disappointment. But Miss Crocker continued to beam as she called each fourth grader to her desk and, recording a number in her roll book, handed him or her a book.

As I returned from my trip to her desk, I noticed the first graders anxiously watching the disappearing pile. Miss Crocker must have noticed them too, for as I sat down she said, "Don't worry, little ones, there are plenty of readers for you too. See there on Miss Davis's desk." Wide eyes turned to the covered teacher's platform directly in front of them and an audible sigh of relief swelled in the room.

I glanced across at Little Man, his face lit in eager excitement. I knew that he could not see the soiled covers or the marred pages from where he sat, and even though his penchant for cleanliness was often annoying, I did not like to think of his disappointment when he saw the books as they really were. But there was nothing that I could do about it, so I opened my book to its center and began browsing through the spotted pages. Girls with blond braids and boys with blue eyes stared up at me. I found a story about a boy and his dog lost in a cave and began reading while Miss Crocker's voice droned on monotonously.

Suddenly I grew conscious of a break in monotonous tone and I looked up. Miss Crocker was sitting at Miss Davis's desk with the first-grade books stacked before her, staring fiercely down at Little Man, who was pushing a book back upon the desk.

"What's that you said, Clayton Chester Logan?" she asked.

The room became gravely silent. Everyone knew that Little Man was in big trouble for no one, but no one, ever called Little Man "Clayton Chester," unless she or he meant serious business.

Little Man knew this too. His lips parted slightly as he took his hands from the book. He quivered, but he did not take his eyes from Miss Crocker. "I—I said may I have another book please, ma'am," he squeaked. "That one's dirty."

"Dirty!" Miss Crocker echoed, appalled by such temerity. She stood up, gazing down upon Little Man like a bony giant, but Little Man raised his head and continued to look into her eyes. "Dirty! And just who do you think you are, Clayton Chester? Here the county is giving us these wonderful books during these hard times and you're going to stand there and tell me that the book's too dirty? Now you take that book or get nothing at all."

Little Man lowered his eyes and said nothing as he stared at the book. For several moments he stood there, his face barely visible above the desk, then he turned and looked at the few remaining books and, seeming to realize that they were as badly soiled as the one Miss Crocker had given him, he looked across the room at me. I nodded and Little Man, glancing up again at Miss Crocker, slid the book from the edge of the desk, and with his back straight and his head up returned to his seat.

Miss Crocker sat down again. "Some people around here seem to be giving themselves airs. I'll tolerate no more of that," she scowled. "Sharon Lake, come get your book."

I watched Little Man as he scooted into his seat beside two other little boys. He sat for a while with a stony face looking out the window; then, evidently accepting the fact that the book in front of him was the best that he could expect, he turned and opened it. But as he stared at the book's inside cover, his face clouded, changing from sulky acceptance to puzzlement. His brows furrowed. Then his eyes grew wide, and suddenly he sucked in his breath and sprang from his chair like a wounded animal, flinging the book onto the floor and stomping madly upon it.

Miss Crocker rushed to Little Man and grabbed him up in powerful hands. She shook him vigorously, then set him on the floor again. "Now, just what's gotten into you, Clayton Chester?"

But Little Man said nothing. He just stood staring down at the open book, shivering with indignant anger.

"Pick it up," she ordered.

"No!" defied Little Man.

"No? I'll give you ten seconds to pick up that book, boy, or I'm going to get my switch."

Little Man bit his lower lip, and I knew that he was not going to pick up the book. Rapidly, I turned to the inside cover of my own book and saw immediately what had made Little Man so furious. Stamped on the inside cover was a chart which read:

Property of the Board of Education
Spokane County, Mississippi
September, 1922

Chronological Issuance	Date Of Issuance	Condition of Book	Race of Student
1	September 1922	New	White
2	September 1923	Excellent	White
3	September 1924	Excellent	White
4	September 1925	Very Good	White
5	September 1926	Good	White
6	September 1927	Good	White
7	September 1928	Average	White
8	September 1929	Average	White
9	September 1930	Average	White
10	September 1931	Poor	White
11	September 1932	Poor	White
12	September 1933	Very Poor	nigra
13			
14			
15			

The blank lines continued down to line 20 and I knew that they had all been reserved for black students. A knot of anger swelled in my throat and held there, but as Miss Crocker directed Little Man to bend over the "whipping" chair I put aside my anger and, jumped up.

"Miz Crocker, don't, please!" I cried. Miss Crocker's dark eyes warned me not to say another word. "I know why he done it!"

"You want part of this switch, Cassie?"

"No'm," I said hastily. 'I just wanna tell you how come Little Man done what he done."

"Sit down!" she ordered as I hurried toward her with the open book in my hand.

Holding the book up to her, I said, "See, Miz Crocker, see what it says. They give us these ole books when they didn't want 'em no more."

She regarded me impatiently, but did not look at the book. "Now how could he know what it says? He can't read."

"Yes'm, he can. He been reading since he was four. He can't read all them big words, but he can read them columns. See what's in the last row. Please look, Miz Crocker."

This time Miss Crocker did look, but her face did not change. Then, holding up her head, she gazed unblinkingly down at me.

"S-see what they called us," I said, afraid she had not seen.

"That's what you are," she said coldly. "Now go sit down."

I shook my head, realizing now that Miss Crocker did not even know what I was talking about. She had looked at the page and had understood nothing.

"I said sit down, Cassie."

I started slowly toward my desk, but as the hickory stick sliced the tense air, I turned back around. "Miz Crocker," I said, "I don't want my book neither."

The switch landed hard upon Little Man's upturned bottom. Miss Crocker looked questioningly at me as I reached up to her desk and placed the book upon it. Then she swung the switch five more times and, discovering that Little Man had no intention of crying, ordered him up.

"All right, Cassie," she sighed, turning to me, "come on and get yours."

By the end of the school day I had decided that I would tell Mama everything before Miss Crocker had a chance to do so. From nine years of trial and error, I had learned that punishment was always less severe when I poured out the whole truth to Mama on my own before she had heard anything from anyone else.

I knew that Miss Crocker had not spoken to Mama during the lunch period, for she had spent the whole hour in the classroom preparing for the afternoon session.

As soon as class was dismissed I sped from the room, weaving a path through throngs of students happy to be free. But before I could reach the seventh-grade class building, I had the misfortune to collide with Mary Lou's father. Mr. Wellever looked down on me with surprise that I would actually bump into him, then proceeded to lecture me on the virtues of watch'n where one was going. Meanwhile Miss Crocker briskly crossed the lawn to Mama's class building. By the time I escaped Mr. Wellever, she had already disappeared into the darkness of the hallway. Mama's classroom was in the back. I crept silently along the quiet hall and peeped cautiously into the open doorway. Mama, pushing a strand of her long, crinkly hair back into the chignon at the base of her slender neck, was seated at her desk watching Miss Crocker thrust a book before her. "Just look at that, Mary," Miss Crocker said, thumping the book twice with her forefinger. "A perfectly good book ruined. Look at that broken binding and those foot marks all over it."

Mama did not speak as she studied the book.

"And here's the one Cassie wouldn't take," she said, placing a second book on Mama's desk with an outraged slam. "At least she didn't have a tantrum and stomp all over hers. I tell you, Mary, I just don't know what got into those children today. I always knew Cassie was rather high-strung, but Little Man. He's always such a perfect little gentleman."

Mama glanced at the book I had rejected and opened the front cover so that the offensive pages of both books faced her. "You say Cassie said it was because of this front page that she and Little Man didn't want the books?" Mama asked quietly.

"Yes, ain't that something?" Miss Crocker said, forgetting her teacher-training-school diction in her indignation. "The very idea! That's on all the books, and why they got so upset about it I'll never know."

"You punish them?" asked Mama, glancing up at Miss Crocker.

"Well, I certainly did! Whipped both of them good with my hickory stick. Wouldn't you have?" When Marna did not reply, she added defensively, "I had a perfect right to."

"Of course you did, Daisy," Mama said, turning back to the books again. "They disobeyed you." But her tone was so quiet and noncommittal that I knew Miss Crocker was not satisfied with her reaction.

"Well I thought you would've wanted to know, Mary, in case you wanted to give them a piece of your mind also."

Mama smiled up at Miss Crocker and said rather absently, "Yes, of course, Daisy. Thank you." Then she opened her desk drawer and pulled out some paper, a pair of scissors, and a small brown bottle.

Miss Crocker, dismayed by Mama's seeming unconcern for the serious-ness of the matter, thrust her shoulders back and began moving away from the desk. "You understand that if they don't have those books to study from, I'll have to fail them in both reading and composition, since I plan to base all my lessons around—" She stopped abruptly and stared in amazement at Mama. "Mary, what in the world are you doing?"

Mama did not answer. She had trimmed the paper to the size of the books and was now dipping a gray looking glue from the brown bottle onto the inside cover of one of the books. Then she took the paper and placed it over the glue.

"Mary Logan, do you know what you're doing? That book belongs to the county. If somebody from the superintendent's office ever comes down here and sees that book, you'll be in real trouble."

Mama laughed and picked up the other book. "In the first place no one cares enough to come down here, and in the second place if anyone should come, maybe, he could see all the things we need—current books for all of our subjects, not just somebody's old throwaways, desks, paper, blackboards, erasers, maps, chalk . . ." Her voice trailed off as she glued the second book.

"Biting the hand that feeds you. That's what you're doing, Mary Logan, biting the hand that feeds you."

Again, Mama laughed. "If that's the case, Daisy, I don't think I need that little bit of food." With the second book finished, she stared at a small pile of seventh-grade books on her desk.

"Well, I just think you're spoiling those children, Mary. They've got to learn how things are sometime."

"Maybe so," said Mama, "but that doesn't mean they have to accept them . . . and maybe we don't either!"

Miss Crocker gazed suspiciously at Mama. Although Mama had been a teacher at Great Faith for fourteen years, ever since she had graduated from the Crandon Teacher Training School at nineteen, she was still considered by many of the other teachers as a disrupting maverick. Her ideas were always a bit too radical and her statements a bit too pointed. The fact that she had not grown up in Spokane County but in the Delta made her even more suspect and the more traditional thinkers like Miss Crocker were wary of her. "Well, if anyone ever does come from the county and sees Cassie's and Little Man's books messed up like that," she said, "I certainly won't accept the responsibility for them."

"It will be easy enough for anyone to see whose responsibility it is, Daisy, by opening any seventh grade book. Because tomorrow I'm going to 'mess them up' too."

Miss Crocker, finding nothing else to say, turned imperiously and headed for the door. I dashed across the hall and awaited her exit, then crept back.

Mama remained at her desk, sitting very still. For a long time she did not move. When she did, she picked up one of the seventh-grade books and began to glue again. I wanted to go and help her, but something warned me that now was not the time to make my presence known, and I left.

I would wait until the evening to talk to her. There was no rush now. She understood.

PART VII

Myths and Stereotypes About Teaching

18. Selection From *To Teach: The Journey of a Teacher*
    William Ayers

19. Selections From *School Is Hell*: Lesson 6: The 9 Types of Grade School
    Teachers and Lesson 13: The 9 Types of High School Teachers
    Matt Groening

Teaching is a profession that is fraught with myths and stereotypes. Interestingly, many of these myths have a grain of truth in them. Among the most common, for example, is the myth of schoolteachers being female and being either very young or middle-aged and graying. In fact, historically, teachers did fit this profile well into the 20th century. It is not, however, accurate anymore. Other stereotypes include the idea that the typical teacher is single, sexless, temperate, not entirely comfortable with the world of adults, and politically unengaged if not politically naïve.

The origins of this second stereotype can be explained by looking at the historical data about teachers in American society. Starting in the 1830s, young women began to be heavily recruited into the teaching profession. As noted in the introduction of this work, this led to the profession becoming "feminized." Female teachers in most parts of the country were not allowed to marry. In

Missouri, for example, until 1948 a female teacher could not be married and work in the schools. (No corresponding laws existed for men.) As a result of this restriction, many teachers left the profession after relatively brief careers. Those who stayed generally stayed for life. Hence, the stereotypes emerged of teachers being either old or young with very little exception in between. Female teachers were often restricted by local standards of propriety in terms of what they could wear or whether they could drink alcohol. In Dade County, Florida, for example, during the mid-1930s, teachers were not allowed to wear lipstick when they taught. Drinking, at least in public, was also considered an inappropriate type of behavior. Hence, the myth of temperance emerged.

Many of these restrictions are still quietly enforced in many communities. For example, a few years back, one of the editor's female students who had gone to teach in a small rural town in central Florida came back to visit in Miami and explained how her principal had made it very clear that if she was going to drink, she should do it privately, and that if she had a boyfriend and he "slept over," she should be discreet about it. It was explained that the small town she lived in had "expectations and rules" for its teachers.

What does the typical or "model" teacher in the United States look like? If she is an elementary school teacher, she is a woman in her mid-30s, is well educated, holds a master's degree, is married with two children, is not very politically active, and is supervised by a man. She has taught for 12 years. This contradicts the model of the very young or aging teacher.

Another myth or stereotype about teaching is that teachers are frequently thought to work less hard than other workers because they have long vacations and a three-month break during the summer. This is not accurate. When school is in session, the average teacher works about 46 hours per week. This includes grading and preparation time. Compare this to 35 hours per week for the average industrial worker. Thus, the typical teacher works about the same number of hours as any other worker, just in more concentrated segments of time.

The readings in this section explore some of the myths and stereotypes that are commonly held about educators in the United States. William Ayers' (2001) essay provides an analysis of 12 commonly held myths about teachers, while Matt Groening's (1987) cartoons humorously present stereotypes of teacher "types" at the elementary and secondary levels of schooling.

Further Readings: In addition to Matt Groening's *School Is Hell* cartoons, there are many other comics that portray schools and what it is like to "suffer" through them as a student. One of the very best cartoonists to deal with being in the classroom as a student is Bill Watterson. His *Calvin and Hobbes* series includes numerous depictions of teachers as dinosaurs and of Calvin's boredom in day-to-day life at school.

Linking to Popular Culture: There are numerous movies that include stereotypes of teachers, many of them comedies. Among the best are *Fast Times at Ridgemont High* (1982), *Porky's I–III* (1982–1985), and *Ferris Bueller's Day Off* (1986). Stereotypes about the condition of inner-city schools can be seen in films such as *The Principal* (1987) and *Lean on Me* (1989).

References

Ayers, W. (2001). *To teach: The journey of a teacher.* New York: Teachers College Press.
Groening, M. (2007). *School Is Hell.* New York: Random House.

18

Selection From *To Teach*

The Journey of a Teacher

William Ayers

Bill Ayers (2001) is a professor at the University of Illinois at Chicago. He was a radical and political activist during the 1960s and has taught in both K–12 and higher-education classrooms. An accomplished writer and teacher educator, he was a major source of controversy in the 2008 presidential campaign. Republican critics questioned then candidate Obama's association with Ayers, who had known him professionally in Chicago.

Consider the following questions:

1. According to Ayers, "teaching is instructing, advising, counseling, organizing, assessing, guiding, goading, showing, managing, modeling, coaching, disciplining, prodding, preaching, persuading, proselytizing, listening, interacting, nursing, and inspiring." How does this type of analysis contradict the idea of teaching being simply the delivery of a preplanned curriculum?

2. What are the reasons not to be a teacher? What are the reasons to be a teacher?

3. Look at each one of Ayers's 10 myths about teaching. Ask yourself whether Ayers's argument that they are myths is true. If you feel Ayers is wrong, indicate why.

NOTE: Reprinted by permission of the Publisher. From William Ayers, To Teach: The Journey of a Teacher, New York: Teachers College Press. Copyright © 2001 by Teachers College, Columbia University. All rights reserved.

Before I stepped into my first classroom as a teacher, I thought teaching was mainly instruction, partly performing, certainly being in the front and at the center of classroom life. Later, with much chaos and some pain, I learned that this is the least of it—teaching includes a more splendorous range of actions. Teaching is instructing, advising, counseling, organizing, assessing, guiding, goading, showing, managing, modeling, coaching, disciplining, prodding, preaching, persuading, proselytizing, listening, interacting, nursing, and inspiring. Teachers must be experts and generalists, psychologists and cops, rabbis and priests, judges and gurus. And that's not all. When we face ourselves, we face memories of our own triumphs and humiliations, of our cowardice and bravery, our breakthroughs and breakdowns, our betrayals as well as our fidelity. When we characterize our work—even partially, even incompletely—straightforward images and one-dimensional definitions dissolve, and teaching becomes elusive, problematic, often impossibly opaque.

One thing becomes clear enough. Teaching as the direct delivery of some preplanned curriculum, teaching as the orderly and scripted conveyance of information, teaching as clerking, is simply a myth. Teaching is much larger and much more alive than that; it contains more pain and conflict, more joy and intelligence, more uncertainty and ambiguity. It requires more judgment and energy and intensity than, on some days, seems humanly possible. Teaching is spectacularly unlimited.

When students describe us, the picture becomes even denser and more layered. Teachers are good and bad, kind and mean, unjust and fair, arbitrary and even-handed, thoughtful and stupid. For elementary school students, we embody the adult world and we are, next to parents, the strongest representatives of and guides into that world. The hopes and dreams of youth are in our hands; their goals and aspirations are shaped through their encounters with us. Positive memories of teachers are reserved for particular and special people: the teacher who touched your heart, the teacher who understood you or who cared about you as a person, the teacher whose passion for something—music, math, Latin, kites—was infectious and energizing. In any case, teachers are a large presence in the lives of students; we take up a lot of space and we have a powerful impact. This is why I chose teaching: to share my life with young people, to shape and touch the future.

* * *

Teachers are asked hundreds, perhaps thousands of times why they choose teaching. The question often means: "Why teach, when you could do something more profitable?" "Why teach, since teaching is beneath your skill and intelligence?" The question can be filled with contempt and cynicism or it can be simply a request for understanding and knowledge: "What is there in teaching to attract and keep you?" Either way, it is a question worth pursuing, for there are good reasons to teach and equally good reasons not to teach. Teaching is, after all, different in character from any other profession or job or occupation, and teaching, like anything else, is not for everyone.

There are many reasons not to teach, and they cannot be easily dismissed, especially by those of us who love teaching. Teachers are badly paid, so badly that it is a national disgrace. We earn on average a quarter of what lawyers are paid, half of what accountants make, less than truck drivers and shipyard workers. Romantic appeals aside, wages and salaries are one reflection of relative social value; a collective, community assessment of worth. There is no other profession that demands so much and receives so little in financial compensation; none in which the state stipulates such extensive and specific educational requirements, for example, and then financially rewards people so sparingly. Slight improvements in pay and benefits in some districts serve only to highlight how out of step we really are when it comes to valuing and rewarding teaching.

Teachers also suffer low status in many communities, in part as a legacy of sexism: Teaching is largely women's work, and it is constantly being deskilled, made into something to be performed mechanically, without much thought or care, covered over with layers of supervision and accountability and bureaucracy, and held in low esteem. Low pay is part of that dynamic. So is the paradox of holding teachers up as paragons of virtue (the traditional pedestal) while constraining real choices and growth.

Teachers often work in difficult situations, under impossible conditions. We are usually isolated from other adults and yet have no privacy and no time for ourselves. We teach youngsters who are compelled by law to attend school, many of whom have no deep motivation or desire to be there. We sometimes work in schools that are large, impersonal, and factory-like; sometimes in schools that resemble war zones. We are subject to the endless and arbitrary demands of bureaucracies and distant state legislatures. Teachers are expected to cover everything without neglecting anything, to teach reading and arithmetic, for example, but also good citizenship, basic values, drug and alcohol awareness, AIDS prevention, dating, mating, and relating, sexuality, how to drive, parenting skills, and whatever else comes up.

The complexity of teaching can be excruciating, and for some that may be a sufficient reason not to teach (for others, it is one of teaching's most compelling allures). Teachers must face a large number of students: thirty or more for typical elementary school teachers, a hundred and fifty for high school teachers. Each youngster comes to us with a specific background, with unique desires, abilities, intentions, and needs. Somehow, we must reach out to each student; we must meet each one. A common experience of teachers is to feel the pain of opportunities missed, potential unrealized, students untouched. Add to this the constancy of change and the press of time, the lack of support and the scarcity of resources, and some of the intensity and difficulty of teaching becomes apparent. It is no wonder that many of us retreat into something certain and solid, something reliable, something we can see and get our hands around—lesson plans, say, or assertive discipline workshops—because we fear burning out altogether.

These are some of the reasons not to teach, and, for me at least, they add up to a compelling case. So, why teach? My own pathway to teaching began long ago in a large, uniquely nurturing family, a place where I experienced the ecstasy of intimacy and the irritation of being known, the power of will and the boundary of freedom, both the safety and the constraints of family living. I was the middle child of five children and I had opportunities to learn as well as opportunities to teach. In my family, I learned to balance self-respect with respect for others, assertiveness with compromise, individual choice with group consciousness.

I began teaching in an alternative school in Ann Arbor, Michigan, called the Children's Community. It was a small school with large purposes; a school that, we hoped, would change the world. One of our goals was to provide an outstanding, experience-based education for the young people we taught. Another was to develop a potent model of freedom and racial integration, a model that would have wide impact on other schools and on all of society. We thought of ourselves as an insurgent, experimental counter-institution; one part of a larger movement for social change.

The year was 1965, and I was twenty years old. For many young people, teaching was not only respectable, it was one of the meaningful, relevant things a person could do. Many schools then, as now, were inhumane, lifeless places. We felt that we could save the schools, create life spaces and islands of compassion for children and, through our work, help create a new social order. We were intent on living lives that did not make a mockery of our values, and teaching seemed a way to live that kind of life. We were hopeful and altruistic and we were on a mission of change.

Today, teaching may not seem so attractive, nor so compelling in quite the same way. Not only are the schools in even worse shape than before, and the problems seemingly more intractable, but there is a narrow, selfish spirit loose in the land. Idealists are "suckers" in the currency of the day, and the notion that schools should be decent, accessible, and responsive places for all children is just more pie-in-the-sky. With a combative social

Darwinism setting the pace in our society, and a cynical sense that morality has no place in our public lives, teaching today can seem a fool's errand.

But it is not. Teaching is still a powerful calling for many people, and powerful for the same reasons that it has always been so. There are still young people who need a thoughtful, caring adult in their lives; someone who can nurture and challenge them, who can coach and guide, understand and care about them. There are still injustices and deficiencies in society, in even more desperate need of repair. There are still worlds to change— including specific, individual worlds, one by one—and classrooms can be places of possibility and transformation for youngsters, certainly, but also for teachers. Teaching can still be world-changing work. And this, I believe, is finally the reason to teach. People are called to teaching because they love children and youth, or because they love being with them, watching them open up and grow and become more able, more competent, more powerful in the world. They may love what happens to themselves when they are with children, the ways in which they become their best selves. Or they become teachers because they love the world, or some piece of the world enough that they want to show that love to others. In either case, people teach as an act of construction and reconstruction, and as a gift of oneself to others. I teach in the hope of making the world a better place.

While practically every teacher I have known over many years came to teaching in part with this hope, only a few outstanding teachers are able to carry it fully into a life in teaching. What happens? To begin with, most of us attend colleges or preparation programs that neither acknowledge nor honor our larger and deeper purposes—places that turn our attention to research on teaching or methods of teaching and away from a serious encounter with the reality of teaching, the art and craft of teaching, the morality of teaching, or the ecology of childhood. Our love of children, our idealism, is made to seem quaint in these places. Later, we find ourselves struggling to survive in schools structured in ways that make our purposes seem hopeless and inaccessible. We may have longed for child-centered communities of shared values and common goals, but mostly we settle for institutions, procedure-centered places characterized by hierarchy, control, and efficiency. We may have imagined the kind of wonderful teachers we could become in an ideal world, but we had no idea of the obstacles that would be scattered along our pathway to teaching.

One common obstacle is the pressure not to teach. Family and friends question the choice to teach, and even experienced teachers advise young people to search somewhere else. One elementary school teacher I know, while in graduate school, worked as an assistant to a prominent education professor who told her repeatedly that she was too bright and too able to be a teacher. She found herself defending her choice against a person she thought would be an obvious ally but was not, and she learned an important lesson: The profession is full of people who don't respect its purposes. If teaching is to become vital and honorable again, it is teachers who will have to make it so. It is the voice of the teacher that must at last be heard.

Another obstacle is the chorus of references to the "real world," as in, "Now this school is the real world." The point is to tell you that you are naive and foolish and that this school is immutable, that it has always been as it is and that it can never be changed. School, in this view, is not an institution of society or history, not something created by people, but rather something outside of history, agency, and choice. Teachers and students alike are supposed to compromise, accommodate, and adjust; to be compliant, conformist, and obedient.

There is a related, even more subtle sapping of your energy and mind as you submit to the structure of schooling. I observed a principal recently welcoming a group of new teachers to his school. Indoctrinating may be a more accurate word. He began by praising these teachers, by admiring their commitment and acknowledging their youthful energy and idealism. There were smiles and a sense of worth and pride all around. Then, without changing tone or expression, he began to caution them about the families and the children they would encounter, warning them that they should not expect too much from these youngsters. "Your idealism is wonderful, just what our school needs," he concluded. "But don't blame yourselves if you can't teach these kids to read. It will be enough if you can get them to listen."

All the praise of youth and admiration of idealism turns out to be a cover for cynicism. These teachers are being told to accept something that is really unacceptable, to "grow up," to lower their expectations for learners. It is true that teachers need to grow in experience, skill, and judgment. But that growth does not need to be based on narrowing goals, aspirations, and ideals, as this principal would have it. It is true that teaching is the kind of activity that develops and flowers over time, that there is no way to be an experienced teacher without first being a new teacher. But that development can be constructed on the basis of high ideals, hope, realism, and compassion for others. Teachers do, indeed, need to be forgiving of their own inevitable shortcomings, but always in the context of being critical and demanding of themselves as well.

Finally, a major obstacle on the pathway to teaching is the notion that teaching is essentially technical, that it is easily learned, simply assessed, and quickly remediated. Students of teaching spend an inordinate amount of time learning how to make lesson plans (an astonishingly simple, entirely overblown, and not very useful skill) or reading the research on classroom management. We are encouraged to attend to the voice of the supervisor and the administrator, the academic and the researcher, and not to the more immediate and important voices of children and their parents. This is, perhaps, the most difficult obstacle to overcome, and resistance and reconciliation are major themes in the act of effective teaching.

I know that I celebrate a kind of teaching that is exceedingly rare. I know that becoming an outstanding teacher is an heroic quest: One must navigate turbulent and troubled waters, overcome a seemingly endless sea of obstacles, and face danger and challenge (often alone), on the way toward an uncertain reward. Teaching is not for the weak or the faint-hearted; courage and imagination are needed to move from myth to reality.

Teaching is entombed in myth—there are literally thousands of tiny ones clinging like barnacles to teaching, while others perch on it like giant, fire-breathing creatures. These myths are available in every film about teaching, in all the popular literature, and in the common sense passed across the generations. Here is a sample:

MYTH 1: Good Classroom Management is an Essential First Step Toward Becoming a Good Teacher

This myth is central to the everyday lore of teaching. It is the old "don't-smile-until-Christmas" wisdom. Some teachers say, "I get tough in September to gain their respect, and then I can ease up without losing control." Others say, "I play 'bad cop' first so they know who's boss, and then I can afford to be 'good cop.'"

There is a sleight-of-hand involved here, for it is true that an out-of-control classroom is dysfunctional for everyone. But what makes this a myth is (1) its linearity—the assumption that classroom management precedes teaching in time and (2) its insularity—the notion that classroom management can sensibly be understood as an event separated from the whole of teaching. The classroom management myth represents, in a sense, the triumph of narrow behaviorism and manipulation over teaching as a moral craft.

The ability to work productively with a large group of students is a skill that comes with experience. The development of that skill is not aided by focusing on techniques from the pantheon of classroom management: "positive reinforcement," "anticipatory set," "wait time," and all the rest. Those simply turn a teacher's attention in the wrong direction. Nor is it useful to assume that once in control, teaching can begin. There are a lot of quiet, passive classrooms where not much learning is taking place, and others where children's hearts and souls are being silently destroyed in the name of good management.

Working well with a group of youngsters is something learned in practice. And it is best learned not as a set of techniques to shape behavior without regard to persons or values, but while attempting to accomplish larger goals and purposes. This means focusing on three essentials: youngsters (Are they active? Are they pursuing questions and concerns of importance to them and us?); the environment (Is it appropriate? Does it offer sufficient challenge? Are there multiple opportunities to succeed?); and curriculum (Is it engaging? Does it connect the known to the unknown?). While this will not yield instant "results," it will allow for the emergence of more authentic and productive teachers and teaching relationships, and questions of group coherence and standards of behavior can then be worked out in context.

MYTH 2: Teachers Learn to Teach in Colleges of Education

This myth floats pervasively (if uneasily) on the surface of society as a whole, but teachers don't believe it for a minute. Teachers know that they learned to teach on the job (and unfortunately, some of what is learned on the job is never subjected to serious scrutiny), and that their journey through teacher education was painfully dull, occasionally malevolent, and mostly beside the point. Some teachers believe that a few college courses could have been useful if they had been offered during the first years of actual classroom experience, instead of being dished out as "truth" disconnected from the messy reality of schools.

When teacher education programs structure the separation of theory and practice, this message alone is enough to degrade teaching. When we imply that teaching is quickly learned and easily fixed (like learning the fox trot); that it is based on methods and techniques or on little formulas; that it is generic, in the sense that learning to teach in Hannibal equips a teacher for teaching in Harlem—then teaching can be killed off entirely.

Teaching is an eminently practical activity, best learned in the exercise of it and in the thoughtful reflection that must accompany that. This reflection should be structured into the teaching day, and should be conducted with peers, and with more experienced people who can act as coaches or guides, and can direct a probingly critical eye at every detail of school life. The complexity of real teaching can then be grasped, and the intellectual and ethical heart of teaching can be kept in its center.

MYTH 3: Good Teachers Make Learning Fun

Fun is distracting, amusing. Clowns are fun. Jokes can be fun. Learning can be engaging, engrossing, amazing, disorienting, involving, and often deeply pleasurable. If it's fun, fine. But it doesn't need to be fun.

MYTH 4: Good Teachers Always Know the Materials

This is tricky. On the one hand, teachers need to know a lot, and good teachers are always reading, wondering, exploring—always expanding their interests and their knowledge. Who would argue for knowing less? On the other hand, since knowledge is infinite there is simply no way for any teacher to know everything. The game some teachers play of trying to stay one step ahead in the text in order to teach the material is ludicrous. That game assumes that knowledge is finite and that teaching is a matter of conveying the same limited stuff to students, who are themselves beneath respect, incapable of thinking outside the informational realm of "one step forward at a time."

Many fine teachers plunge into the unknown alongside their students, simultaneously enacting productive approaches to learning and demonstrating desirable dispositions of mind, like courage and curiosity. A unit on machines in elementary school might involve bringing in broken household appliances and working together to understand how they function. A unit on Asian immigration in high school might involve a collective search through newspaper archives or interviews in the community. Learning with students can be a powerful approach to teaching. Good teachers often teach precisely so that they can learn.

MYTH 5: Good Teachers Begin With the Curriculum They Are Given and Find Clever Ways to Enhance It

Good teachers begin with high expectations for learners and struggle to meet those expectation in every instance. Too often the question is, "Is it practical?" when the question ought to be, "Is it passionate?" The given curriculum can be a guide or an obstacle, a framework or a hindrance, a resource or a barrier. The point is to get the job done, and sometimes that means starting elsewhere and circling back to the official curriculum simply to satisfy administrators.

MYTH 6: Good Teachers Are Good Performers

Sometimes. But just as often, good teachers are not charismatic and are not exhibitionists. Certainly they are not "center stage," because that place is reserved for students.

When I taught preschool, much of my work was behind the scenes, quiet, unobtrusive. One year, a student teacher paid me a high compliment: "For two months, I didn't think you were doing anything. Your teaching was indirect, seamless, and subtle, and the kids' work was all that I could see."

This myth of teachers as performers strips teaching of much of its depth and texture and is linked to the idea that teaching is telling, that teaching is delivering lessons or dispensing knowledge. This is a tiny part of teaching, and yet in myth it is elevated to the whole of it.

MYTH 7: Good Teachers Treat all Students Alike

It is important for teachers to be fair, to be thoughtful, to be caring in relation to all students. If all students were the same then a good teacher would treat them all the same. But here is Sonia with an explosive anger that can take over the room, and she needs more; here is James, whose mother died recently, and he needs more; here is Angel, who cannot speak English, and he needs more. Needs shift and change. When I was a new teacher and Kevin showed up one day without lunch money, I gave him the necessary fifty cents; several colleagues encouraged me to let him go hungry or I'd "be buying every kid's lunch every day." It never happened.

In a family, the nighttime fears of one child might take considerable focus and energy for a time, and then the struggle of another child to read takes over. Helping the two children in kindergarten who are having difficulty separating from their mothers assures all children that this is a safe and friendly place. Good teachers spend time and energy where they must, and expect that positive results will spread laterally among the group.

MYTH 8: Students Today Are Different From Ever Before

Every generation of adults tells of a golden age of teaching or parenting when youngsters were well-behaved and capable. This misty-eyed view is typically a highly edited version of their own youth. Some teachers claim to have been outstanding early in their careers, but now assert: "I can't teach these kids." Today, the justifications for this are put in terms of "cocaine babies" and "households headed by women," where once it was the "culture of poverty" and "cultural deprivation," and before that, "immigrants who didn't care about their children."

The fact is that kids come to school with a range of difficult backgrounds and troubling experiences. They come from families, each of which has strengths and weaknesses. Teachers, as always, must resist the idea that there is some ideal child with whom they would be brilliant; they must reject the notion that a child's success is determined by family background or circumstance; they must respond to the real children coming through the door and find ways to teach them. That has always been a complex and difficult goal and it will always be so.

MYTH 9: Good Teaching Can Be Measured by How Well Students Do on Tests

Besides the many problems related to standardized testing, there are also problems that revolve around the connection of teaching to learning. Learning is not linear; it does not occur as a straight line, gradually inclined, formally and incrementally constructed. Learning is dynamic and explosive and a lot of it is informal; much of it builds up over time and connects suddenly.

MYTH 10: A Good Teacher Knows What's Going on in the Classroom

Teachers know one story of what's going on, but not the only story nor even the "true story." True stories are multitudinous because there are thirty-some true stories. Kids are active interpreters of classroom reality and their interpretations are only sometimes synonymous with their teacher's interpretations. Classrooms are yeasty places, where an entire group comes together and creates a distinctive and dynamic culture; sometimes things bubble and rise; sometimes they are punched down or killed off.

* * *

Teaching is a human activity, constrained and made possible by all the limits and potential that characterize any other human activity. Teaching depends on people—people who choose to teach and other people who become students, by choice or not. There are these two sides to teaching, and on each side there are human beings, whole people with their own unique thoughts, hopes, dreams, aspirations, needs, experiences, contexts, agendas, and priorities. Teaching is relational and interactive. It requires dialogue, give and take, back and forth. It is multi-directional. This explains in part why every teaching encounter is particular, each unique in its details.

When Jakob learned to read, for example, he was five years old, a student in my class, and he accomplished this feat without formal instruction. He felt strong and independent and important as a person, and he approached most things with courage and confidence. Reading was no different. He loved hearing stories read, and he had many favorites. He dictated his own stories to accompany pictures he painted. And he could read bits and pieces from his environment: "stop," "pizza," "fruit." One day, he announced he could read. He read a couple of familiar stories, moved on with occasional help, and never looked back. He was reading.

Molly read at six. She watched from a distance when she was in my class as others learned to read, and she looked hard at her own books. She never asked for help, and when help was offered she pushed it away. And then she apparently made a decision that she could do it, that the time had come. She asked me to teach her to read. We sat down and read for two hours. We recognized easy words together and then more difficult ones. We discussed letter sounds and the mystery of phonics. Within a few days she felt like she, too, was a reader.

Shawn learned to read independently at eight, some years after he had been my student. Reading had been a goal for years, but it seemed out of reach to him. He struggled hard to get it, and I struggled to help, both by making him comfortable and by offering a range of reading strategies and opportunities. He found phonics both an incredibly helpful aid and a consistent betrayer. Slowly, painstakingly, he broke the code in the second grade, and read. When he was nine, he was as sophisticated a reader as any of his classmates, and the early frustration was a distant memory.

Each of these learners was different, each had his or her own specific talents, styles, obstacles, and needs. Each demanded a teacher who could invent an appropriate response to a unique encounter.

A powerful, perhaps dominant, view of teaching, holds that teaching is little more than the simple and efficient delivery of curriculum. There is little need for adjustment, no need for dialogue. In the dominant view, teachers are glorified clerks or line employees, functionaries whose job it is to pass along the wisdom and the thinking of some expert, academic, or policy-maker: here is the literary canon; here is the truth of history; here is the skill of reading. The teacher is near the base of the educational hierarchy, just above the student, who is the very bottom of the barrel. Years ago, there was serious talk of making the curriculum "teacher proof," creating packages that even thoughtless, careless people could pass along. The idea behind "new math," for example, was that teachers would transmit something they neither experienced nor understood, and that a generation of brilliant math students would somehow emerge, bypassing teachers altogether. This was, of course, a monumental failure, and that talk has been largely discredited. Today teachers are expected to develop "critical thinking" and "ethical reflection" in youngsters without opportunities to think critically or reflect on values in their own lives. These approaches to reform are folly. The current enthusiasm for some imagined artificial intelligence that will replace the need for thinking, committed teachers in classrooms is only the most recent high-tech version of the old idea of teacher-as-clerk.

I have been a teacher for over twenty years. In that time, I have taught at every level, from preschool to graduate school: I have taught reading, math and social studies, research methodology, and philosophy. I have cared for infants in a day care center and for juvenile "delinquents" in a residential home. In every instance, there has been discovery and surprise, for me as much as for my students. Human relationships are just that way; surprising, idiosyncratic, unique, and marked by variety. Over time, a basic understanding about teaching has emerged and become deeply etched in my own consciousness: Good teaching requires most of all a thoughtful, caring teacher committed to the lives of students. So simple and, in turn, somehow so elegant. Like mothering or parenting, good teaching is not a matter of specific techniques or styles, plans or actions. Like friendship, good teaching is not something that can be entirely scripted, preplanned, or prespecified. If a person is thoughtful, caring, and committed, mistakes will be made, but they will not be disastrous; if a person lacks commitment, compassion, or thought, outstanding technique and style will never really compensate. Teaching is primarily a matter of love. The rest is, at best, ornamentation, nice to look at but not of the essence; at worst it is obfuscating—it pulls our attention in the wrong direction and turns us away from the heart of the matter.

Of course, we cannot love what we neither know nor understand. Nor can we teach someone entirely outside our capacity for empathy or comprehension. No one can teach someone they hate, or despise, or find unworthy; someone completely alien or apart from some sense of a shared humanity. On the other hand, sustained interest in and deep knowledge of another person is in itself an act of love, and a good preparation for teaching.

19

Selections From
School Is Hell

Lesson 6: The 9 Types of
Grade School Teachers
Lesson 13: The 9 Types of
High School Teachers

Matt Groening

Matt Groening is most well known for his television cartoon series *The Simpsons*. Groening began his career, however, in 1978 with a print cartoon series called *Life in Hell*. *School Is Hell* is his satirical take on going to school. The main character of the collection is Bongo, a one-eared character, who clearly has in him the seeds of the future Bart Simpson.

Among the funniest of Groening's (2007) Lessons are his portraits of elementary, high school, and college teachers. Look at "Lesson 6: The 9 Types of

NOTE: Groening, M. (2007). *School is Hell*. New York: Random House.

Grade School Teachers" and "Lesson 13: The 9 Types of High School Teachers."
Answer the following questions:

1. Do any of these descriptions actually remind you of teachers who have taught you?

2. Are these representations stereotypes of teachers, or do these representations reflect some of the actual types of teachers found in American classrooms?

3. Which teachers are the ones you would like to be taught by?

4. Which type of teacher do you think you most likely resemble?

"Lesson 6: The 9 Types of Grade School Teachers." © 1987 Matt Groening. Reprinted from School is Hell, © 1987 Pantheon Books.

"Lesson 13: The 9 Types of High School Teachers." © 1987 Matt Groening. Reprinted from <u>School is Hell</u>, © 1987 Pantheon Books.

PART VIII

Teaching and Sexuality

20. "The Teacher" From *Winesburg, Ohio*
    Sherwood Anderson

21. Selection From *Socrates, Plato, & Guys Like Me: Confessions of a Gay Schoolteacher*
    Eric Rofes

————————————

Teaching and sexuality are not terms that are commonly spoken or written about together. Yet teachers, like everyone else, are sexual beings. In American society, heterosexuality has been defined as "normal." Closely related to the idea of sexuality is gender. Schools have historically maintained normative values involving sexuality and gender. As a result, teachers are expected to conform to the society's notion of normal sexual behavior. This means that not only in terms of what they teach but also in terms of their public if not their private lives, teachers are bound by a much more conservative set of sexual standards than the more general population.

Until the late 1940s, in many states female teachers were not allowed to be married. The rationalization was that married teachers would be distracted from their work by their involvement with their own families and children. Less clear was the notion that the children should be protected from teachers who might also be sexually active beings. Even into the 1970s, when teachers were allowed to marry, pregnant teachers could not remain in their jobs once they began to "show."

Individuals defining themselves as lesbian, gay, bisexual, transgender, transsexual, or intersexual were excluded from working in schools—at least if their orientations were public. As late as 1977, a national poll said 65% of the American population objected to the idea that homosexual teachers be allowed to teach in elementary schools. At this time, prominent national figures such as Anita Bryant, an evangelical spokesperson and former Miss America, took on the elimination of homosexuals working in public schools. Rallying conservative Christians to overcome a nondiscrimination ordinance in Dade County, Florida, that protected homosexuals from housing and employment discrimination, Bryant argued that homosexual teachers would encourage the students they taught to adopt a homosexual lifestyle.

Eventually, gay activists were able to overcome these discriminatory practices. Often this involved overcoming stereotypes of queer adults as potential child molesters. Although being a gay teacher is not an issue of importance in many more liberal communities, in more conservative enclaves, it is still an issue. Much like the question of whether teachers should be able to teach when they're married, it is likely that the question of whether homosexual teachers should be allowed in the classroom will become a nonissue in years to come.

In this section is included a classic story by the American master Sherwood Anderson (1921) from his collection *Winesberg, Ohio,* in which the sexual longings and repression of a high school teacher are explored at length. In the section from Eric Rofes' (1985) *Socrates, Plato, & Guys Like Me: Confessions of a Gay Schoolteacher,* Rofes, a well known gay activist, refuses to hide his homosexuality as a requirement of employment and loses his job as a result.

Further Readings: Sexuality is a steady undercurrent for the teachers and students in the previously discussed novel *The Prime of Miss Jean Brodie* (Macmillan, 1961), which was made into a stage play in 1968 and a film starring Maggie Smith in 1969. Personal accounts by gay teachers are included in *One Teacher in Ten: Gay and Lesbian Educators Tell Their Stories,* edited by Kevin Jennings (Alyson Books, 1994). Themes discussed in the book include student–teacher relationships, teacher–teacher relationships, AIDS, support groups, the process of coming out, and community reactions.

Linking to Popular Culture: Many popular songs that focus on teachers and how they are viewed by students as sexual objects can be found at Web sites such as Songlyrics.com (http://www.songlyrics.com/). Search for words such as *teacher* and *school*. Artists singing songs about teachers include Jethro Tull, *Teacher* (1970); Abba, *When I Kissed the Teacher* (1975); and Van Halen, *Hot for Teacher* (1984). Go to YouTube for music videos of these songs. Particularly interesting is Van Halen's *Hot for Teacher* video. On YouTube, also search for videos in which teachers express their sexuality and contradict some of the traditional stereotypes we have about them. Search for *teacher videos* and *teachers rap*.

In the 2006 British film *The History Boys,* homosexual relationships between teachers and students are explored. In the 1997 film *In & Out,* a midwestern teacher is challenged about his sexuality by a former student.

References

Anderson, S. (1921). *Winesburg, Ohio: A group of tales of Ohio small town life.* New York: W. B. Huebsch.

Rofes, E. (1985). *Socrates, Plato, & guys like me: Confessions of a gay schoolteacher.* New York: Alyson.

20

"The Teacher"
From *Winesburg, Ohio*

Sherwood Anderson

"The Teacher" is included the American author Sherwood Anderson's (1876–1941) most famous work. Published in 1919 as a novel, the book is in fact a collection of short stories that focus on the fictional inhabitants of the town of Winesburg, Ohio. The book, which consists of 22 short stories, includes a chapter about a high school teacher named Kate Swift.

Swift is a lonely woman, 30 years old, not entirely healthy, seemingly destined to be a spinster. Close to her students, she is also perceived as stern. She is in love with a former student of hers, George Willard, a young newspaper reporter, perhaps 15 years her junior.

1. What does Anderson mean when he says about Kate Swift that "she was a teacher but she was also a woman"?

2. Why is it that teachers are often stereotyped by society as being sexually neutral and lacking the passion for ideas and life that other people often have?

3. Would it have been all right for Kate Swift to have had George Willard as a lover? To have married him? Would there have been repercussions for her doing so?

NOTE: Anderson, S. (1921). *Winesburg, Ohio: A group of tales of Ohio small town life*. New York: W. B. Huebsch.

Snow lay deep in the streets of Winesburg. It had begun to snow about ten o'clock in the morning and a wind sprang up and blew the snow in clouds along Main Street. The frozen mud roads that led into town were fairly smooth and in places ice covered the mud. "There will be good sleighing," said Will Henderson, standing by the bar in Ed Griffith's saloon. Out of the saloon he went and met Sylvester West the druggist stumbling along in the kind of heavy overshoes called arctics. "Snow will bring the people into town on Saturday," said the druggist. The two men stopped and discussed their affairs. Will Henderson, who had on a light overcoat and no overshoes, kicked the heel of his left foot with the toe of the right. "Snow will be good for the wheat," observed the druggist sagely.

Young George Willard, who had nothing to do, was glad because he did not feel like working that day. The weekly paper had been printed and taken to the post office Wednesday evening and the snow began to fall on Thursday. At eight o'clock, after the morning train had passed, he put a pair of skates in his pocket and went up to Waterworks Pond but did not go skating. Past the pond and along a path that followed Wine Creek he went until he came to a grove of beech trees. There he built a fire against the side of a log and sat down at the end of the log to think. When the snow began to fall and the wind to blow he hurried about getting fuel for the fire.

The young reporter was thinking of Kate Swift, who had once been his school teacher. On the evening before he had gone to her house to get a book she wanted him to read and had been alone with her for an hour. For the fourth or fifth time the woman had talked to him with great earnestness and he could not make out what she meant by her talk. He began to believe she must be in love with him and the thought was both pleasing and annoying.

Up from the log he sprang and began to pile sticks on the fire. Looking about to be sure he was alone he talked aloud pretending he was in the presence of the woman, "Oh, you're just letting on, you know you are," he declared. "I am going to find out about you. You wait and see."

The young man got up and went back along the path toward town leaving the fire blazing in the wood. As he went through the streets the skates clanked in his pocket. In his own room in the New Willard House he built a fire in the stove and lay down on top of the bed. He began to have lustful thoughts and pulling down the shade of the window closed his eyes and turned his face to the wall. He took a pillow into his arms and embraced it thinking first of the school teacher, who by her words had stirred something within him, and later of Helen White, the slim daughter of the town banker, with whom he had been for a long time half in love.

By nine o'clock of that evening snow lay deep in the streets and the weather had become bitter cold. It was difficult to walk about. The stores were dark and the people had crawled away to their houses. The evening train from Cleveland was very late but nobody was interested in its arrival. By ten o'clock all but four of the eighteen hundred citizens of the town were in bed.

Hop Higgins, the night watchman, was partially awake. He was lame and carried a heavy stick. On dark nights he carried a lantern. Between nine and ten o'clock he went his rounds. Up and down Main Street he stumbled through the drifts trying the doors of the stores. Then he went into alleyways and tried the back doors. Finding all tight he hurried around the corner to the New Willard House and beat on the door. Through the rest of the night he intended to stay by the stove. "You go to bed. I'll keep the stove going," he said to the boy who slept on a cot in the hotel office.

Hop Higgins sat down by the stove and took off his shoes. When the boy had gone to sleep he began to think of his own affairs. He intended to paint his house in the spring and sat by the stove calculating the cost of paint and labor. That led him into other calculations. The night watchman was sixty years old and wanted to retire. He had been a soldier in the Civil War and drew a small pension. He hoped to find some new method of making a living and aspired to become a professional breeder of ferrets. Already he had four of the strangely shaped savage little creatures, that are used by sportsmen in the pursuit of rabbits, in the cellar of his house. "Now I have one male and three females," he mused. "If I am lucky by spring I shall have twelve or fifteen. In another year I shall be able to begin advertising ferrets for sale in the sporting papers."

The nightwatchman settled into his chair and his mind became a blank. He did not sleep. By years of practice he had trained himself to sit for hours through the long nights neither asleep nor awake. In the morning he was almost as refreshed as though he had slept.

With Hop Higgins safely stowed away in the chair behind the stove only three people were awake in Winesburg. George Willard was in the office of the *Eagle* pretending to be at work on the writing of a story but in reality continuing the mood of the morning by the fire in the wood. In the bell tower of the Presbyterian Church the Reverend Curtis Hartman was sitting in the darkness preparing himself for a revelation from God, and Kate Swift, the school teacher, was leaving her house for a walk in the storm.

It was past ten o'clock when Kate Swift set out and the walk was unpremeditated. It was as though the man and the boy, by thinking of her, had driven her forth into the wintry streets. Aunt Elizabeth Swift had gone to the county seat concerning some business in connection with mortgages in which she had money invested and would not be back until the next day. By a huge stove, called a base burner, in the living room of the house sat the daughter reading a book. Suddenly she sprang to her feet and, snatching a cloak from a rack by the front door, ran out of the house.

At the age of thirty Kate Swift was not known in Winesburg as a pretty woman. Her complexion was not good and her face was covered with blotches that indicated ill health. Alone in the night in the winter streets she was lovely. Her back was straight, her shoulders square, and her features were as the features of a tiny goddess on a pedestal in a garden in the dim light of a summer evening.

During the afternoon the school teacher had been to see Doctor Welling concerning her health. The doctor had scolded her and had declared she was in danger of losing her hearing. It was foolish for Kate Swift to be abroad in the storm, foolish and perhaps dangerous.

The woman in the streets did not remember the words of the doctor and would not have turned back had she remembered. She was very cold but after walking for five minutes no longer minded the cold. First she went to the end of her own street and then across a pair of hay scales set in the ground before a feed barn and into Trunion Pike. Along Trunion Pike she went to Ned Winters' barn and turning east followed a street of low frame houses that led over Gospel Hill and into Sucker Road that ran down a shallow valley past Ike Smead's chicken farm to Waterworks Pond. As she went along, the bold, excited mood that had driven her out of doors passed and then returned again.

There was something biting and forbidding in the character of Kate Swift. Everyone felt it. In the schoolroom she was silent, cold, and stern, and yet in an odd way very close to her pupils. Once in a long while something seemed to have come over her and she was happy. All of the children in the school-room felt the effect of her happiness. For a time they did not work but sat back in their chairs and looked at her.

With hands clasped behind her back the school teacher walked up and down in the schoolroom and talked very rapidly. It did not seem to matter what subject came into her mind. Once she talked to the children of Charles Lamb and made up strange, intimate little stories concerning the life of the dead writer. The stories were told with the air of one who had lived in a house with Charles Lamb and knew all the secrets of his private life. The children were somewhat confused, thinking Charles Lamb must be some-one who had once lived in Winesburg.

On another occasion the teacher talked to the children of Benvenuto Cellini. That time they laughed. What a bragging, blustering, brave, lovable fellow she made of the old artist! Concerning him also she invented anec-dotes. There was one of a German music teacher who had a room above Cellini's lodgings in the city of Milan that made the boys guffaw. Sugars McNutts, a fat boy with red cheeks, laughed so hard that he became dizzy and fell off his seat and Kate Swift laughed with him. Then suddenly she became again cold and stern.

On the winter night when she walked through the deserted snow-covered streets, a crisis had come into the life of the school teacher. Although no one in Winesburg would have suspected it, her life had been very adventurous. It was still adventurous. Day by day as she worked in the schoolroom or walked in the streets, grief, hope, and desire fought within her. Behind a cold exterior the most extraordinary events transpired in her mind. The people of the town thought of her as a confirmed old maid and because she spoke sharply and went her own way thought her lacking in all the human feeling that did so much to make and mar their own lives. In reality she was the most eagerly passionate soul among them, and more than once, in the five years since she had come back from her travels to settle in Winesburg and become a school teacher, had been compelled to go out of the house and walk half through the night fighting out some battle raging within. Once on a night when it rained she had stayed out six hours and when she came home had a quarrel with Aunt Elizabeth Swift. "I am glad you're not a man," said the mother sharply. "More than once I've waited for your father to come home, not knowing what new mess he had got into. I've had my share of uncertainty and you cannot blame me if I do not want to see the worst side of him reproduced in you."

Kate Swift's mind was ablaze with thoughts of George Willard. In something he had written as a school boy she thought she had recognized the spark of genius and wanted to blow on the spark. One day in the summer she had gone to the *Eagle* office and finding the boy unoccupied had taken him out on Main Street to the Fair Ground, where the two sat on a grassy bank and talked. The school teacher tried to bring home to the mind of the boy some conception of the difficulties he would have to face as a writer. "You will have to know life," she declared, and her voice trembled with earnestness. She took hold of George Willard's shoulders and turned him about so that she could look into his eyes. A passer-by might have thought them about to embrace. "If you are to become a writer you'll have to stop fooling with words," she explained. "It would be better to give up the notion of writing until you are better prepared. Now it's time to be living. I don't want to frighten you, but I would like to make you understand the import of what you think of attempting. You must not become a mere peddler of words. The thing to learn is to know what people are thinking about, not what they say."

On the evening before that stormy Thursday night when the Reverend Curtis Hartman sat in the bell tower of the church waiting to look at her body, young Willard had gone to visit the teacher and to borrow a book. It was then the thing happened that confused and puzzled the boy. He had the book under his arm and was preparing to depart. Again Kate Swift talked with great earnestness. Night was coming on and the light in the room grew dim. As he turned to go she spoke his name softly and with an impulsive movement took hold of his hand. Because the reporter was rapidly becoming a man something of his man's appeal, combined with the winsomeness of the boy, stirred the heart of the lonely woman. A passionate desire to have him understand the import of life, to learn to interpret it truly and honestly, swept over her. Leaning forward, her lips brushed his cheek. At the same moment he for the first time became aware of the marked beauty of her features. They were both embarrassed, and to relieve her feeling she became harsh and domineering. "What's the use? It will be ten years before you begin to understand what I mean when I talk to you," she cried passionately.

On the night of the storm and while the minister sat in the church waiting for her, Kate Swift went to the office of the *Winesburg Eagle,* intending to have another talk with the boy. After the long walk in the snow she was cold, lonely, and tired. As she came through Main Street she saw the light from the printshop window shining on the snow and on an impulse opened the door and went in. For an hour she sat by the stove in the office talking of life. She talked with passionate earnestness. The impulse that had driven her out into the snow poured itself out into talk. She became inspired as she sometimes did in the presence of the children in school. A great eagerness to open the door of life to the boy, who had been her pupil and who she thought might possess a talent for the understanding of life, had possession of her. So strong was her passion that it became something physical. Again her hands took hold of his shoulders and she turned him about. In the dim light her eyes blazed. She arose and laughed, not sharply as was customary with her, but in a queer, hesitating way. "I must be going," she said. "In a moment, if I stay, I'll be wanting to kiss you."

In the newspaper office a confusion arose. Kate Swift turned and walked to the door. She was a teacher but she was also a woman. As she looked at George Willard, the passionate desire to be loved by a man, that had a thousand times before swept like a storm over her body, took possession of her. In the lamplight George Willard looked no longer a boy, but a man ready to play the part of a man.

The school teacher let George Willard take her into his arms. In the warm little office the air became suddenly heavy and the strength went out of her body. Leaning against a low counter by the door she waited. When he came and put a hand on her shoulder she turned and let her body fall heavily against him. For George Willard the confusion was immediately increased. For a moment he held the body of the woman tightly against his body and then it stiffened. Two sharp little fists began to beat on his face. When the school teacher had run away and left him alone, he walked up and down the office swearing furiously.

It was into this confusion that the Reverend Curtis Hartman protruded himself. When he came in George Willard thought the town had gone mad. Shaking a bleeding fist in the air, the minister proclaimed the woman George had only a moment before held in his arms an instrument of God bearing a message of truth.

George blew out the lamp by the window and locking the door of the printshop went home. Through the hotel office, past Hop Higgins lost in his dream of the raising of ferrets, he went up and into his own room. The fire in the stove had gone out and he undressed in the cold. When he got into bed the sheets were like blankets of dry snow.

George Willard rolled about in the bed on which he had lain in the afternoon hugging the pillow and thinking thoughts of Kate Swift. The words of the minister, who he thought had gone suddenly insane, rang in his ears. His eyes stared about the room. The resentment, natural to the baffled male, passed and he tried to understand what had happened. He could not make it out. Over and over he turned the matter in his mind. Hours passed and he began to think it must be time for another day to come. At four o'clock he pulled the covers up about his neck and tried to sleep. When he became drowsy and closed his eyes, he raised a hand and with it groped about in the darkness. "I have missed something. I have missed something Kate Swift was trying to tell me," he muttered sleepily. Then he slept and in all Winesburg he was the last soul on that winter night to go to sleep.

21

Selection From *Socrates, Plato, & Guys Like Me*

Confessions of a Gay Schoolteacher

Eric Rofes

Eric Rofes (1954–2006) was a teacher and gay activist who has been described by the anthropologist and community historian Gayle Rubin as "a massive presence whose influence was felt across a broad range of constituencies and issues and organizations." (Rofes, 2009). He died of a heart attack in June 2006.

Rofes was a graduate of Harvard University and became involved in gay issues in Boston during the 1970s. Rofes published more than a dozen books and numerous scholarly essays and popular articles. In *Socrates, Plato, & Guys Like Me: Confessions of a Gay Schoolteacher,* he recounts being forced out of his teaching job because he was gay. After leaving teaching, he became a member of the Gay Community News collective, started several queer youth groups in Boston (Out Here for Gay Youth and the Committee for Gay Youth), and founded the Boston Lesbian and Gay Political Alliance. In 1980, he went as a delegate to the White House Conference on the Family. Rofes was fired from his sixth-grade public

NOTES: Rofes, E. (1985). *Socrates, Plato, & guys like me: Confessions of a gay schoolteacher.* New York: Alyson; Rofes, E. (2009). Biographies. Retrieved October 9, 2009, from http://www.ericrofes.com/bio/general.php.

school teaching job after he came out of the closet. He was later hired by the progressive Fayerweather Street School in Cambridge and eventually founded the Boston Area Gay and Lesbian Schoolworkers.

In this selection, Rofes (1985) describes his dismissal from the Shawmutt Hills schools. Rofes is offered the opportunity to keep working in the school system as long as he does not make his homosexuality public. This approach is basically the same as the American military's recent Don't Ask, Don't Tell policy, which says that homosexuals can keep their positions if they do not make their sexual orientation public. Rofes refused to do this, maintaining that he needed "to come clean with everyone and live an honest life."

Reading this selection from *Socrates, Plato, & Guys Like Me* raises a number of interesting questions:

1. To what extent should teachers, whether straight or gay, have the right to be political and social activists in their lives outside of school?

2. Is a Don't Ask, Don't Tell approach to dealing with a teacher's sexual orientation inherently discriminatory?

3. Is it fair to consider gay teachers as being more likely than heterosexual teachers to sexually abuse their students?

4. Are gay teachers likely to cause students to become gay?

5. Do gay students need to receive counseling from gay teachers as well as to have them as role models?

I stood waiting by the front door for Alice and Marie to arrive and escort me to the board meeting. Aware that I'd be a wreck inside despite a composed public appearance, I had arranged to have friends accompany me this evening. Alice served as the faculty representative to the board, so she was expected to attend in any case. Marie had been granted special permission to be present at the meeting and lend silent support to her friend on trial. Thus I stood at the door, gazing out at dusk settling onto the streets of Somerville, waiting for my ride to Shawmut Hills, feeling like a convict about to walk his final mile.

Holly came bounding down the stairway with her hand behind her back. Arriving at the front door, she drew out a small bouquet of spring flowers and pressed it into my hand. "Here, honey," she said smiling. "My best wishes go with you. I really wish I could be there to watch this performance. You'll do all of us proud, I'm sure."

I smelled the flowers and my spring allergies brought tears to my eyes. "Do I look all right?" I asked. "This is a difficult occasion to dress for. None of the fashion books give any indication of what to wear to an execution. I spent about an hour going through the closet and trying to decide what I could wear that would give me some degree of integrity, but not seem too blatant."

Holly looked me over from head to toe. "You look like the perfect preppie schoolteacher. The khakis, the oxford shirt and those loafers are strictly prepster. No one could challenge you tonight. The only thing that's missing is this," she said, reaching into her pocket and pulling out a metallic button which she pinned to my shirt. I looked down and saw the bright pink "Gay and Proud" button against my white shirt. Instinctively, I reached down to take it off, but Holly's hand caught mine.

"No," she said quietly. "Leave it on, at least till you arrive at school. It'll be comforting to know that it's there and you can be sure that—even in the madness of the night—you won't leave it on when you walk into the judge's chambers."

The phone rang and Holly rushed into the kitchen to answer it. I peered out the window, glanced nervously at my watch, and began to pace.

"It's for you," she called to me from the other room.

I directed my pacing toward the phone and grabbed it from Holly. "Hello?" I said, my voice cracking for the first time in years.

"It's just me, Eric." I heard Paul's voice at the other end of the line. "Just calling to send you best wishes for a pleasant evening on Firing Line."

"Thanks, I need all the support I can get."

"Remember, no matter what happens, you have the satisfaction of knowing you've handled this whole thing with a great deal of integrity."

"That's not going to keep me employed, Paul."

"No, it's not. And you might lose your job tonight, although I think they'd be crazy to let you go. But I think you've got to keep in mind that—no matter what happens—you've handled a difficult situation with a great deal of pride and dignity. This could have been a real mess for you and for the school. You've done the responsible thing."

I heard a car honking for me out front. "They're here!" I exclaimed. "I've got to go, Paul. Thanks for calling and call me at midnight and I'll let you know what happened!"

I dropped the phone onto the receiver, kissed Holly good-bye, grabbed my sweater and dashed down the walkway to the car.

The school library had always seemed to be one of the warmer, homier rooms of the school. Located in the center of the building and accessible to every classroom, it easily had become a reflection of Alice's personality over the last dozen years. Stacks of books and periodicals made it clear that this was a room that saw heavy use on a daily basis. The brightly colored finger paintings by first-grade children gave the room a down-to-earth feeling and the wood-stained panels added to the sense of formality and tradition that served to remind the viewer that this was—despite the warmth—an institution of learning.

Tonight as I entered the library, the formality of the wood-stained panels loomed large. The room took on a new feeling, a feeling of conservatism and seriousness. Only Miss Clarkson had arrived and she was carefully arranging the library chairs into a circle in the center of the room.

"Good evening," she said in an unusually awkward tone. "We're all a bit early for the meeting."

Alice and Marie took off their coats and tossed them onto one of the library tables. Plates of Fig Newtons sat on one of the desks, and a coffee machine was beginning to perk. I looked quickly around the room, wondering where I would be sitting when my final judgment was pronounced—by a jury that was distinctly not comprised of my peers.

Before I had a chance to ask, Miss Clarkson answered my question. "I think it's best for you to sit over there, Eric," she said, indicating a chair at the edge of the circle. "And Alice and Marie may sit wherever they'd like."

Marie came up beside me. "I'd like to sit next to you," she said, trying to sound cheery. "Is that okay?"

"It sure is," I responded.

"Are you sure you want to keep that button on all night?" she asked, indicating the pink button that I'd forgotten to remove.

I became flustered and took it off quickly, and we settled into our seats just as the clock struck eight. The trustees slowly entered, one-by-one, and greeted us. Several of them were unfamiliar to me, and they introduced themselves and shook my hand. One of them—Peter Larkin—was the man responsible for connecting me to Shawmut Hills just two years earlier. He was one of my professors at Harvard, my thesis advisor, and a friend whom I'd never told about this side of my life. He greeted me and smiled in a way that seemed to express a shared sense of naughtiness—as if Peter and I had together sprung this controversy on the school. The smile was encouraging—the formality and seriousness of the other board members was beginning to feel unduly fatalistic.

When all twelve trustees had taken their seats, Doug Cabot began the meeting. "You all know why we're here tonight," he began, "and I thank you very much for arranging your schedules so that this meeting could take place on such short notice. I know that the last few weeks have been difficult for Eric, as they have been difficult for all of us who are in a situation that is unique and troublesome. As I've told all of you on the telephone, Eric, Miss Clarkson and I met last week and discussed a letter he'd written and enclosed with his contract for next year. In the letter, he explained that, not only is he gay, but he is a political activist and a writer. I think what we're here to discuss tonight is whether or not there is a future for Eric at Shawmut Hills knowing these additional pieces of information."

He paused here and I looked up from the floor where my eyes had been riveted since Mr. Cabot began to speak. I looked from one trustee to another. Serious faces all. One woman, a teacher of anthropology at a nearby high school, seemed troubled to the point of facial contortion. Her son Arthur had been my student during my first year in the school, and I always found her to be supportive and friendly. Her roles as a mother, board member and thinking person seemed to conflict in this situation.

Another trustee, a noted psychiatrist at Massachusetts General Hospital and the father of two young students at the school, seemed to be attempting to maintain a non-judgmental look on his face. Showing no reaction to Doug Cabot's statements, nor any semblance of emotion, he sat through the initial statement with a studied, earnest look on his face.

My eyes glanced from one trustee to another. Only Alice was able to shoot me an occasional smile or wink, and I worked to control my own reaction.

"What I want to make clear from the start of this discussion," Cabot continued, "is that we're not here to judge Mr. Rofes as a teacher. The offer of a contract for a third year at our school indicates that Miss Clarkson finds him to be a commendable teacher and, indeed, most of us have heard very positive feedback from parents and students since his arrival at the school. His ability to challenge the students, as well as maintain strict discipline in the classroom, are what we've wanted to have at the sixth grade level for a long time. There is no doubt in my mind that we'd like to keep Eric at the school and what this meeting is trying to determine is if it is possible for him to continue with us, despite these recent revelations."

Cabot laid out the ground rules for the evening. It would be strictly question and answer for an hour or so, and then I would be asked to leave while the trustees discussed the matter and voted on my continued presence in the school. I was to receive a phone call from Cabot probably late that evening to inform me of their decision.

The discussion began with a question from Doug Cabot. "Why don't you tell us about how you arrived at the point where you decided to send this letter to Miss Clarkson," he suggested.

This seemed like an innocuous starting point, I thought to myself. "I sent the letter after two years of soul-searching," I began. "During my first two years at the school, I have had a lot of conflicting feelings about parts of my life. While I've been developing my abilities to teach children and have been enjoying my teaching experiences, I have also been feeling more and more comfortable as a gay person. I've started to become involved in gay community activities, including some political work. Thus I've found myself torn between two lives that seem incompatible. I'm trying to find a way to survive with them both as comfortably as possible."

"Have you deliberately kept these lives separate up until this point?" Cabot asked.

"Until now," I continued, "I was able to do my work as an activist under a pseudonym. I'd write articles under a fake name, stay out of pictures when the newspapers or television cameras covered an event in which I was involved, and I'd tell lies to people in the gay community about the work I did professionally.

"Even in this school, I'd allow parents and other staff members to attempt to set me up on blind dates with women, permit my students to have the impression that every woman I was seen with was my girlfriend, and I'd even find myself lying about my life to other teachers. I don't want to do these things anymore. I don't want to live with the lies and the deception and I don't want to feel split into two directions. I need to come clean with everyone and live an honest life."

I had spoken this speech in an unusually quiet tone of voice, attempting to keep my remarks free from the strident tones for which I had a tendency. While several trustees nodded, indicating their understanding of my predicament, others looked puzzled or disturbed. The psychiatrist was the only one eager to ask a question.

"Are there other teachers anywhere who are open about this kind of thing?" he asked. "If there are, I haven't heard about it."

"At this point, there are not any openly gay teachers in this part of the country below the college level," I answered. "However, in other parts of the country, teachers of young children, as well as junior high and high school teachers, are openly gay. In some cities teachers are actually protected in their contracts from losing their jobs because they're gay. There aren't hundreds of teachers who are open about this, but there are quite a few and most of them maintain that they simply address questions from their students when and if they come up and then they go about their teaching. It doesn't seem to have such a dramatic effect on the school or on their teaching as one would expect."

Arthur's mother had her hand raised and seemed to be troubled by something I'd said. "I guess what I'm most concerned with," she said, "are the ramifications of this matter for the children. I think all of us are aware of the possible influence this could have on the children's sexual orientation."

I was annoyed at this concern but I tried to keep my perspective. "What influence do you think this will have on the children?" I asked quietly.

"You are teaching children at a very formative age, Eric. Early adolescence is an important time for the kids. I'm concerned with the way this might influence them. Now, you have chosen to be this way yourself and that's your right and your business. But when you go public about it, you influence other people and this concerns me."

"Are you asking me if I think my talking to the children about my sexual orientation will influence them and encourage them to be gay?"

The woman thought for a moment. "I suppose that's what I'm afraid of. I've been told that you work with a group called Committee for Gay Youth, and it seems to me that you're encouraging our young people to be this way. I'm not comfortable with that at all."

"I appreciate your expressing your concern," I said, attempting to appear in control of the matter while, in fact, I was enraged inside at the assumptions she was making. "Committee for Gay Youth does not encourage children or teenagers to have any particular sexual orientation."

Doug Cabot jumped in. "What does this group do, Eric?" he asked.

"We support kids when they choose to identify themselves as gay. We're not rigid at all and we support teens who evolve from one sexual orientation to another. While some adolescents seem to experience a great deal of confusion concerning their sexual orientations, I think it's important to acknowledge that some of them don't. We work primarily with those rare kids who are fifteen or sixteen years old and able to say to themselves 'I'm gay and I need to find some other kids like me.' Otherwise they would probably end up on the streets, without money, in some fairly desperate situations."

Arthur's mother wanted to pursue some points. "What you haven't answered in a way that satisfies me, is whether your coming out, as you call it, would influence our children later in life."

"Most of the studies I've read over the past few years seem to agree that sexual identity is formed during the first few years of life," I said, sounding like a schoolteacher. "By the time a child is in the sixth grade, his or her orientation is pretty well-formed. I think having a gay teacher would allow students who are gay to feel more comfortable with themselves, but I don't think it will cause students to have gay feelings if they wouldn't have had them otherwise."

"But what about these other students?" another woman asked quickly. I'd never before met her, but I knew that she was the director of a nearby hospital and the parent of a fourth-grade girl. She dressed conservatively and seemed a bit older than the other trustees. I had been warned that she might be hostile. "If your other students are primarily heterosexually oriented, in the normal fashion, shouldn't they be able to feel some support? If you tell them that you're homosexual, this might make them feel wrong or out of place."

"I'm sorry," I said, "but I feel there's already a lot of support within this school and within our society for kids who are heterosexual. From the wedding rings we see on teachers' fingers, to the ads we see on television, to most kids' parents, I feel that heterosexual teenagers receive a lot of support and validation."

I wasn't going to get off easy. She continued her hostile line of questioning. "I think this is clearly a question of values," she said in a serious tone.

"The question for me is, do the parents of children at Shawmut Hills School want their children to be told that it is okay to choose to be a homosexual? Because that's what we'd be doing if we condone this kind of activity on the part of our teachers."

I looked at Alice, needing a supportive face in my line of vision at the moment. Alice was peering over her spectacles, staring with angry eyes at the woman, but she managed to sit quietly without letting her anger erupt.

I decided to follow suit and let the bigotry speak for itself while I awaited the next rational question.

Doug Cabot sensed the tension in the room and changed the focus of the discussion. "I was wondering," he said, "whether it would be possible for you to continue doing your political work, as well as working with that youth project, and not let people know that you're a school teacher. You wouldn't necessarily have to tell people that you teach school, and I certainly think it would be fairly easy for you to keep the name of the school private. Would that be possible, Eric?"

While his suggestion was certainly possible, I wondered what he was getting at. If Cabot hoped to keep me at the school by having me hide my professional identity, it was a compromise that I could probably try to make. I told him so and then added, "I think it's highly unlikely that some people will not connect the gay activist Eric Rofes with the schoolteacher Eric Rofes. If I had a name like 'Doug Cabot,' or any name more common than my own, I could see people not assuming they were the same person. But with my name, it seems likely that someone could connect the employee of this school to the activist quoted in the *Globe.*"

It was my former professor, Peter Larkin's turn for a question. "What kinds of things can you foresee doing over the next year that would get your name into the *Boston Globe?*" he asked.

"I'm not sure that my name will end up in papers like that," I answered, "But it might. This summer and this fall I'll be doing some organizing work related to gay teachers, especially around the Briggs Initiative in California. That initiative is going to be on the ballot in November throughout the state of California, and would mandate that schools fire any employee who is supportive of gay rights. In my opinion, this is a very frightening thing and we've formed a committee here in Boston to do support work for the people organizing against it in California."

"What kind of work will you be doing?" Larkin continued.

"I'll be doing some public speaking on the issue, possibly as a gay school-teacher. I don't think I have to announce where I teach school, but I think it's important for teachers around the country to speak out publicly against this initiative."

"Do you mean to say that any schoolteacher in California who speaks positively about gays would be fired under this law?" The question came from a trustee I hadn't noticed before who was sitting in the back of the room, puffing on his pipe. "I find that incredible."

"Yes, it would cause such firings," I answered. "I think this helps you to realize why it's important for me to get involved. This kind of thing is pretty dangerous. Any teacher—gay or straight—who simply said it was okay for gays to have rights, could legally lose their jobs."

"If you were allowed to continue to teach here," interjected Doug Cabot, "how would you deal with the subject with the children? Would you allow the issue to come up in the classroom?"

"The subject comes up anyway," I said. "I'm afraid that many of you don't realize that, with sixth graders, at least, homosexuality comes up all the time. When I walked into the classroom two years ago, I vowed never to raise the subject. It came out of the kids all the time. Whether it's questions in health class, current event articles brought in about Anita Bryant, taunts on the playing field, or books in the classroom, homosexuality has found its way into the classroom. Any teacher could tell you that."

Alice spoke up. "What do you mean by books in the classroom?" she asked curiously.

I'd never talked with Alice about this, but I supposed now was as good a time as any for her to find out. "When I began teaching here, I took home copies of all the reading books we had for sixth graders in multiple copies. One of them is a wonderful book called *The Man Without a Face*, which has won all kinds of awards. It's a moving story about a boy from a troubled family and the man who befriends him and becomes his tutor.

"Well, the climax of the book involves the two of them sleeping together in quite an ambiguous manner that leaves the boy confused and disturbed. Now I've never had my students read the book, but I assume that if we have 22 copies of it in my classroom, some teacher has. I raise this issue only to let you know that whether or not I'm teaching this class, homosexuality is a subject that will be dealt with in one way or another. It was here before I got to this school, and it will be here long after I'm gone."

Doug Cabot still seemed concerned. "That is helpful for us to know, Eric, but you didn't answer my question. How would you discuss the matter with the children?"

I paused for a moment while I thought about my response. "I would have to do a little research before I talked to the kids about being gay. Just off the top of my head, I think I'd want to explain to them that I was gay and tell them what it meant. I'd make sure to explain it in more than sexual terms, since too often kids see relationships between adults purely in terms of sex. I'd explain that being gay means that my deepest feelings go toward other men. Then I'd ask them if they had any questions. It would probably be a good idea to break into smaller groups at this time and have the groups develop questions. Then we'd come back and hear their questions."

"What would you tell them about sex, if they asked about it?" the psychiatrist asked.

"I suppose I'd want to make sure that they realized that sex was more than just genital contact, that it involved hugging and kissing and touching."

"Then you'd answer their questions about sex," he continued incredulously.

I knew it was the wrong thing to say but I took a deep breath, glanced at Marie, and answered, "Yes. I believe that children's questions about sex should be answered honestly."

I think it was at this point that several of the trustees made up their mind that I was a lost cause. Both the psychiatrist and the hospital director grew silent for the next forty minutes while the other trustees shifted into discussions about homosexuality and children which ranged from discussing the stereotypes about child molestation to the current far-fetched sociobiological theory that nature created homosexuals to care for children of other people while the parents were busy reaping harvests or killing dinosaurs. I was asked quite personal questions about when I'd come out, my relationship with my parents, and whether or not I had a "partner."

I felt many of the trustees were sincerely struggling to grasp the issues and I was pleased with the range of questions asked. I had a difficult time stomaching some of the off-the-cuff comments from the committee's liberals (one even worked into the conversation the line, "Some of my best friends are gay), but I felt that they served to balance the hostile looks and well-timed guffaws of the administrator.

After about two hours, the discussion began to wane. I remained keyed up, ready for anything, although the intensity of the discussion had drained me somewhat. "It's getting rather late," Doug Cabot said, glancing at his watch. "I'd like to start bringing this discussion to a close and allow Eric to get home before dawn. Are there any final questions?"

I glanced around the room. There were a few somber faces, a few smiles. Then the hospital administrator raised her voice again.

"I have one final question for Mr. Rofes," she said. "Have you seen a psychiatrist about your problem?"

I was caught a little off guard. As I caught my breath and began to formulate a response, I noticed that many of the other trustees were obviously put off by her question.

"I don't believe I have a problem," I said. "I did see a psychiatrist while I was in college who helped me adjust to being gay, but currently I do not see one."

"Then my follow-up question is," she continued her hostile line of questioning, "Why are you doing this to us?"

Before I could answer, Doug Cabot jumped in. "I don't believe that this question merits a response from Eric. I apologize for—"

I cut him off. "Excuse me, Mr. Cabot," I said, "but I would like a moment to respond to the question. I am not doing anything to you or to the school. I could have returned next year, written my gay articles under my own name, and have a major scandal come over the school without any preparation on the part of Miss Clarkson or the trustees. Or I could have walked away from education, robbing the school of another teacher simply because I didn't have the courage to discuss this difficult issue with all of you. I believe that I've chosen an honorable process by which to pursue the matter. I care about this school and I've tried to respond professionally and with sensitivity to everyone involved. I came here tonight prepared to answer questions as best as I could, however difficult and personal they might be. I also came here to be honest with you and not to cover up my political involvement or deceive you about my true thoughts on these matters.

"However, I did not come here to be insulted and I thank the rest of the trustees for their kindness and consideration this evening. It is one thing to find oneself in honest disagreement with others. It is quite another matter to find oneself insulted and I shall not accept any more of your questions."

With that off my chest, I sat there, red-faced, drained, angry and exhausted. I missed Doug Cabot's closing remarks as he summarized the evening's discussion and explained that I would now leave and the trustees would remain and discuss the issue. Since Alice was a part of the discussion, I would leave with Marie. I found myself shaking hands with my judges and being whisked by Marie out the door and into the cool night air.

Marie drove me home and came in to join me for a cup of coffee while I waited for the phone call from the school. Holly had a fresh pot of coffee ready for us when we walked in the door and she eagerly listened to Marie and me recount our tales of the inquisition.

"That hospital director sure sounds like the Anita Bryant of Shawmut Hills," Holly said. "I suppose there's going to be one in every crowd, but I'm glad you spoke your mind at the end."

"She was just terrible," Marie said shaking her head, "just terrible. I could tell that you were sitting there, trying to be polite, holding your feelings in and sitting on your temper. I don't know how you controlled yourself for as long as you did. You deserve some kind of medal for that performance, sweetie."

"So what are the odds that they'll keep you?" Holly asked. "I know it's hard to tell, especially since the phone might ring at any moment, but what is your prediction?"

I hesitated for a moment. "I think I made it crystal clear that this boy is going to be out-loud and proud-if he continues as a schoolteacher. The question will be whether they're willing to take the risk for the school. The way I see it, they need to weigh having a popular teacher who has somehow managed to earn a pretty decent reputation for academic competence against the fears that the conservative Shawmut Hills establishment might stop sending their kids to the school because a fag is on the faculty."

"What odds do you give me that they'll never find the chutzpah to keep you?" Holly asked. "I mean Shawmut Hills School just doesn't have a reputation for innovation and integrity."

"I don't know," Marie said slowly. "I think they might surprise us. I mean, I'm surprised that they're even considering the question, aren't you, Eric?"

"I guess deep inside me, I am. It really is a big step for the school to even allow the topic into the forum for discussion. And the fact that they're taking it seriously, considering the possibilities, is certainly a step, even if they decide against me."

"I'll bet they're just doing that because they're afraid you'll sue their asses off," Holly said, pouring coffee into our half-empty mugs.

"I'm not so sure of that," I responded quickly. "I give them more credit than that . . . but you might be right."

"It's difficult to call this one, Holly," Marie said. "Clearly there were some pretty cool characters at the meeting tonight who wouldn't care a bit about a homosexual teaching their kids. But there were some pretty hostile folks as well. In my mind, Cabot's going to be the swing vote. He's a pretty cagey guy and I don't think he showed his cards at all throughout the meeting."

Just then the telephone rang. I rushed to the front foyer and grabbed it before the third ring.

"Hello," I whispered into the receiver, clearly out of breath.

"Hello, is this Eric?"

"Yes it is. Who's calling please?" I asked in my most courteous tone of voice.

"This is Doug Cabot. We've just concluded our meeting and I've been asked to call you and let you know the decision of the committee."

His voice was calm, quiet, and I couldn't sense whether he was about to transmit good news or bad.

"We discussed the matter for about an hour. First of all, everyone was very appreciative of your willingness to answer our questions. We found the discussion to be quite informative. We thought that you conducted yourself in a mature and responsible manner throughout the evening."

He paused here. Get to the point, I thought, my mind racing madly.

"Thank you," I responded. "Did the committee reach a decision?"

"I'm getting to that," Cabot said slowly. "We would very much like to see you return to Shawmut Hills. Everyone feels that you're an excellent teacher and that we should do everything within our power to keep you here. We do feel, however, that—while it would be fine for you to be open about these things within our school community—we really couldn't allow you to use your real name in your writings, nor could we allow you to be photographed at gay events. We'd want you to keep your political activism low-key and away from controversy."

Again he paused, waiting for my reaction. I held my silence this time, forcing him to continue.

"You see, Eric, this school really couldn't stand the public attention that would come if word got out that we had a homosexual teacher. People would withdraw their children and our enrollment would fall. The entire financial stability of the school would be undermined. It's a risk that we could not take and still be a responsible board of trustees, even if we support you in principle.

"Thus we're hoping that you will return to the school next year, but without the same degree of activism."

I didn't know what to say. Yes, the school had made a major step by allowing me to return next year as a gay man, even if they were unwilling to allow me to be a public gay activist. On the other hand, the specific issues which I'd raised—leaving the pseudonyms behind, ending my enforced schizophrenia, feeling comfortable with media exposure—had been circumvented.

"It sounds as if you'd want me to come back, but on your own terms, not on mine," I said quietly.

"We prefer to think of it as, not in our terms or your terms, but in terms that have the best interests of the children in mind."

He was beginning to sound patronizing. "We don't want you to feel that you have to decide about this overnight. Take some time to think about it, maybe discuss it with your friends. But do let us know within the week."

I needed to clarify what he'd told me. This was all happening too quickly and my heart was pounding a mile a minute in my chest.

"If I return to Shawmut Hills," I asked, "what you're saying is that I still have to maintain two separate identities."

"You might choose to see it that way," Cabot acknowledged. "Your activist activities would have to be kept fully separate from your teaching."

"I'd still have to avoid photos and use a fake name?"

"I think you're correct in saying that," Cabot responded formally.

"Then what you're saying is that you don't want me to return next year, since I have made it very clear to you—both in my letter to Miss Clarkson and in the meeting this evening—that I intend to write under my own name next year."

"That's your decision, Eric."

"But it's *not* my decision. You're trying to absolve yourself and your board of trustees from this decision. You want me to be the one who decided not to return to the school. You don't even have the courage to tell me about your decision directly." I was beginning to shout.

"Now wait a minute, Eric. That's unfair -"

"No, you wait a minute, Mr. Cabot. I want you to answer me one question, and this time you listen carefully. I, Eric Rofes, am going to be an openly gay person next year, in my writing, in my political work, and in my teaching. Am I welcome to return to Shawmut Hills School next year, Mr. Cabot?"

There was a silence at the end of the line. I allowed him a moment to make the decision.

"Under those conditions, Eric, you would not be welcome back," he said slowly and quietly. Then he added, "But take a few days and think about it. We don't need your decision tonight."

"Thank you," I said. "I'm afraid I need to get off the phone now. I appreciate your call."

With that comment, I hung up the receiver, walked directly up the flight of stairs, went into my bedroom, and started to cry.

Index

"Accident, Awareness, and
    Actualization" (Noddings),
    selection from, 25–30
Advantage, unearned, 130
American Dilemma, An (Myrdal), 195
American Mind, The (Commager), 193
Americans, The (Spencer), 193
America's Country Schools
    (Gulliford), 46
Andersen, Margaret, 127
Anderson, Sherwood, 7, 228, 231–237
Art, teaching as, 1
Art as Experience (Dewey), 18n1
Artistry, teaching as, 1
Attractions, to teaching, 10, 147
Ayers, William, 9, 206, 209–221

Baldacci, Leslie, 148
"Ballad of the Landlord" (Hughes), 186
Becker, Carl, 194
Bent, William Rose, 192
Black culture, 101n
Black Teachers on Teaching
    (Foster), 148
Border-crosser, teacher as, 6, 50, 93
Braithwaite, E. R., 46
Branscombe, Amanda, 107–108
Bridenbaugh, Carl, 193
Bruner, Jerome, 28–29
Burgess, Tony, 117

Calvin and Hobbes (Watterson), 206
Care, teaching themes of, 135–145
Caring, why teach, 136–138
Caring for self, 138

Cazden, Courtney, 117
Children of a Lesser God, 94–95
Classroom behavior, and fairness, 43
Cloud, Howard, 118
Codell, Esmé Raji, 46, 67–73
Combahee River Collective, 132
Commager, Henry Steele, 193
Committee for Gay Youth, 245
Compulsory Mis-education
    (Goodman), 76
Compulsory schooling, hidden
    curriculum of, 77–84
Conant, James, 143
Conferred dominance, 130
"Confessions of a Gay Schoolteacher"
    (Rofes), 6, 239–252
Conrack, 46, 94
Conroy, Pat, 46
Conscientization, 86
Core black culture, 101n
Counts, George S., 175, 176,
    189–195
Cousins, Norman, 192
Cultural capital, 104
Cultural lag, 193
Culture of power, 97, 105, 113
    aspects of, 100–102
Curriculum, hidden, 77–84
Cushman, Kathleen, 10, 31–43

Dangerous Minds, 46–47, 147, 161
"Dare the Schools Build a New Social
    Order?" (Counts), 175
Dauphin, Gary, 90
Dead Poets Society, 11, 76

Death at an Early Age (Kozol),
    selection from, 177–188
Debs, Eugene, 17
Declaration of Independence, 195
Delpit, Lisa D., 4–6, 94, 97–120
Demientieff, Martha, 114
Democracy, 14
Democracy and Education
    (Dewey), 30
Deschooling Society (Illich), 76
Dewey, John, 14, 18n1, 30, 190
Dialect readers, 104
Dickens, Charles, 19
Discrimination, 197
Distar, 103, 105
Downing, Lucia, 46
Du Bois, W. E. B., 24, 46, 49–57
Dumbing Us Down (Gatto), selection
    from, 77–84
Durkheim, Emile, 76

Educating Esmé (Codell), selection
    from, 46, 67–73
Education, liberatory, 88–90
Emperor's Club, The, 11
"Engaged Pedagogy" (hooks), 85–92
Entitlement, unearned, 130
Erickson, Fred, 103
Ethnographic analysis, 100
*Être et Avoir (To Be and
    To Have),* 148
Evans, Marnie, 131

Fairness, 31–43
    building trust and respect,
        36–37
    classroom behavior and, 43
Fast Times at Ridgemont High, 207
Fayerweather Street School, 240
Featherstone, Joseph, 10, 13–24,
    75, 176
Ferris Bueller's Day Off, 207
Fields, Karen, 127
Fields, Mamie, 127
Fires in the Bathroom (Cushman),
    selection from, 31–43
Foster, Michele, 148
Franklin, Benjamin, 183

Freedom and Civilization
    (Malinowski), 191, 194
Freedom and Responsibility in
    the American Way of Life
    (Becker), 194
Freedom Writers, 148
Freedom Writers Diary, The
    (Gruwell), 76
Freire, Paulo, 76, 85–86, 89

Gatto, John Taylor, 75, 77–84
Gay Community News, 239
Generation gap, 193
Gibson, William, 94
Girls in the Back of the Class, The
    (Johnson), 148, 161
Giroux, Henry, 6, 50, 93
Goodbye, Mr. Chips (Hilton), 148
Goodman, Paul, 76
Good Morning, Miss Dove, 148
Groening, Matt, 76, 206, 223–229
Growing Up Absurd (Goodman), 76
Gruwell, Erin, 76
Gulliford, Andrew, 46
Gurnperz, John, 103
Gwaltney, John, 106

Hand, Learned, 194
Hanh, Thich Nhat, 85–87
Hard Times (Dickens), 19
Heath, Shirley Brice, 108
Hilton, James, 148
History Begins at Sumer (Kramer), 3
History Boys, The, 229
hooks, bell, 75, 85–92
Horace's Compromise (Sizer),
    prologue from, 147, 149–160
"How to Run the Yard"
    (Dauphin), 90
Hughes, Langston, 186

Illich, Ivan, 76
In & Out, 229
Inside Mrs. B's Classroom
    (Baldacci), 148
"Interrupting the Calls for Student
    Voice in Liberatory Education"
    (Orner), 91

Jefferson, Thomas, 193
Jennings, Kevin, 228
Johnson, LouAnne, 46–47, 147,
    161–169
Junell, Joe, 190

Kaufman, Bel, 46
Keats, John, 17–18
Keller, Helen, 94
Killers of the Dream (Smith), 127
Kohl, Herbert, 46, 59–65, 67
Kozol, Jonathan, 4, 11, 176,
    177–188
Kramer, Noah, 3

Lean on Me, 207
Lemon Swamp (Fields and
    Fields), 127
Letters to a Young Teacher (Kozol),
    11, 176
"Letter to a Young Teacher"
    (Featherstone), 13–24, 176
Levy, H., 191
Liberatory education, 88–90
Life in Hell, 223
Liking, 31–43
Lopez, Georges, 148
Lortie, Dan, 4, 10, 147
Lunacharsky, Anatole, 191

Maldonado, Milagros, 82–84
Male privilege, 121–133
Mali, Taylor, 147, 171–173
Malinowski, Bronislaw, 191, 194
Mann, Horace, 16, 193
Man without a Face, The, 148, 247
McIntosh, Peggy, 121–133
Middle-class, 101n
Minnich, Elizabeth, 124
Miracle Worker, The (Gibson), 94
Mohanty, Chandra, 91
Montesquieu (Charles-Louis de
    Secondat), 193
Mr. Holland's Opus, 148
Mumford, Lewis, 192
My Posse Don't Do Homework
    (Johnson), selection from, 147,
    161–169

Myrdal, Gunnar, 195
Myth of the Machine,
    The (Mumford), 192
Myths, about teaching, 205–221

"Negro Schoolmaster in the
    New South, A" (Du Bois), 46,
    49–57
Neutrality, and teaching, 189–195
Nieto, Sonia, 11, 176
Ninth Annual Report (Mann), 193
Noddings, Nel, 10–11, 25–30, 94,
    135–145

Ogburn, William F., 193
One Teacher in Ten (Jennings), 228
"On Race and Voice"
    (Mohanty), 91
On the Spirit of the Laws
    (Montesquieu), 193
Orner, Mini, 91
Our Social Heritage (Wallas), 191

Pedagogy
    engaged, 85–92
    in teaching, 97–120
Pedagogy of the Oppressed, The
    (Freire), 76
Poetry of Freedom, The (Bent and
    Cousins), 192
Popular culture, and teaching, 11,
    46–47, 76, 94–95, 148, 176, 207,
    228–229
Porky's I–III, 207
Power
    culture of, 97, 100–102, 105, 113
    in teaching, 97–120
Practice of freedom, teaching as,
    75–92
Praxis, 86
Prime of Miss Jean Brodie, The
    (Spark), 11, 228
Principal, The, 207
Privilege, white and male,
    121–133
Process-oriented approaches,
    99, 106
Profession, teaching as a, 3–4

Queen of Education,
    The (Johnson), 161

"Racism without Racists" (Massey,
    Scott, and Dornbusch), 118
Reflection-in-action, 2
Reflective practice, 1
Reflective practicum, 2
"Respect, Liking, Trust, and Fairness"
    (Cushman), 31–43
Responsibility, 27
Rich, Adrienne, 127–128
Rofes, Eric, 6, 228, 239–252
Roll of Thunder, Hear My Cry
    (Taylor), selection from, 197–207
Rubin, Gayle, 239

Savage Inequalities (Kozol), 178
Schön, Donald, 1
Schooling, compulsory, 77–84
School Is Hell (Groening), selections
    from, 76, 206, 223–229
Schoolteacher (Lortie), 10
Self-actualization, 82, 87–88, 90
Self-respect, importance of, 36
Sexuality, and teaching, 227–252
Shawmutt Hills Schools, 240, 246
"Should the Teacher Always Be
    Neutral?" (Counts), 189–195
"Silenced Dialogue, The" (Delpit),
    97–120
Simpsons, The, 223
Sizer, Theodore R., 147, 149–160
"Skills and Other Dilemmas of a
    Progressive Black Educator"
    (Delpit), 99–100, 107, 111
Slick Boys rap group, 71
Smith, B. Othanel, 9
Smith, Horace, 150
Smith, Lillean, 127
Social activism, and teaching, 175–204
Social Frontier, The, 189
Social reconstructivist movement, 189
Socrates, Plato, & Guys Like Me
    (Rofes), selection from, 6, 228,
    239–252
Souls of Black Folk, The (Du Bois), 24
Spark, Muriel, 11

Spencer, Herbert, 193
Stand and Deliver, 176
Stereotypes, about teachers, 223–225
Students, and teachers, 31–43. See also
    Teacher(s); Teaching
Sullivan, Annie, 94

Taylor, Mildred D., 176, 197–207
Teacher(s)
    as border-crosser, 6, 50, 93
    being a, 9–47
    neutrality and, 189–195
    reflective exercise for, 39–40
    stereotypes of, 223–225
    students and, 31–43
"Teacher, The" (Anderson), 231–237
Teacher! Teacher!, 171
Teachers, 148, 176
Teaching
    as a profession, 3–4
    as art, 1
    as practice of freedom, 75–92
    as social activism, 175–204
    as work, 147–173
    attractions to, 10
    beginning, 45–73
    myths about, 205–221
    others, 93–145
    popular culture and, 11, 46–47, 76,
        94–95, 148, 176, 207, 228–229
    power and pedagogy in, 97–120
    sexuality and, 227–252
"Teaching in the Keeler 'Deestrict'
    School" (Downing), 46
Teaching Outside of the Box
    (Johnson), 161
"Teaching Themes of Care"
    (Noddings), 135–145
Teaching to Transgress (hooks),
    selection from, 85–92
Themes of care, 147
    choosing and organizing,
        138–142
    supporting structures, 143–145
36 Children (Kohl), selection from,
    46, 59–65
To Sir, with Love (Braithwaite),
    46, 94

To Teach (Ayers), selection from, 209–221

Trust, 31–43

Unamuno, Miguel, 28

Unearned advantage and entitlement, 130

Universe of Science, The (Levy), 191

Up the Down Staircase (Kaufman), 46

Village English, 114

Vulnerability, 177–178

Wallas, Graham, 191

Washington, Booker T., 46

Water Is Wide, The (Conroy), 46, 94

Watterson, Bill, 206

Ways with Words (Heath), 108

"What Teachers Make" (Mali), 147, 148, 171–173

Whitehead, Alfred North, 193

"White Privilege and Male Privilege" (McIntosh), 121–133

White teachers, 94, 121–133

Whitman, Walt, 18

Why We Teach (Nieto), 11, 176

Wilde, Oscar, 190

Winesburg, Ohio (Anderson), selection from, 7, 228, 231–237

Women's Studies, 87, 121–133

Wordsworth, William, 186

Work, teaching as, 147–173

Writing-process advocates, 99

About the Editor

Eugene F. Provenzo, Jr. is one of the nation's leading scholars in the foundations of education. He is a professor at the University of Miami, where he has taught since 1976. He has won numerous awards throughout his career in both teaching and research and sits on a wide range of editorial boards. He is the author or editor of more than 60 books on different aspects of education, culture, and history, as well as many articles and book chapters in a wide range of areas in education. His recent projects include serving as the editor-in-chief for the three-volume *Encyclopedia of the Social and Cultural Foundations of Education* (Sage Publications, 2009) and as editor of the four-volume *Foundations of Educational Thought*. His online vita can be viewed at the following address: http://www.education.miami.edu/ep/vita/.

Supporting researchers for more than 40 years

Research methods have always been at the core of SAGE's publishing program. Founder Sara Miller McCune published SAGE's first methods book, *Public Policy Evaluation*, in 1970. Soon after, she launched the *Quantitative Applications in the Social Sciences* series—affectionately known as the "little green books."

Always at the forefront of developing and supporting new approaches in methods, SAGE published early groundbreaking texts and journals in the fields of qualitative methods and evaluation.

Today, more than 40 years and two million little green books later, SAGE continues to push the boundaries with a growing list of more than 1,200 research methods books, journals, and reference works across the social, behavioral, and health sciences. Its imprints—Pine Forge Press, home of innovative textbooks in sociology, and Corwin, publisher of PreK–12 resources for teachers and administrators—broaden SAGE's range of offerings in methods. SAGE further extended its impact in 2008 when it acquired CQ Press and its best-selling and highly respected political science research methods list.

From qualitative, quantitative, and mixed methods to evaluation, SAGE is the essential resource for academics and practitioners looking for the latest methods by leading scholars.

For more information, visit **www.sagepub.com**.